Th   n

G

POLITY PRESS
in association with

TheOpen

Cover illustration: Greenpeace's Rainbow Warrior *en route to Moruroa to protest against French nuclear tests is juxtaposed with the USA's Stealth Fighter (117A)*

The Open University, Walton Hall, Milton Keynes MK7 6AA
© The Open University 1997
First published in 1997 by Polity Press in association with The Open University

Polity Press,
65 Bridge Street,
Cambridge, CB2 1UR.

Published in the USA by
Blackwell Publishers Inc.,
Commerce Place, 350 Main Street,
Malden, MA 02148, USA.

A CIP catalogue record for this book is available from the British Library.

Library of Congress Cataloging-in-Publication Data
The transformation of democracy? globalization and territorial democracy / edited by
    Anthony McGrew.
        p. cm. — (Democracy — from classical times to the present:
3)
    Includes bibliographical references and index.
    ISBN 0-7456-1816-2. — ISBN 0-7456-1817-0 (p)
    1. Democracy. 2. International organization. 3. International economic relations.
    4. Human rights. I. McGrew, Anthony G. II. Series.
JC423.T65   1997
320.9'09'049—dc21   97–572
                                                                           CIP

Edited, designed and typeset by the Open University.
Printed in the United Kingdom by Halstan & Co. Ltd., Amersham, Bucks.
This text forms part of an Open University course D316 *Democracy: From Classical Times to the Present*. Details of this and other Open University courses can be obtained from the Course Enquiries Data Service, P.O. Box 625, The Open University, Dane Road, Milton Keynes, MK1 1TY. For availability of other course components, contact Open University Educational Enterprises Ltd, 12 Cofferidge Close, Stony Stratford, Milton Keynes MK11 1BY.
1.1
15665B/d316b3pi1.1

Contents

CONCLUSION

Democracy: From Classical Times to the Present

Open University Course Team

David Held, *Faculty of Social Sciences and Course Team Chair*
Mandy Anton, *Designer*
Richard Bessel, *Faculty of Arts*
David Calderwood, *Project Control*
Stephen Clift, *Editor*
Lene Connolly, *Print Buying Controller*
Jeremy Cooper, *Producer, BBC*
Jonathan Davies, *Graphic Designer*
Michael Dawson, *Course Manager, Faculty of Social Sciences*
Margaret Dickens, *Print Buying Co-ordinator*
Donna Dickenson, *School of Health and Social Welfare*
Mary Dicker, *Secretary, Faculty of Social Sciences*
Martin Ferns, *Editor*
Bram Gieben, *Staff Tutor, Faculty of Social Sciences*
David Goldblatt, *Faculty of Social Sciences*
Anne Hunt, *Secretary, Faculty of Social Sciences*
Tom Hunter, *Editor*
Margaret Kiloh, *Staff Tutor, Faculty of Social Sciences*
Valerie Kirby, *Secretary, Faculty of Social Sciences*
Simon Lawson, *Producer, BBC*
Paul Lewis, *Faculty of Social Sciences*
Richard Maidment, *Faculty of Social Sciences*
Anthony McGrew, *Faculty of Social Sciences*
Eleanor Morris, *Producer, BBC*
Ray Munns, *Cartographer*
David Potter, *Faculty of Social Sciences*
Paul Smith, *Media Librarian*
Grahame Thompson, *Faculty of Social Sciences*
Kathy Wilson, *Producer, BBC*

External Academic Consultants for this book

Robert Cox, *York University, Toronto*
Tony Evans, *Southampton University*
James Goodman, *University of Sydney*
Mark Imber, *University of St Andrews*
Martin Shaw, *University of Sussex*

External Assessor

Adrian Leftwich, *University of York*

Preface

Globalization - the growing interconnectedness of national societies - has important ramifications for the liberal democratic polity. This volume offers a systematic enquiry into how globalization is transforming the very conditions under which modern liberal democratic states operate. It also explores the prospects for a more democratic world order under conditions of contemporary globalization.

This book is one of three produced for the Open University course: *Democracy: From Classical Times to the Present*. The other two books are David Held's *Models of Democracy* (second edition) and *Democratization* edited by David Potter *et al*. All three are published by Polity Press. Open University courses are put together by a course team consisting of academic authors and experienced tutors, editors and designers, BBC producers, academic administrators and secretaries, and an external academic assessor. The course team and the external academic consultants that helped to write this book are listed on the opposite page.

The process of producing this book involved bringing together a wide range of academic talent. Most of us met initially at a one-day workshop in mid 1995 when agreement was reached on a common framework and a set of detailed chapter outlines. Both first and second drafts of each chapter subsequently received critical evaluation by the entire course team during 1996. These procedures helped to produce a book with an overall coherence not normally found in collaborative volumes.

I want to thank the external contributors for the splendid way in which they responded so patiently, during a long collaborative process, to the course team's numerous criticisms and suggestions for improvement. They took on board a lot while preserving the integrity of their initial conception of their chapter. I would also like to acknowledge the excellent work of Adrian Leftwich, our external assessor, for his careful reading and constructive criticism of all the chapters as well as his contribution to ensuring the intellectual coherence of the volume.

Many people within the Open University helped to produce this book and I wish in particular to express my appreciation to Mary Dicker, Anne Hunt and Valerie Kirby for typing speedily and cheerfully all the various and quite different drafts that were involved; Michael Dawson who as course manager kept us all on schedule and sustained the essential links with others in the Open University; David Potter and Paul Lewis for their thorough and helpful comments on all drafts; and David Held for his intellectual stimulus and encouragement at every stage of the process.

Finally my thanks to Christine, Francesca, Naomi and Kathryn for their forbearance during the completion of the manuscript in the Summer and Autumn of 1996.

Tony McGrew
Walton Hall, November 1996

cation of global interconnectedness – presents liberal democratic states especially with a profound challenge since it appears to rob them of the means of self-governance, the very essence of democratic politics. In an epoch of intense globalization the most urgent question confronting democrats, and democratic theory, is how, or indeed whether it is even feasible, to reconcile effective national democratic governance with the global and transnational scale of contemporary social and economic organization. This question, and the other fundamental issues to which it gives rise, is the primary concern of this volume.

1.1   Themes and structure

In subsequent chapters we will explore the nature and consequences of globalization for the liberal democratic state. Part I (*Global transformations*) investigates whether, or in what ways, globalization is transforming the conditions of democratic politics and governance. This will embrace not only a discussion of the problems and dilemmas of liberal democracy, buffeted by the powerful forces of globalization, but also the new democratic energies nurtured by globalizing imperatives, from the growth of transnational social movements, such as Greenpeace and Amnesty International, to the international diffusion of democratic ideas and forms of governance as evidenced most recently in the 'Third Wave' of 'global democratization' (Potter *et al.*, 1997) Part II (*Democratizing world order*) builds upon the analysis of globalization from Part I. It explores the possibilities for the democratization of existing structures of global governance, from the United Nations (UN) to the multinational corporation. But the democratization of world order is subject to powerful countervailing forces which are also interrogated in Part II. The final chapter reflects upon all these issues and so returns to the meaning of democracy in an era of globalization. It poses, and considers, the critical question of whether we need to re-think conventional accounts of liberal democracy to fit the new political circumstances in which we find ourselves on the eve of the twenty-first century.

   This chapter reviews the main theoretical debates and controversies which inform the concerns of subsequent parts. These debates have their origins in both international relations theory and democratic theory. The chapter commences with an account of how liberal democracy came to be associated almost exclusively with the territorial nation-state, as a political form, and why, under conditions of globalization, this continuing association might be considered increasingly problematic. How far globalization prefigures the erosion or transformation of liberal democracy comes under scrutiny in Section 1.4. The penultimate section describes four distinctive accounts of world order and global governance. The final section returns to the question of the meaning of democracy today.

Introduction

CHAPTER 1

Globalization and territorial democracy: an introduction

Anthony McGrew

Introduction

Addressing, from the steps of Her Majesty's Treasury in September 1992, the assembled reporters from the world's media on the escalating 'sterling crisis', the British Chancellor of the Exchequer appeared dimly aware that, a continent away in New York and Tokyo, foreign exchange dealers had sealed the fate of the government's economic strategy. Reaffirming the government's staunch commitment to Britain's membership of the European Exchange Rate Mechanism (ERM) the Chancellor returned, within 24 hours on 'Black Wednesday', to acknowledge a humiliating 'defeat' in the confrontation with global financial markets. Despite achieving a fourth general election victory, fought on a manifesto which promised continuity of economic policy, the forced withdrawal from the ERM, and the consequent devaluation, was testament to the fickleness of electoral commitments in an era of global financial markets. Times of crisis pose awkward questions about prevailing political orthodoxies. Not long after the ERM debacle the G7 governments, the 'club' of rich nations, proposed measures to deal with currency speculation recognizing that financial globalization imposed significant constraints upon national economic autonomy. In this respect globalization – simply the intensifi-

Chancellor Norman Lamont arrives for a Cabinet meeting at 10 Downing Street

1.2 Democracy, the nation-state and world order

When Pope Innocent X learnt the details of the peace settlement of 1648, which brought to an end the Thirty Years War in Europe, he denounced it angrily: '[The Peace of Westphalia] is null, void, invalid, unjust, damnable, reprobate, insane, empty of meaning and effect for all time' (Holsti, 1991, p.25). Over three centuries later, despite Pope Innocent's denouncements, this 'reprobate and insane' peace settlement is still regarded as the normative foundation of the modern international order. For the Treaties of Westphalia '... fostered a world view in which discrete, quasi-independent territorial units were seen as the primary building blocks for social and political life' (Murphy, 1996, p.82). In opposition to the medieval view of Western Europe, as a universal Christian kingdom, the Westphalian order codified a new set of normative principles upon which the international states system has been constructed and which are now such a familiar aspect of modern social life that they appear to define natural features of the political landscape.

The Westphalian world order

The central principles of the Westphalian order, as it has evolved over the last three centuries, are fourfold:

1 *Territoriality* – States have fixed territorial boundaries which define the limits to their legal jurisdiction and the scope of their political authority. Thus the authority of the British government only extends to the people and resources within its territorial borders. Territoriality thus represents a central principle of modern political organization namely that humankind is divided into political units defined in terms of fixed and exclusive territorial spaces.

2 *Sovereignty* – Within these fixed territorial spaces the state, or government, claims effective supremacy; it claims the undisputed and exclusive right to rule and so represents the ultimate source of legal and political authority over the people within a delimited territory. Moreover, that supreme authority is indivisible in that 'Sovereignty over the same territory cannot reside simultaneously in two different authorities' (Morgenthau, 1967, p.307). Accordingly, humanity is organized today into over 185 sovereign territorial states which recognize no higher political or legal authority than themselves.

3 *Autonomy* – States are entitled to conduct their own internal and external affairs in a manner which only they are competent to decide and free from external intervention or control (Osiander, 1994).

4 *Legality* – Relations between sovereign states may be subject to international law but only in so far as each state consents to being so bound. There is no legal authority beyond the state which can impose legal duties upon it or its citizens. Thus, when the International Court of Justice recently ruled that the use of nuclear weapons might, in some circumstances, be contrary to humanitarian international law the world's nuclear powers gave notice of their right, under international law, to ignore its ruling.

These four principles constitute the bedrock of the modern international system of states and the defining characteristics of the modern territorial state as a form of political rule or governance. However, this Westphalian order did not simply appear in 1648, rather it has evolved over the centuries into its present form.

The Westphalian order and the sovereign state evolved in a symbiotic 'partnership'. As rulers recognized each other's sovereignty the Westphalian order was expanded and consolidated. In turn the consolidation of the Westphalian states system reinforced the primacy of the sovereign territorial state. In this respect the modern state and the modern inter-state system have developed in a coeval relationship over the last three centuries. The growth of nationalism, in the nineteenth and twentieth centuries, contributed significantly to the consolidation of the modern state and the modern international system of states. Nationalism reconstituted the state as an expression of the nation and state sovereignty as an expression of popular sovereignty. It underwrote the nationalization of politics as subjects were transformed into citizens and the nation-state became an exclusive, territorially bounded political community. With the collapse of Empires and the championing of national self-determination, the nation-state has become the principal form of modern political organization. Despite Pope Innocent's predictions, the sovereign territorial nation-state, and the Westphalian international order in which it is embedded, have come to define the architecture of modern political life. This has had important implications for liberal democracy as we have come to understand it today.

King Gustavus Adolphus of Sweden whose military campaigns in the Thirty Years War helped bring about the Peace of Westphalia (1648)

The Westphalian order and territorial democracy

Liberal democracy, as Huntington observes, is '... not simply democracy of the village, the tribe, or the city-state; it is democracy of the nation-state and its emergence is associated with the development of the nation-state' (Huntington, 1991, p.13). Historical, as well as theoretical, accounts of liberal democracy overwhelmingly take for granted the nation-state as the primary 'container' of democratic politics. This is not surprising since throughout the modern era the story of democracy has been intimately associated with the evolution and consolidation of the sovereign, territorial nation-state.

During the 'long nineteenth century' the institutional form of modern democracy was crystallized in the 'shell' of the territorial nation-state. Industrialization, the integration of local economies into a nation-wide economic order, and the nationalization of political life underwrote a corresponding nationalization of democratic politics. Moreover, whether in late nineteenth century Europe, or post-colonial Africa, processes of democratization have been deeply implicated in the strengthening of the institution of sovereign statehood and nation-building. This correspondence between liberal democracy and the territorial nation-state is not purely coincidental; on the contrary, the modern nation-state has proved, over the *longue durée* (the very long term), an effective incubator for the democratic project. The reasons for this are complex and a huge literature exists on the dynamics of democratization (see Potter *et al.*, 1997). Of significance is the role of the bounded sovereign state form in providing the relatively pacified, territorially delimited political space within which the struggles for democracy, the nurturing of social solidarities, and constitutional forms of government could develop within a framework of the rule of law. Moreover, the modern state has proved remarkably adaptable as the history of the nineteenth, early and late twentieth century waves of democratization illustrate (Potter *et al.*, 1997).

Today the fundamental principles and practices of liberal democracy – the nature of the demos, the definition of democratic citizenship, the ideas of self-governance, consent, representation, popular sovereignty – are almost exclusively associated with the institutions of the sovereign territorial nation-state (Held, 1995, 1996). As Walker comments, it is only in the context of the sovereign nation-state '... that we have come to understand what is meant by democracy' (Walker, 1988, p.83). For instance, the modern 'demos' is understood exclusively in terms of the peoples, the nation, within a delimited territory; the interests of citizens are expressed through the ballot box by which means government secures the consent of the nation; self-governance is defined in terms of the sovereignty and autonomy of the nation-state; and popular sovereignty is elided with exclusive control of a bounded territorial state (Held, 1995). In essence modern democratic theory and democratic politics assume a symmetrical correspondence between the democratic political community and the modern nation-state; a self-contained, self-governing, territorially delimited 'national community of fate'. Furthermore this '... territorialization of democratic politics' is predicated upon a world order based upon Westphalian norms and principles (Connolly, 1991). But what if that world order, and sovereign statehood, are no longer so 'fixed' or immutable as has been assumed? What if globalization is challenging the foundations and political principles upon which the 'Westphalian temple' is constructed? What then are the potential consequences for the liberal democratic polity?

1.3   Globalization and the Westphalian order

In some tangible respects our everyday activities as consumers, from the food we eat to the clothes we wear, are manifestations of globalization. Put another way, 'Multinational corporations are as close as the next meal' (Walker, 1988, p.141). Modern existence depends upon complex chains of production and exchange which stretch across the globe and which link the fate of communities in one location to the prosperity of others a continent away. But such global interconnectedness is not only evident in the economic domain but in virtually every aspect of contemporary social life.

What is globalization?

Information, pollution, migrants, arms, ideas, images, news, crime, narcotics, disease, amongst other things, readily and frequently flow across national territorial boundaries. In addition, global transport and communications infrastructures, from airlines to the internet, facilitate the emergence of global and transnational networks linking peoples and organizations in different parts of the world. 'Central Bankers' within the world's richest states regularly attempt to co-ordinate their activities and policies through their own elite networks. Professional groups of all kinds have developed their own transnational networks, from scientists studying AIDS to engineers designing bridges. The '50 Years is Enough' networks bring together radical groups in the affluent North with grassrooots development movements in the South to oppose World Bank development projects. But by themselves these illustrative examples fail to capture the sheer density, growing intensity and scale of contemporary global and transnational flows, activities, networks and systems of interaction. Perhaps some selective statistics will make this point more forcefully:

– Over $1 trillion flows across the world's foreign exchange markets every day; over 50 times the size of world trade and dwarfing the collective foreign exchange reserves of the world's richest states.

– In 1960 there were 70 million international tourists; by 1995 there were nearly 500 million.

– Multinational corporations now account for between 25–33 per cent of world output, 70 per cent of world trade and 80 per cent of international investment; in 1992 the top 100 multinationals controlled sales almost equal in size to the world's largest economy, the USA.

– In 1993 the UN calculated that there were 28,900 citizen, or non-governmental, organizations with an international dimension compared with 176 at the turn of the century.

- Global warming, ozone depletion and deforestation represent environmental problems with serious global impacts.

- In 1990, 95 per cent of the world's nations were members of the global trading system whilst world trade has more than doubled since the 1950s and become increasingly important to national economic survival in the majority of states.

Accordingly, there is much evidence to suggest that, as a consequence of contemporary globalization, 'Virtually all countries in the world, if not all parts of their territory and all segments of their society, are now functionally part of that larger [global] system in one or more respects' (Nierop, 1994, p.171).

Globalization can be defined quite simply as growing global interconnectedness. But this definition needs a little elaboration for globalization has a number of distinctive attributes. Firstly, it implies that social, political and economic activities are becoming 'stretched' across national frontiers such that events, decisions and activities in one part of the world come to have immediate significance for individuals and communities in distant parts of the globe. For instance, failure of the rice crop in China translates into higher rice prices in our local supermarket. Secondly, globalization involves an intensification, or increasing density, in the flows and patterns of interaction or interconnectedness which transcend the states and societies which constitute the modern world system. As indicated above, all states are now part of the global trading order and world trade has grown extensively in the post-war period. Thirdly, the growing extensity and intensity of global interactions is associated with a deepening enmeshment of the local and global so that the distinction between what is internal and what is external is increasingly blurred. Alongside the 'stretching' goes a 'deepening' such that even though '...everyone has a local life, phenomenal worlds for the most part are truly global' (Giddens, 1991, p.187). Thus, a so called 'domestic' decision by the German Bundesbank to raise interest rates in Germany can lead to houseowners in the UK paying more for their mortgages. Fourthly, growing interconnectedness generates a host of transnational problems, from the proliferation of weapons of mass destruction to global trafficking in narcotics, which cannot be resolved by the action of individual governments but only through multilateral or international co-operation. Thus globalization stimulates the growth of international organizations and multilateral mechanisms for regulating areas of transnational activity, from telecommunications to nuclear power station safety standards. Fifthly, the density and intensity of patterns of global and transnational interconnectedness weave ever tighter and more complex webs of relations between the states, international institutions, communities, non-governmental organizations, and multinational corporations which make up the global system generating systemic constraints upon all their activities and their autonomy. Thus the operation of the global financial system determines the market conditions which, as the 1992 ERM crisis demonstrated, defines the scope which individual governments have to conduct an autonomous economic policy.

Accordingly, we can conceive of globalization as a process which involves something more than simply flows and connections across nation-states and national territorial boundaries. Indeed globalization denotes a *significant shift in the spatial form of human social organization and activity to transcontinental or inter-regional patterns of relations, interaction and the exercise of power* (Goldblatt *et al.*, forthcoming). This definition advertises the fundamental historical shift in the scale of contemporary social and economic organization which globalization entails. Moreover, if globalization is understood as transcontinental interconnectedness it is distinguished clearly from more delimited processes, such as regionalization which can be conceived as the intensification of patterns of interconnectedness between geographically contiguous states. Thus flows of trade and finance between the world's three major economic regions – North America, Asia-Pacific, and Europe – constitute globalization, whilst flows within them constitute regionalization.

Furthermore, it is important to understand that globalization is evident in all the key institutional domains of modern life, including the economic, the cultural, the technological, the political, the legal, the military, the environmental and the social. Accordingly, globalization should not be conceived as a singular condition. It refers to the patterns of growing global interconnectedness across all these different domains. But in each of these domains, from the economic to the social, the scale, intensity, and impact of global interconnectedness may be rather different. To understand the dynamics and consequences of globalization therefore demands some knowledge of the differential patterns and intensity of global interconnectedness in each of these domains. For instance, the patterns of global ecological interconnectedness are quite different from the patterns of global cultural or military interaction. Any general account of the process of globalization must therefore acknowledge that, far from being a singular condition, it is best conceived as a multi-dimensional process.

Globalization too necessarily involves the organization and exercise of social power on a transnational and intercontinental scale. In an increasingly interconnected global system the exercise of power through the decisions, actions, or inaction of agencies on one continent can have significant consequences for nations, communities, and households on other continents. Deforestation in the Amazon, for instance, has long-term environmental consequences which extend well beyond Brazil's sovereign territory; a decision by the New York financiers Moody's to alter Zimbabwe's or Poland's international credit rating will have immediate consequences for the livelihoods and prosperity of communities and households in those countries; whilst multinational corporations organize relations of production on a transnational scale affecting the economic security of nations and communities across the globe.

Globalization is associated with a 'stretching' of power relations such that sites of power and the exercise of power become increasingly distant from the subjects or locales which experience its consequences. In this respect inequality and hierarchy are deeply inscribed in the very processes of globalization. States, communities, and nations are differentially enmeshed in global and transnational flows and networks (Hurrell and Woods, 1995). Patterns of hierarchy and stratification mediate access to sites of power whilst the consequences of globalization are unevenly experienced (Johnston *et al.*, 1995). Political and economic elites in the world's major metropolitan areas are much more tightly integrated into, and have much greater control over, global networks than do the subsistence farmers of Burundi. Moreover, the uneveness of globalization simultaneously stimulates processes of global fragmentation and global integration.

The globalization debate

Early in the twentieth century Norman Angell argued that the intensification of international interdependence '...cutting athwart frontiers, is largely the work of the last forty or fifty years' (Angell, 1909, p.147). What is therefore unique about contemporary globalization? World historical studies indicate that the 'discrete civilizations' of the first millennium, and their antecedents, were not without direct contact (Mann, 1986; Watson, 1992; Fernandez-Armesto, 1995). In the middle ages, there was a century's long luxury trade in slippers, silk and silver between China and Europe alongside a trade in arms and merchandise between major civilizations (Chase-Dunn, 1986; Abu-Lughod, 1988; Krause, 1992). Europe's global empires, beginning with the voyages of discovery in the fifteenth century and ending in the division of Africa in the nineteenth century, are also testament to the long history of globalization. However, what is undoubtedly distinctive about globalization today is that it unfolds in a world of nation-states, a Westphalian world order, not a world of Empires or discrete civilizations. It is this fact which has stimulated a vigorous academic debate concerning the consequences of contemporary globalization both for the sovereign, territorial nation-state and the Westphalian order itself.

This debate is characterized by enormous theoretical diversity. But there are broadly two intellectual 'fault-lines' around which the discourses of globalization arguably can be said to cluster. The first 'fault-line' is that of key causal processes: accounts differ dramatically as to whether globalization is conceived as a single process driven by a dominant logic (e.g. capitalism, technological change, or imperialism) or as a multidimensional process driven by several interrelated causal logics (e.g. technological, economic, cultural and political change). Put simply, the difference is largely between mono-causal and multi-causal accounts of globalization. The second 'fault-line' concerns the issue of continuity and change: accounts differ markedly as to whether the contemporary phase of globalization is argued to engender a radical break with the past (*the transformationalists*), constituting a transformation or restructuring of the global political economy, or alternatively represents historical continuity (*the sceptics*) rather than a discontinuity, and so is not without historical precedents (see Figure 1.1 The globalization debate: a summary). A brief elaboration of these contrasting positions is called for.

At the core of the 'transformationalist' case is a reasoned conviction that contemporary globalization fundamentally compromises the insti-

	Mono-causal/uni-dimensional accounts	**Multi-causal/multi-dimensional accounts**	
Historical continuity	Globalization as a product of economic, political, or technological change Limits to globalization. Not historically unique.	Globalization as a product of economic and technological and political forces. Limits to globalization mainly political and ecological	**SCEPTICS**
Historical transformation	Globalization as a product of economic, political, or technological change Contemporary globalization historically unprecedented	Globalization as a product of a combination of economic, technological and political change Contemporary globalization historically unprecedented	**TRANSFORMA-TIONALISTS**

Figure 1.1   The globalization debate: a summary

tution of sovereign statehood upon which the Westphalian order is constructed (Cox, 1981; Walker, 1988; Rosenau, 1990; Cammilleri and Falk, 1992; Linklater and MacMillan, 1995). For in a 'globalized' world, territorial boundaries are increasingly porous such that governments no longer control what transpires within their own national boundaries. Moreover, since states are locked into global systems of trade, finance, security etc., their scope for autonomous action is constrained and in some cases involves infringements upon national sovereignty, as in the case of membership of the European Union (EU). In these circumstances the Westphalian institution of sovereign statehood no longer appears as robust as it may once have done. Globalization, in this account, is therefore associated with an erosion or transformation of the Westphalian order. But what are we to understand by the term 'transformation'?

In his thorough review of the concept of change in international relations Barry Jones identifies the notion of transformation with the emergence of '...qualitatively novel conditions' (Barry-Jones, 1981, p.27). But how can the flux of daily events be distinguished from processes of qualitative change or transformation? Braudel devised a taxonomy of change in which he differentiated forms of change according to their historical tempo. Thus he distinguished between everyday events which are transitory; cyclical change such as business or economic cycles; and the *longue durée* which involves underlying structural change, as in the shift from medieval non-territorial systems of rule to the modern Westphalian order of sovereign territorial states (Spruyt, 1994). It is this third dimension of change which is absolutely central to the concept of transformation. Indeed, the argument of the 'transformationalists' is that globalization is associated not only with the erosion of the Westphalian order of the sovereign territorial nation-state but also with the emergence of new non-territorial forms of economic and political organization in the global domain e.g., multinational corporations, transnational social movements. In this sense the emerging world order is a post-Westphalian order which is no longer purely state-centric.

For the 'transformationalists' there are strong reasons for assuming that globalization and regionalization are restructuring sovereign statehood and contributing to the emergence of a post-Westphalian order. In particular globalization erodes the boundaries between the foreign and the domestic, the national and the international; inside and outside the state respectively. Thus electricity generation in the UK contributes to the acid rain which despoils the forests of Norway and Sweden; it is thus simultaneously a domestic and international matter and one in which the distinction between inside/outside has only administrative significance. In this respect states no longer retain sole control over what occurs within their own territorial boundaries whilst the intensification of societal and governmental enmeshment in global and regional systems restricts the scope for the exercise of state autonomy or self-governance. Furthermore, the proliferation of multilateral institutions and international regulatory mechanisms designed to manage common problems (e.g., acid rain), generated by globalizing imperatives, compromises further the state's sovereign and autonomous capacities. Globalization, the transformationalists argue, is thereby demolishing the 'Pillars of the Westphalian Temple' (Zacher, 1992).

Such a conclusion is regarded as hyperbole by the 'sceptics'. Despite diverse theoretical assumptions the sceptics nevertheless share deep reservations about the extent to which globalization, or regionalization, prefigures the emergence of a new, less state-centric world order (Bozeman, 1984, Gilpin, 1987; Gordon, 1988; Krasner, 1993; Cable, 1996; Hirst and Thompson, 1996). They dispute the view that globalization necessarily involves a diminution in the power, functions, or authority of the nation-state. Far from regarding states as becoming immobilized the sceptics point to their growing importance in regulating and facilitating processes of globalization. Furthermore, some argue that globalization is a product of the policy of hegemonic powers, such as Britain in the nineteenth century and the USA in the twentieth century, to create the necessary conditions for a liberal (free trade) international political economy (Gilpin, 1987).

In general the sceptics take issue with the claim that contemporary globalization is historically unique, pointing to the comparatively greater levels of economic interdependence at the beginning of the century (Gilpin, 1981; Krasner, 1993). Moreover, they reject the notion that state sovereignty or state autonomy today is any more compromised, or under threat, than it was in the past (Krasner, 1995). Indeed, they argue that, rather than constituting a descriptive statement of political reality, sovereignty has always involved a normative claim to supreme authority. What unites these very different approaches is a deeply held scepticism both towards the empirical evidence concerning globalization as well as the 'transformationalist' conviction that it is historically unprecedented and invites the demise of the Westphalian order.

We will return to consider this debate more fully in the concluding chapter, with the benefit of the discussion in the chapters in Parts I and II. Its significance, at this point, is that it underpins and informs the controversies which surround the relationship between globalization and (territorial) liberal democracy. For if globalization is transforming the Westphalian order it might therefore logically be argued that it is also transforming the institutional conditions which have so far ensured the historical correspondence (discussed in Section 1.2) between liberal democracy and the nation-state.

1.4   Globalization and the transformation of territorial liberal democracy

For the 'transformationalists' accelerating global and regional interconnectedness poses distinct challenges to liberal democratic forms of governance. Liberal democracy, as discussed earlier, is organized on the principle of the accountability of sites of power within the exclusive, delimited territory of the sovereign nation-state. Since globalization involves a profound shift in the scale of human economic and social organization, the exercise of power can readily transcend or bypass existing forms of democratic accountability which remain organized on an exclusively national and territorial basis. By destabilizing the political foundations of the Westphalian order, globalization problematizes the historical and analytical correspondence between modern liberal democracy and the sovereign nation-state. This is a complex argument which requires further elaboration.

If, as the transformationalists argue, globalization is reconstituting the nature of sovereign statehood this has the most profound implications for modern democratic theory and practice which are constructed upon Westphalian foundations (Held, 1995). For if state sovereignty is no longer conceived as indivisible but shared with international agencies; if states no longer have control over their own territories; and if territorial and political boundaries are increasingly permeable, the core principles of liberal democracy – that is self-governance, the demos, consent, representation, and popular sovereignty – are made distinctly problematic. As noted earlier, liberal democracy assumes a direct and symmetrical correspondence between government and the (demos) governed (Held, 1996). But under conditions of globalization this correspondence is disrupted since, in an increasingly interconnected world system, sites of power can be a continent away from the communities or constituencies which are the subjects of its exercise. Thus a decision by the Singapore government to ban the import of British beef directly affects the livelihoods of people and rural communities in the British beef industry. Significantly the latter have no voice in the former's decision whilst the former are not accountable to the latter. Under conditions of globalization the (non)decisions and (in)actions of the powerful can readily acquire a transnational impact affecting the welfare and security of peoples across the globe; yet they are not subject to corresponding mechanisms of democratic accountability. As a consequence of globalization, territorial systems of democratic accountability no longer necessarily coincide with the spatial reach of sites of power. In these circumstances the principles of consent, representation and the very idea of the democratic political community (should it be national, regional, or global?) become decidedly problematic (Held, 1995).

Furthermore, the intensity of transnational flows of trade, finance, information, capital, technology, culture, amongst other things, erode the distinctions between the internal and the external, domestic policy and foreign policy. The capacity of democratic governments to control or manage their own internal affairs is thereby decidedly weakened. In establishing global and international forms of governance, from the IMF (International Monetary Fund) to the WHO (World Health Organization), to regulate these transnational activities new concentrations of power are created which lack democratic credentials and which further compromise the democratic autonomy of individual states. This is particularly evident in the case of the European Union. Additionally, the existence of fundamental global problems, from security to the environment, demand global solutions which imply negotiated restrictions upon state sovereignty and limit the scope for self-governance. In these circumstances the ideal of the liberal democratic state as a self-governing, autonomous, 'national community of fate', in which government is conducted in general accordance with popular sovereignty, seems somewhat removed from 'really existing' historical conditions.

However, the transformationalists also argue that globalization is associated with the emergence of new progressive political forces and energies. Its capacity to stimulate new kinds of political organization, political solidarities and the mobilization of democratic forces both across and within states is evident in the massive growth of international nongovernmental organizations (INGOs) and transnational social movements, such as Greenpeace, Amnesty International, the women's movement and the environmental movement. In this respect the 1995 Beijing UN World Conference on Women demonstrated how the forces of globalization are generating a global women's response which seeks, through a more democratized world order, to advance and empower women across the world. Similarly in 1993, some 2,721 representatives of 529 INGOs, from every region of the world, attended the UN World Conference on Human Rights in Vienna. These developments suggest the emergence of a 'global civil society' in which citizens groups, social movements, non-governmental organizations, and new forms of political association (the virtual communities of the internet) are redefining the boundaries of democratic political space (Falk, 1994).

'Global civil society' is a term which embraces those organizations, associations and movements which exist '...above the individual and below the state but across national boundaries' (Wapner, 1995). Organizations, such as Greenpeace and Amnesty International, effectively conduct their own 'foreign policies', engage in activities which bypass the state, and participate in many aspects of global governance. They seek to make states and the 'international society of states' accountable for their actions. Furthermore, they also mobilize political solidarities across terri-

torial boundaries, challenging existing structures of national and international power, pursuing a politics of emancipation which transcends
national frontiers. This evolving 'global civil society' therefore stands in an
ambiguous relationship to established territorial forms of democratic
governance.

In short, the transformationalists reason that in eroding the
foundations upon which liberal democracies have been constructed,
namely the Westphalian order of sovereign territorial states, globalization
is also contributing to a transformation of democratic politics itself. But
the 'sceptics' remain unconvinced.

Their scepticism arises, in part, from a conviction that, irrespective of
globalization, serious disjunctures between the principles of liberal
democracy and its substantive realization have always existed in liberal
democratic polities. In his later writings Robert Dahl expressed a growing
concern with the 'limits' imposed upon democratic governance by the
nature of late capitalism and, in particular, with how the growing concentration of corporate, financial, and political power was effectively
'distorting' the democratic process (Dahl, 1985, 1989). To many Marxist
and radical critics of liberal democracy this appears a somewhat surprising 'conversion' given their own long-standing analyses of the
fundamental contradictions between modern capitalism and 'real' democracy. Contemporary democratic theory is extremely conscious of the
disjunctures between the principles of liberal democracy and the powerful forces which render its substantive realization problematic. In this
respect globalization does not represent a unique or even primary constraint upon the liberal democratic polity.

Furthermore, the sceptical position stresses the resilience and adapta-
bility of the nation-state. Sceptics dispute the claim that the modern sovereign nation-state is in decline or that its autonomous capacities are any
more compromised today than in the past (Krasner, 1995; Hirst and
Thompson, 1996). Globalization in this respect is thus not conceived as a
fundamental restriction upon democratic autonomy, nor a fundamental
threat to the liberal democratic state. Since the 'sceptics' reject the proposition that globalization presents a unique challenge to the Westphalian
order they remain deeply unconvinced by the argument that it is also
transforming the conditions under which liberal democracies operate.

The chapters in Part I explore aspects of this debate more fully. In
particular, following the conception of globalization as a multi-
dimensional process, they explore its dynamics in respect of four key
domains: the military; the economic; the environmental; and the social
(gender divisions). In doing so they address two fundamental questions:

1   *To what extent is globalization transforming the conditions under
    which liberal democracy operates?*
2   *How far is globalization associated with new 'limits' to, or alternatively
    'new forms' or expressions of, democratic politics?*

Part I therefore offers a mapping, in each of these key domains, of the
pattern and consequences of globalization for existing forms of liberal
democracy.

1.5   Democratizing global governance and world order

⌊While the principles and practice of liberal democracy find their expression in the institutional structures and domestic politics of the nation-state the global system appears defiantly undemocratic.⌉ Since the sovereign, liberal democratic state is required to obey no other authority than that of its citizens '...the people have acquired with democracy the right to create their own authority, in international relations the right to deny all and every authority' (Mitrany, 1932). It is this contradiction, between democracy within states and the 'state of nature' outside, which is deeply embedded in the Westphalian model of world order.

If the nineteenth and twentieth centuries represent the era of the 'nationalization of democracy', for some the twenty-first century, as the age of globalization, holds out the prospect of the 'globalization of democracy'. For if, as the transformationalists argue, the Westphalian order is undergoing profound change and liberal democracy is thereby being transformed, then the requirement for the democratization of world order becomes more urgent. This is necessarily so since, in order to bring to account those global and transnational forces which presently escape the jurisdiction of territorial liberal democracy, world order and the institutions of global governance themselves have to be democratized. But what precisely do the terms 'global governance' and 'world order' mean?

Global governance (or geo-governance) is a term which refers to those formal and informal mechanisms for managing, regulating, and controlling international activity and international systems of interaction (e.g., the trade system). Whereas in the domestic realm, government defines a system of rule, backed by constitutional authority, and an administrative and enforcement apparatus, in the international realm there exists no formal authority above the individual sovereign states. But although there is no government or formal authority *per se*, in co-operating with each other, and with non-governmental agencies, states do engage in a process of global governance. For instance, through the World Trade Organization (WTO) and the G7, the global trading order is highly regulated or governed. As Rosenau observes, '...it is possible to conceive of governance without government – of regulatory mechanisms in a sphere of activity which function effectively even though they are not endowed with formal authority' (Rosenau, 1992, p.5). Global governance is a process which is closely associated with the reproduction of world order.

Hedley Bull, in his brilliant study of world politics, declares that: 'World order is wider than international order because to give an account of it we have to deal not only with order among states but also with order within the wider world political system of which the states system is only part' (Bull, 1977, p.22). The concept of world order therefore embraces more than simply how the inter-states system is governed but, in addition, includes how human civilization, as a whole, is organized politically and economically. With this distinction in mind any historical world order can be analysed in respect of three constitutive elements:

1   *its 'deep structure'* – defined by its fundamental organizing principles and rules e.g., the Westphalian order of sovereign territorial states versus the medieval order of non-territorial rule (Buzan *et al.*, 1993; Spruyt, 1994);

2   *the primary forms and institutions of global governance* which regulate and reproduce order e.g. hegemonic (great power) governance versus world government;

and

3   *its dominant ideology(ies) and political practices* which legitimize (1) and (2) e.g., nationalism, liberal-capitalism etc.(Cox, 1981).

In the contemporary debate about the democratization of world order these constitutive elements figure prominently in both the descriptive analyses and the normative claims of the major theoretical discourses found in the literature. Broadly speaking there are four dominant traditions of thinking about democracy and world order: realism; liberal-internationalism; radicalism; and cosmopolitanism. Since the notion of democratizing world order is deeply contentious these traditions offer distinctive, although by no means contradictory, reflections upon three key issues, namely:

1   the desirability and feasibility of extending the 'democratic project';

2   the political form which a more democratic world order might take;

and

3   whether existing structures of global and international governance are amenable to democratic practices.

A short resume of each of these traditions follows.

Realism

Hans Morgenthau, one of the founding 'fathers' of the American realist tradition, believed that 'In politics, the nation and not humanity is the ultimate fact' (quoted in Modelski, 1972, p.228). World order, for realists, is synonymous with international order. Despite differing assessments of the significance of contemporary globalization, there is an overwhelming consensus that it does not pose a challenge to the deep structure of international order, namely the modern Westphalian system of sovereign territorial states (Gilpin, 1981; Krasner, 1995). For realists geo-governance is primarily a matter for the great powers (hegemons) of the day. In short the exercise of hegemonic power, whether unilaterally or through political control of the institutions of global governance, such as the UN or the G7, constitutes a core principle of effective geo-governance. This sits uneasily alongside the logic of democracy which, by definition, is subversive of the principle that 'might equals right'. This is not to argue that realism posits or even promotes the idea of a world order devoid of any norms or rules of behaviour. Rather, it is a recognition that the rule of law in an international society of sovereign states is very different from that found within domestic society in which government can enforce the 'law'. This absence of a centralized, legitimate authority defines the 'real' condition of international society. Accordingly, realism exhibits a sceptical attitude towards the idea that world order can be made subject, as in domestic politics, to the rule of law and democratic decision making.

This scepticism is based upon an understanding of the historical 'laws' of international politics which confirm that no powerful state has ever voluntarily relinquished its hegemonic status without some compulsion and none have ever sought a more democratic world order. Furthermore realists link this with a normative objection in that in a volatile and violent world, the nation-state continues to remain the natural 'home' of the 'good (democratic) political community'.

Although there is some acknowledgement that, in the arenas of global governance, governments act as a representative of their peoples this semblance of representative democracy is only weakly observed. Of course this is not to argue that realists *per se* are not committed democrats, on the contrary Morgenthau for example was a firm believer in liberal democracy. Rather the foundation of their scepticism stems from a conviction that democracy, as a system of political rule, is not transferable to the international 'society of states'.

Liberal-internationalism

In contrast to realism, the proponents of liberal-internationalism acknowledge that globalization is bringing into existence a post-Westphalian order in which the institution of sovereign statehood is being reconstituted. In this new context states and societies are becoming increasingly interdependent and therefore less able to manage their own domestic and foreign affairs without resort to international co-operation. Accordingly, there is a proliferation of international institutions, regulatory regimes and informal networks of geo-governance to manage this more interdependent world. In addition, a whole range of actors, from multinational corporations, non-governmental organizations, international pressure groups, individuals, and citizen groups are viewed as important participants in these processes of global governance. World order is therefore conceived more as a polyarchy – a decentralized and pluralistic system – in contradistinction to the realist view of a hierarchy of states. Although the state remains of crucial importance as a key player in world order its formal sovereignty is becoming increasingly fictive.

For liberal-internationalists the growth and expanding jurisdiction of international governance represents a historic (but not necessarily permanent) institutionalization of world politics. Geo-governance, in this account, is much less a product of the exercise of hegemonic power than a product of necessity: for states, in a world of growing interconnectedness, are forced to acquiesce to internationally agreed rules because it is in their immediate self-interest, and the interests of their citizens, to do so. The costs of failing to create some form of global governance often far outweigh the benefits of failing to do so. Moreover, on many global issues (e.g. global warming) there is no alternative to collective action.

Such is the intensity of interdependence and the degree of institutionalization of relations between the Western advanced states that some have suggested that it represents an emerging 'zone of peace' in which inter-state relations are becoming 'domesticated' (Keohane, 1995). This is most apparent in the case of the EU which represents a distinctive model of a law-governed partially democratic 'international polity' (Ruggie, 1993). However, contemporary variants of liberal-internationalism recognize the limits to the democratization of world order in a global system in which states remain of central importance. Thus liberal-internationalism tends to emphasize the gradual reform of global structures of geo-governance to accord with more democratic practices rather than revolutionary change. As Mitrany stated, 'It is not an unprincipled or an unwise compromise to err, if need be, on the side of working democracy [consensus] rather than voting democracy' (Mitrany, 1943, p.132).

Radicalism

Rooted in a Marxist analysis of world politics, radicalism seeks to move beyond appearances to isolate the underlying social forces which shape global destiny. Furthermore, this tradition retains a strong commitment to knowledge as critical enquiry; that is, to knowledge as an instrument of human emancipation from oppression of all kinds.

Radical accounts identify in the post-war phase of globalization the emergence of a new form of capitalism: transnational or global capitalism (Cox, 1996). This new phase of capitalism is characterized by the growing globalization of production, finance and consumption, and the growing polarization between rich and poor in world society and within domestic societies. In this new order the formal institutions and mechanisms of geo-governance primarily reflect the interests of the economic and political elites of the dominant capitalist states and those of global capital. Together with the key officials of international organizations these social forces constitute a 'transnational class' which exerts hegemonic control over the formal institutions and informal networks of geo-governance. States remain important but only to the extent they are the primary 'disciplinary institutions' for global market capitalism.

This new order has significant implications for democracy since global capitalism delivers a powerful assault upon the social, economic and political fabric of liberal democracy. This is compounded by the enormous power of global capital, the growth of transnational elite networks, and the institutions of geo-governance all of which are beyond national democratic control or accountability. As Gill argues this 'new world order' therefore requires '... a double democratization of forms of state and civil society in both global and local dimensions of political life' (Gill, 1995). But the prospects for this kind of radical democratic project, animated as it is by ideas of socialist democracy and direct democracy, appear extremely limited. On the other hand, the political mobilization of the marginalized, alongside the contradictions of economic globalization (such as increasing social polarization and inequality as well as the environmental limits to growth) suggest there are countervailing forces at work which represent an on-going struggle for a more democratic world order (Ekins, 1992).

Cosmopolitanism

In the cosmopolitan account of world order, humanity is viewed both as a 'universal community' – the citizens of a single ecumen – and also as organized political communities, namely states (Brown, 1992, p.24). World order, for cosmopolitans, is therefore an order of both states and peoples. Globalization reinforces this vision in as much as '... in the modern world, communities and solidarities have to be grasped as a dialectical moment, as a sense of participation both in large-scale global processes and in particular communities' (Walker, 1988, p.102). Cosmopolitans therefore identify in the contemporary conjuncture the emergence of a post-Westphalian order in which sovereign statehood and territoriality are loosening their grip on modern political life.

At the same time, however, these global forces escape any form of national democratic control and so undermine the efficacy of liberal democracy. Existing mechanisms of geo-governance too fail to address these 'democratic deficits' because they remain to a great extent captives of the powerful states and other elite interest groups. Global governance therefore operates in a way which is fundamentally at odds with democratic principles and continues to reflect existing asymmetries in global power relations. However, cosmopolitanism identifies in processes of globalization and regionalization a transformative potential. For these processes also stimulate new forms of transnational associations, solidarities, identities, communities and organizations which in combination define an emerging 'global civil society' (Falk, 1994). Accordingly there is a degree of cautious optimism that the political dynamics of the emerging post-Westphalian order mean that the possibilities for substantive democracy have not been entirely extinguished.

Underlying the cosmopolitan account is a powerful normative commitment to democratic forms of global governance; a factor which distinguishes it from liberal-internationalism. But there is also a recognition that democracy needs to be re-thought and reconstructed if it is to sustain its relevance under the conditions of contemporary globalization – a factor which distinguishes it from the radical tradition. In this respect Held proposes the transnationalization of democracy, in that '... the possibility of democracy today must ... be linked to an expanding framework of democratic institutions and procedures – to what I have called the cosmopolitan model of democracy' (Held, 1995, p.267).

These distinctive traditions (see Table 1.1 for a summary) inform the discussion in Part II which explores the prospects for extending democratic principles and practices to the global domain. More specifically, the chapters in Part II build upon the analyses of globalization in Part I to enquire into the changing nature of the contemporary world order and the prospects, under conditions of globalization, for its democratization. Accordingly, Part II explores *two* key questions:

1   *How far are existing structures of global governance responsive to democratic control or reform?*

2   *What are the primary obstacles to the democratization of world order?*

Table 1.1 Democracy and world order: traditions of international thought – a summary

	Realism	Liberal-Internationalism	Radicalism	Cosmopolitanism
Key Actors	States and International Organizations	States and International Organizations	Transnational capital, states, and international economic agencies	States, international organizations, corporations, social movements
Deep Structure of World Order	Westphalian Order	Emerging Post-Westphalian Order	Global capitalism	Post-Westphalian Order
Who governs?	Hegemonic states (Great Powers)	States, international agencies, corporations, NGOs etc.	Transnational capitalist class, elites through states and international agencies	States, peoples, corporate power, international organizations, communities, NGOs etc.
A Democratic World Order?	No – but some representation/accountability through governments	No – requires democratic reform of global governance	No – requires double democratization of local and global life	No – requires transnational democracy
Democratic Heritage	Representative (Protective) Democracy	Liberal-democracy	Direct democracy	Liberal-democracy Direct Democracy Participatory Democracy
Vision of World Order	Hierarchical State-centric	Polyarchy	Rule of capital	Cosmopolitan – states and peoples
Ethic of Global Governance	Power politics	Consensus politics	Humane governance	Cosmopolitan democracy
Globalization – Cause and effect	Politically determined – enhances power of nation-states	Multi-causal process – generates interdependence and 'zones of peace'	Economically driven – subject to contradictions	Multi-causal process with transformative potential

Individual chapters explore these questions in relation to the key structures of global and regional governance including the UN system, multinational corporations, and the EU. In addition, the democratization of global civil society is also analysed through an examination of human rights. Each chapter brings out starkly the tensions which exist between different conceptions of world order reflecting different theoretical and normative traditions. Together they also review the evidence concerning the emergence of a post-Westphalian world order of peoples and states. This discussion lays the empirical and analytical foundations for the concluding chapter of the volume which attempts to draw together the 'stories' of Parts I and II through a critical reflection upon the meaning of democracy, and the prospects for the 'democratic project', under conditions of contemporary globalization.

1.6   Rethinking democracy

In the final quarter of the twentieth century liberal democracy, as a form of political rule, has acquired apparent global primacy. The dramatic events of 1989, the birth of a new democratic South Africa, the return to democracy in Argentina and Chile, and democratic transitions in the Philippines, South Korea and elsewhere, represent historic moments in a remarkable process of global democratization. But the 'triumph' of liberal democracy has coincided with a developing conviction that the global and transnational scale of contemporary economic and social organization presents a unique challenge to the liberal democratic state. Fukuyama's declaration of the victory of liberal democracy, and thus the 'end of history', has proved to be somewhat premature and ill-judged (Fukuyama, 1992). For today the re-thinking and revitalization of democracy have become dominant themes in contemporary political and academic discourse (Held, 1996; Sandel, 1996).

Just as liberal democracy appears to have acquired the status of a political standard for global civilization, the forces of globalization appear to be rendering it obsolete. But is this so? Is globalization bringing about the 'end of liberal democracy' as we have come to understand it? Can the forces of globalization be made subject to democratic control? Is a more democratic world order a utopian ideal? What should democracy mean today? In the following pages the authors begin to address these questions and the prospects for the democratic project into the twenty-first century.

References

Abu-Lughod, J. (1988) *Before European Hegemony*, Oxford, Oxford University Press.

Angell, N. (1933) *The Great Illusion* (originally published in 1909), London, William Heineman.

Barry-Jones, R.J. (1981) 'Concepts and models of change in international relations' in Buzan, B., and Barry-Jones, R.J.(eds), *Change and the Study of International Relations*, London, Frances Pinter.

Bozeman, A. (1984) 'The international order in a multicultural world' in Bull, H. and Watson, A.(eds), *The Expansion of International Society* Oxford, Oxford University Press.

Brown, C. (1992) *International Relations Theory*, New York, Columbia University Press.

Bull, H. (1977) *The Anarchical Society*, London, MacMillan.

Buzan, B., Jones, C., and Little, R. (1993) *The Logic of Anarchy*, New York, Columbia University Press.

Cable, V. (1996) 'Globalization: can the state strike back?', *The World Today* (May), pp.133–7.

Cammilleri, J.A. and Falk, J. (1992) *The End of Sovereignty: The Politics of a Shrinking and Fragmented World*, Aldershot, Edward Elgar.

Chase-Dunn, C. (1986) *Comparing World-Systems*, unpublished paper.

Commission on Global Governance (1995) *Our Global Neighbourhood*, Oxford, Oxford University Press.

Connolly, W. E. (1991) 'Democracy and territoriality', *Millenium* 20(3), pp.463–84.

Cox, R. (1981) 'Social forces, states and world orders', *Millenium* 10(2), pp.126–55.

Cox, R. (1996) 'Globalization, multilaterlism and democracy' in Cox, R. (ed.) *Approaches to World Order*, Cambridge, Cambridge University Press, pp.524–37.

Dahl, R. (1985) *A Preface to Economic Democracy*, Cambridge, Polity Press.

Dahl, R. (1989) *Democracy and It's Critics*, New Haven, Yale University Press.

Ekins, P. (1992) *A New World Order: Grassroots Movements for Global Change*, London, Routledge.

Falk, R. (1994) *On Humane Governance*, Cambridge, Polity Press.

Fernandez-Armesto, F. (1995) *Millenium*, London, Bantam.

Fukuyama, F. (1992) *The End of History and the last Man*, London, Hamish Hamilton.

Giddens, A. (1991) *Modernity and Self-Identity*, Cambridge, Polity Press.

Gill, S. (1995) 'Globalization, market civilization, and disciplinary neoliberalism', *Millenium* 24(3), pp.399–424.

Gilpin, R. (1981) *War and Change in World Politics*, Cambridge, Cambridge University Press.

Gilpin, R. (1987) *The Political Economy of International Relations*, Princeton, Princeton University Press.

Goldblatt, D., Held, D., McGrew, A. and Perraton, J. (forthcoming) *Global Flows, Global Transformations*, Cambridge, Polity Press.

Gordon, D. (1988) 'The global economy: new edifice or crumbling foundations?', *New Left Review* (168): pp.2465.

Held, D. (1995) *Democracy and Global Order*, Cambridge, Polity Press.

Held, D. (1996) *Models of Democracy*, Cambridge, Polity Press.

Hirst, P. and Thompson, G. (1996) *Globalization in Question*, Cambridge, Polity Press.

Holsti, K.J. (1991) *Peace and War: armed conflicts and international order 1648–1989*, Cambridge, Cambridge University Press.

Huntington, S.P. (1991) *The Third Wave – Democratization in the Late Twentieth Century*, Norman, University of Oklahoma Press.

Hurrell, A. and Woods, N. (1995) 'Globalization and Inequality', *Millenium* 24(3) pp.447–70.

Johnston, R.J., Taylor, P.J. and Watts, M.J. (eds) (1995) *Geographies of Global Change*, Oxford, Blackwell.

Keohane, R. (1995) 'Hobbes dilemma and institutional change in world politics: sovereignty in international society' in Holm, H.H. and Sorensen, G.(eds), *Whose World Order?*, Boulder Col., Westview Press, pp.165–86.

Krasner, S. (1993) 'Economic interdependence and independent statehood' in Jackson, R.H. and James, A. (eds), *States in a Changing World*, Oxford, Oxford University Press, pp.301–22.

Krasner, S. (1995) 'Compromising Westphalia', *International Security*, 20(3), pp.115–51.

Krause, K. (1992) *Arms and the State – Patterns of Military Production and Trade*, Cambridge, Cambridge University Press.

Linklater, A. and MacMillan, J. (1995) 'Boundaries in question' in MacMillan, J. and Linklater, A. (eds) *Boundaries in Question*, London, Frances Pinter, pp.1–16.

Mann, M. (1986) *The Sources of Social Power Vol.1*, Cambridge, Cambridge University Press.

Mitrany, D. (1932) 'The progress of international government' in Taylor, P. (ed.)

Mitrany, D. (1943) 'A working peace system' in Taylor, P. (ed.).

Modelski, G. (1972) *Principles of World Politics*, New York, Free Press.

Morgenthau, H. (1967) *Politics Among Nations*, New York, A.Knopf.

Murphy, A. B. (1996) 'The sovereign state system as political territorial ideal: historical and contemporary considerations' in Biersteker, T. J. and Weber, C. (eds), *State Sovereignty as Social Construct*, Cambridge, Cambridge University Press, pp.81–121.

Nierop, T. (1994) *Systems and Regions in Global Politics*, London, John Wiley.

Osiander, A. (1994) *The States System of Europe*, 1640–1990, Oxford, Clarendon Press.

Potter, D., Goldblatt, D., Kiloh, M. and Lewis, P. (eds) (1997) *Democratization*, Cambridge, Polity Press.

Rosenau, J. (1990) *Turbulence in World Politics*. Brighton, Harvester Wheatsheaf.

Rosenau, J. (1992) 'Governance, order and change in world politics' in Rosenau, J. and Czempiel, E-O (eds), *Governance without Government: Order and Change in World Politics*, Cambridge, Cambridge University Press.

Ruggie, J. (1993) 'Territoriality and beyond', *International Organization*, 41(1), pp.139–74.

Sandel, M. (1996) *Democracy's Discontent*, Cambridge Mass., Harvard.

Spruyt, H. (1994) *The Sovereign State and its Competitors*, Princeton, Princeton University Press.

Taylor, P. (ed.) (1975) *A Functional Theory of Politics*, London, LSE/Martin Robertson.

Walker, R. B. J. (1988) *One World, Many Worlds: Struggles for a Just World Peace*, Boulder Col., Lynne Reinner.

Wapner, P. (1995) 'Politics beyond the state', *World Politics*, vol.47, April, pp.311–40.

Watson, A. (1992) *The Evolution of International Society*, London, Routledge.

Zacher, M. (1992) 'The decaying pillars of the Westphalian temple' in Rosenau, J.N. and Czempiel, O.E. (eds), *Governance without Government*, Cambridge, Cambridge University Press.

PART I
Global transformations

Introduction

Anthony McGrew

Globalization, as discussed in Chapter 1, refers to the changing spatial scale of modern social life. It is a historical process which denotes a shift towards inter-continental or inter-regional patterns and forms of social organization. It is also a multi-dimensional process inasmuch as it finds expression in all the key domains of social activity, from the economic to the political. To understand its implications for liberal democracy it is therefore necessary to separate analytically the process of globalization into its constituent elements. Accordingly the four chapters in Part I explore the dynamics of globalization in respect of four key domains, or clusters, of power relations: the military; the economic; the environmental; and the social (gender). Each chapter is concerned especially with the consequences of globalization for liberal democracy. In particular each chapter addresses these two fundamental questions:

1   To what extent is globalization transforming the conditions under which liberal democracies operate?

2   How far is globalization associated with new 'limits' to, or alternatively 'new forms' or expressions of, democratic politics?

Taken together, the chapters deliver a cogent assessment of the contemporary condition of liberal democracy in the context of powerful globalizing imperatives.

CHAPTER **2**

Globalization and post-military democracy

Martin Shaw

Introduction

Everyday political discussion provides us with contradictory linkages between military power and liberal democracy. Military force, we are told by politicians and media, exists in democratic countries to defend democratic institutions and 'ways of life'. It is also widely agreed, however, that under certain conditions military power can threaten democracy. Thus military regimes and other governments for which military power is a major means of rule are seen as anti-democratic. Many critical writers take this case further and see military power as a threat to democracy even in liberal-democratic states.

The tension between military power and liberal democracy is certainly deep-rooted. The *raison d'être* of military institutions is force, indeed physical coercion, whereas liberal democracy in all its forms is constituted by debate and common decision making. Military power is organized, according to theorists of war like Clausewitz (1831), so that one group may impose its will violently on another. War, he wrote, is 'the continuation of policy by other means'. The important part of this phrase is the reference to 'other means'. Clausewitz makes it clear that war is about the destruction of the enemy's will to resist. While this might fit with authoritarian politics, it is *prima facie* incompatible with the notion of democratic relationships between two parties.

Because military power is organized around the single aim of using superior force to destroy an enemy's will, it is typically highly centralized, hierarchical and monolithic. Liberal democracy, on the other hand, involves the expression of diverse views and implies some degree of decentralization, equality and pluralism. Some radicals have argued that it is possible to have democratic forms of military power, and this has been put into practice in a few revolutionary situations – the Republican militia of the Spanish Civil War, for example. There have also been socialist attempts to theorize centralist forms of democracy – such as Lenin's 'democratic centralism'. Historically, however, neither of these reconciliations has been very successful. Democratic militia have been seen as militarily ineffectual and have tended to be replaced by centralized standing armies. Democratic centralism has been seen as undemocratic and has tended in practice towards bureaucratic centralism.

Despite these contradictions, modern history is littered with cases of wars fought by liberal-democratic states in the name of democracy. The solution to this paradox is simple – and essential to the discussion in this chapter. Liberal democracy is generally understood in modern society to refer to political institutions *within* a single nation-state. War and military power, on the other hand, are understood chiefly as means of resolving disputes *between* two or more nation-states. The tension between war and liberal democracy has been reconciled by the convention of regarding inter- and intra-state relations as two distinct spheres governed by very different rules.

This convention is expressed in the idea of the sovereign nation-state. It is fundamental to the way we usually think about politics and to what is defined as legitimate. Violence against liberal-democratic states, or against other individuals in defiance of the norms of the democratic state, is illegitimate. Democratic governments are expected to manage disputes within the nation-state peacefully and to resort to relatively minimal force only as a last resort. But the same governments may organize violence on an enormous scale in order to prosecute inter-state conflict. Individual behaviour is also governed by these divergent norms. To kill an individual in civilian society will earn one a life (or even a death) sentence in most liberal-democratic states. To kill while under military orders may earn one the state's highest decorations.

The importance of this distinction has been underlined by social theories of the state. The state, according to Weber, is an organization claiming a monopoly of legitimate violence within a given territory (see Mann, 1993, p.55). The implications of this monopoly are twofold. On the one hand, the population within the territory is subjugated by the state, so that relations between the state itself, social groups and individuals are generally pacified. On the other hand, the state may mobilize society for violent conflicts with other states. Giddens (1985) argues that in modern society, nation-states have achieved high levels of pacification of their populations. They manage society by the non-violent means of 'surveillance' (constant monitoring and administration). The violence 'extruded' from society is mobilized by states for inter-state conflicts, which have therefore become more violent as society has become pacified.

This divergence between the two sides of state power applies to liberal-democratic as well as non-democratic states, but many have argued for an important qualification. Liberal democracies, it is contended, fight wars mainly with non-democracies; it is the aggressive actions of authoritarian states which provoke democracies to fight. Relations between liberal-democratic states are largely or (in strong versions) universally peaceful: democracies do not go to war with each other. We shall consider some contemporary problems of this argument below.

The argument of the chapter is that, in the second half and especially at the end of the twentieth century, the relationships between liberal democracy and military power which were forged in the period of total war have been transformed. The chapter first explores the contradictory relationships between liberal democracy and military power in the nineteenth- and twentieth-century nation-state. It looks at how democracy and citizenship have been defined in the context of military and wartime service; how war paradoxically stimulated the extension of democracy; and how liberal democracy was redefined in military conflict with other political forms.

The chapter then examines the changes that have taken place. It argues that militarist definitions of liberal democracy, also paradoxically, declined during the Cold War, and that with globalization there is a fundamental shift in the relationships between state and society which is breaking down the classic division between the domestic and international spheres. The later sections of the chapter examine first the processes of change and second the implications for our understanding of liberal democracy.

─────────────── *Summary of the Introduction* ───────────────

- The tension between military power and liberal democracy is deep-rooted, reflecting their different purposes and organizational imperatives.

- Despite this, liberal-democratic states frequently fight wars in the name of democracy. The explanation is that democracy is generally understood to refer to political institutions within a single nation-state, war and military power as means of resolving disputes between two or more nation-states.

- This convention reflects the nation-state's monopoly of violence, as defined by social theory, but this may no longer hold with globalization.

2.1 Liberal democracy and militarism

In the Introduction, I suggested that liberal democracy and military power were in tension with each other, but that this tension had been resolved in practice through the division between internal and external political spheres. In this section, I go further, and argue that despite the division of the two spheres, they do have important effects on each other. The division is not as clear-cut in social reality as it appears in political theory, and sociological theories have explored a number of linkages. In particular I suggest, following the literature concerning the effects of war on society, that the forms of democracy which have developed in modern society have been strongly conditioned by the character of military power. Modern democracy, I argue, has been to a considerable extent military democracy.

The nineteenth-century model

The connection between democracy and military power is not uniquely modern. Democracy has been linked to war since its origins in ancient Athens, where citizens were also warriors, citizenship implying the duty to fight (Vasillopolus, 1995). But it is in modern times that this connection has been most strongly developed. War played a large part in the origins of the modern liberal-democratic nation-state. In the American and French revolutions, citizens were also expected to fight for their country: the democratic revolution was the struggle of the people in arms against the revolution's foreign enemies. This was the origin of a relationship between democracy and militarism which has been central to modern politics.

From these seminal revolutions came an equation of democratic citizenship and military service which has been at the core of the modern, late nineteenth- and twentieth-century liberal nation-state. In the militia of revolutionary America and the armies of revolutionary France, the *duty* of military service was the corollary of the *rights* of citizenship. Although compulsion had been widely used in military recruitment throughout the ages, the first modern form of conscription, the *levée en masse*, was instituted when revolutionary France was threatened by the armies of Europe's monarchies. The principle of the *levée* was that those who enjoyed the rights of citizens in the republic also had a duty to defend the state when it was threatened.

This equation of the rights and duties of citizenship was standardized in later nineteenth-century European versions of the nation-state. Authoritarian monarchies as well as democratic republics expected military service, not just in crises but as a regular requirement of all male citizens. The Prussian monarchy instituted a system in which all young men underwent a period of military training, and then remained liable to call-up in the event of war throughout their adult lives. This system enabled the state, while maintaining a moderately-sized standing army, to call on virtually its entire adult male population in the event of war. Together with the industrialization of warfare, which took place during the second half of the nineteenth century, mass conscript armies became unprecedentedly powerful armed forces (MacNeill, 1982). But even in Prussia and Imperial Germany the state was obliged to concede some of the rudiments of democracy in return for this mass participation in war. In authoritarian states, however, citizenship rights were more circumscribed than in the more democratic republics, showing that the citizenship equation could be tilted in an authoritarian direction.

This Prussian system became the standard Continental way of organizing military power. It was linked to an idea of the nation-state in which universal military service was regarded as a school of the nation, socializing young men into national values. It must be remembered that most populations remained overwhelmingly agricultural and rural into the twentieth century. There were wide variations between classes and regions. National identity could not be taken for granted: it had to be forged. This was the period in which national traditions – more imperial and monarchical than they were democratic – were invented in many Western countries (Hobsbawm and Ranger, 1983). Military traditions were an important component, often cultivated by governments.

Even in more democratic states, armies remained internally authoritarian institutions. The connection with democracy remained tenuous: the institution of conscription was to play the same nation-integrating role in totalitarian states like Nazi Germany and Stalinist Russia. In fact some of the most liberal states, such as Britain, the British dominions and the USA – which were not Continental European powers – did not enforce conscription in the early twentieth century. But even in these states a military-patriotic culture was developing in the decades before 1914, and the heyday of classical militarism and conscription was to come during the world wars (MacKenzie, 1984).

The First World War and the inter-war crisis of democracy

The first half of the twentieth century saw a many-sided transformation of the quasi-democratic, militarist nation-state bequeathed from the nineteenth. On one level, the always tenuous links between democracy and military power were attenuated still further in the First World War. Although represented ideologically in Britain and America as a struggle of democracy *against* militarism, there was little that was democratic on any side about a war in which everywhere state power was centralized, armies authoritarian and opposition widely suppressed. Even liberal-democratic states conceded few rights to soldiers: Britain and France, for example, shot deserters and mutineers and imprisoned conscientious objectors and anti-war activists. It was the growth of repressive state power in this unprecedented war which provided the main support for Lenin's argument, in his pamphlet *The State and Revolution* (1917), that the capitalist state could not be peacefully reformed by democratic means but only overthrown by violence.

Recruits in 1914: millions of male workers left the industrial work-force to be replaced by new reserves of labour

The effects of the war on democracy were not, however, all so one-sided. Society became the 'home front'. The labour of munitions, transport and even farm workers was recognized as being important alongside that of soldiers and sailors. With millions of male workers siphoned off into armies, reserves of labour in the countryside, among women and minority ethnic groups, were drawn into participation in the industrial work-force. War-stimulated full employment gave labour a greatly improved bargaining position. Although the situation changed after the war – when recession quickly pushed women workers back into the home and men returning from the trenches into the dole queues – there were lasting democratic effects. Social democratic parties became serious contenders for national office in many countries and political rights were extended. In Britain, although the unions were badly weakened by the defeats which culminated in the 1926 General Strike, Labour replaced the Liberals as the Conservatives' rival. Female suffrage, for which women had struggled unsuccessfully before the war, was now conceded: to women over 30 in 1918 and all women over 21 in 1929.

The contradictions of mass militarism also gave rise to a new direct revolutionary democracy, the workers' and soldiers' councils (in Russian, *soviets*) which flourished briefly in several countries at the end of the war. These institutions were seen by Marxists like Lenin as historic alternatives to parliamentary institutions exposed as 'bankrupt' by the war. But whereas liberal democracy was in fact extended in many countries in the war's aftermath, the workers' council model was quickly extinguished by a new revolutionary form of militarism. The Russian civil war provoked by revolutionary successes led to the militarization of the revolution and largely destroyed its democratic element. The new Red Army was highly centralized, and during 'War Communism' (1918–21) was seen as a model for a centralized command model of socialism. This laid the foundations for Stalin's extreme statist, nationalist version of communism, in which democracy was equated with the rule of the proletarian party and its leader.

While overall liberal democracy was much stronger than this fledgling form of direct democracy, parliamentary institutions and liberal freedoms were also overthrown in a number of European countries after the First World War. The national humiliation of defeated states led to the emergence of fascism, a statist, nationalist form of right-wing politics openly denying democracy while claiming legitimacy through representing the nation. Fascism was intrinsically high-militarist, glorifying war as the nation's highest activity. The comradeship of the trenches, in which Hitler had served, was a model for the Nazi movement. Authoritarian military command systems were replicated in the political and economic systems of both fascism and Stalinism, which drew on the totalizing violence and experience of total war in 1914–18.

The First World War was associated, therefore, with a major crisis of the developing system of liberal democracy. While important advances in the liberal-democratic state resulted from war conditions and an alternative democratic model also briefly emerged, new, super-authoritarian (totalitarian) regimes destroyed all democratic forms in major states like Russia, Germany and Italy. Marxist theories explain these developments as a result of the crisis of capitalism and the failure of world revolution. They can also be seen, however, in terms of the 'dialectics of war', in which war-mobilization creates contradictions which give rise to new political conflicts, which in turn feed further wars (Shaw, 1988). Indeed the Marxist writer, Sweezy (1968), analyses fascism as a result of 'war-damaged capitalism'. It was the destabilizing effects of war which heightened the tension between democratic and anti-democratic forces in society.

The Second World War synthesis of democracy and militarism

The crisis of liberal democracy in turn polarized international conflict so that the Second World War, like the First, a struggle for world domination between the great powers, appeared also as a contest between democracy, fascism and communism. In order to mobilize for this, liberal democracy was also redefined and extended. In America, Britain and the British dominions, democracy became essential to the definition of nationalism: fighting for one's nation and fighting for democracy became the same thing.

The Western democracies adopted the conscription system long standard in Continental Europe. While in the Continental superstates, Nazi Germany and the Soviet Union, military duties were de-linked from citizenship rights, in Britain and America the connection was renewed as social groups asserted their expectations of new recognition in return for wartime contributions. Black Americans fought across the world and expected equality and desegregation in return. Women, even more than in 1914–18, filled key economic roles and expected political and social recognition. Labour movements were essential to the delivery of war production and political cohesion and expected not just better wages and bargaining rights but social reform too.

These expectations were part of the general wartime ideological climate and (to varying degrees) informed a growing political consensus in favour of wider and deeper democracy. War-mobilization gave a new significance to *social* definitions of democracy in liberal states. Economic and social as well as political rights were seen as corollaries of military and wartime partici-pation. In the aftermath of war, the role of the state was expanded in all societies and economies, and the idea that the state should regulate social well-being became widespread. Most liberal states (but not the USA) be-came not just liberal democracies, but to some extent social democracies as well. In European states in the 1950s, an updated model of democratic citizenship was widely accepted in which rights to employment, housing, education and welfare were seen as the other side of universal (male) military service.

Britain is perhaps the strongest example of this 'military-democratic' state as a variant of the liberal-democratic model (Shaw, 1987). It had never had conscription (except briefly in the First World War); its continuation in peacetime after 1945 was unprecedented. Interwar Conservative govern-ments had also strongly resisted economic intervention and welfare measures. In the siege atmosphere of the early 1940s, however, the Conservative-led coalition began the process which led to the 'Keynesian welfare-state' consensus of the late 1940s and 1950s. Labour had never had a parliamentary majority; in 1945 it won a landslide victory and consolidated a position as serious contender for power for the rest of the century. These changes were not inevitable; they can be traced to the wartime political upheaval, arguably the most important swing to the left in twentieth-century Britain (Addison, 1975).

The transformation of liberal democracies into interventionist 'welfare states' was not everywhere the direct result of wartime participation: Britain is an extreme case. Most West European welfare states were created during the post-war boom of the 1950s rather than in the immediate aftermath of war. The trend towards Keynesian welfare-statism in the restored post-1945 liberal democracies was strongly influenced, however, by the enhanced role of states in both wartime destruction and post-war reconstruction. In this sense, the social democratic-leaning liberal democracies of the half century after 1945 were all 'military-democratic' states.

Summary of Section 2.1 ─────────

- The forms of democracy which have developed in modern society have been strongly conditioned by the experience of war and the character of military power.

- Citizenship in the Continental European model of the liberal-democratic nation-state was based on an equation between political rights and military duties.

- While the First World War led to a crisis of democracy, the Second World War consolidated a stronger version of the democratic equation, between universal military participation and socio-economic as well as political rights, leading to a form of 'military democracy' in Western liberal-democratic states.

2.2 Globalization and post-military democracy

In the later decades of the twentieth century, the mid-century union of democracy and military power has been fundamentally transformed. On the surface, the Cold War system appeared to maintain the link. 'Western democracy', the battle-cry of 1939–45, was also the watchword in a new ideological struggle against 'totalitarian' communism for four decades between the late 1940s and 1989. Liberal democracy appeared to left-wing critics to be thoroughly militarized, its democratic character compromised by the secretive and unaccountable build-up of nuclear weapons and its association with authoritarian anti-communist regimes in the so-called Third World.

The character of the world which was emerging within the Cold War framework was, however, very different from the world of militarist nation-states which had dominated the first half of the century. The paradox of the Cold War was that while it utilized the old forms of the liberal-democratic nation-state, within its structure radically different social relations were developing. In particular, the key convention, the division between intra- and inter-state politics (which was discussed in the Introduction to this chapter) began to break down. This section deals with the two key changes of the period since 1945 – the development of liberal democracy in a global context because of the military unification of the West, and the de-linking of democracy from military participation – and shows how the end of the Cold War has accelerated these changes.

The liberal-democratic nation-state in the context of blocs

The Second World War was a key transition in the state system, the climax of rivalries which had built up between major nation-states over the previous century. The war was also the high point of states' dominance in society: never before or since have these institutions possessed the same ability to command people and resources, moulding social relations to their ends. During the war years, it appeared that society could only be conceived of in sealed parcels controlled by nation-states. No wonder, then, that the post-war world was seen by the controllers of states in statist terms. But no sooner had this paradigm of nation-statism been realized than it began to dissolve.

This process actually began during the war. Most European nation-states were abolished by conquest during the fighting. Around 1945, they were dutifully restored, but in most cases as shadows of their previous forms. The two main defeated powers, Germany and Japan, were recreated (the former in fragments) only as licensed subordinates of the major victors. Most West European states were restored only by permission and with the financial backing of the USA, and East European states as 'satellites' of the Soviet Union. Even Britain, one of the wartime great powers, which attempted to maintain this status in the post-war world, was in reality dependent on the USA. Outside Europe, as the old empires fell apart, around a hundred new 'nation-states' were created in the quarter-century after 1945, but many of the 'nations' were insecurely founded and the states' control over territory was weak.

Alongside this fragmentation of the state system were dynamic integrating processes, originating in the West, which were reducing the significance of nation-states. The East–West conflict inhibited the re-emergence of intra-West conflicts and fostered the interdependence of Western states under US leadership. In this context, although all Western states recovered the trappings of statehood, only the USA was still a world power. The UK and France still had some capacity and scope for significant independent military action, but the limits of this became apparent in the Anglo-French Suez fiasco of 1956. (The Falklands War of 1982, the UK's only fully-fledged inter-state war since 1945, seems to be the exception that proves the rule, and even this depended partly on US support.) The military power of major states was internationalized, as were (within Europe at least) some areas of military production. Markets in arms grew, not just within alliances but on a global scale, and the great powers (USA, USSR, France, UK) became the major suppliers of a much-expanded world arms trade.

The military unification of the West facilitated other changes which further reduced the role of the nation-state. At the end of the Second World War, Western leaders envisaged a new world order which would overcome the weaknesses of the economic system between the wars. Although the more grandiose hopes were not realized, military unity opened up a combined Western economic space, including most of what became known as the Third World. Within this space, from which only the communist and a few other states were partially separated, international trade and investment grew at unprecedented rates. Western states also evolved new international institutions, such as the European Economic Community (now the European Union) and Group of Seven (G7) major states, in addition to the earlier Organization for Economic Cooperation and Development, General Agreement on Tariffs and Trade (now the World Trade Organization), International Monetary Fund and World Bank, through which to regulate the world economy.

During the Cold War, these Western institutions were balanced symmetrically by the institutions of the Soviet bloc, notably the Warsaw Pact and Comecon. Militarily the East provided the West with real, if generally inferior, competition but economically it was always overwhelmingly weaker. The spectre of communism served better as a catalyst for Western unity than as an alternative model of global organization. By the 1980s the failures of communist economic and political institutions were apparent, and in 1989–91 they collapsed across the Soviet and East European area. The surviving communist states, notably China, were already adapting to the Western-dominated world market economy.

The consolidation of this global economic space, depending on the framework of Western military unity, weakened the autonomy of even the strongest nation-states and thereby brought into question the character of the liberal-democratic nation-state as it had emerged from the Second World War. Within an increasingly internationalized West, national identities remained significant. But nations which were formerly pitted against each other were now allies, whose military activity was mediated through alliances (principally the North Atlantic Treaty Organization). Nationalisms remained the symbolic building blocks of the ideological struggle of the two blocs, but divorced from the old context of nation-state military rivalry, they diminished in strength. The paradox was that liberal democracy was the banner under which both the Cold War and the expansion of the world market were carried out. But because both these developments undermined the autonomous nation-state, in terms of which democracy had been ever more closely defined, classical liberal-democratic thinking was made problematic. The new social-democratic 'settlement' of the late 1940s and early 1950s was particularly threatened. Individual Western democracies could not operate as closed societies, operating national social-democratic policies, when their economics, cultures and even political systems were increasingly part of a global flux.

The Cold War dissolution of democratic militarism

There were also specifically military reasons why post-1945 democratic forms weakened. Military technology and organization, demanding armies and war industries of millions of men and women, had provided the impetus for the new developments in liberal democracy which had emerged from the Second World War. For the first decade after 1945, this model of mass participatory militarism remained dominant. But the war had given rise to new technological spectres: its closing moments had seen the awesome power of the American atomic bomb, while Germany had experimented with rocket technology. By the late 1950s, the USA and USSR had developed large arsenals of nuclear weapons and long-range delivery systems; the arms race was under way. Britain, France and China followed.

The manifest democratic implications of nuclear arms racing involved the centralization of political power. C. Wright Mills (1956, 1959) argued that there was the consolidation of a 'power elite' in the American superpower, monopolizing the 'highest levels' of international military decision making and unaccountable to democratic publics. Even more, the people of other nation-states within the Western alliance effectively lost the possibility of democratic control over their survival since, whatever their general influence on NATO policy, in any major international crisis when a quick decision on the use of the bomb was required, American leaders would prevail.

There were also structural implications for the 'military-democratic' or, as some described it, 'warfare-welfare' state which had emerged from the world war. These implications were also somewhat paradoxical: while at the highest levels the Western system of power appeared to be highly militarized, at other levels forms of demilitarization were taking place. The structural links of democratic forms with the system of military mobilization – which had animated the development of democracy throughout the century and a half up to 1945 – were dissolving. Just when mass military participation appeared to guarantee a strong social-democratic content to the development of liberal democracy, military participation levels declined across the Western world. In the early 1950s, virtually all adult males had military experience, many in war and others in relatively long periods of military service. By the mid 1990s, only small minorities of men had actually been involved in war and a large majority of young men in North America and Britain had no military experience at all.

Theories of the social consequences of military and wartime participation had been developed in the aftermath of the world war. The sociologist Andreski (1954) argued that the extent of the social change caused by war was related to the 'military participation ratio', i.e. the proportion of the population mobilized into the armed forces. The social historian Marwick (1974) modified and extended this claim by arguing that change was related to 'wartime participation', i.e. the proportion of the population, military *and* civilian, participating in the war effort as a whole. For such writers, total war represented war in which, for all its destructive effects, there was a dialectic of democratic advance. Mann (1988) filled out this perspective by describing the era of the world wars as that of 'citizen wars'.

The nuclear wars which the major states were preparing to fight were the opposite of citizen wars. The potential war changed from an all-out struggle of mass armies and national economies to an instantaneous exchange of nuclear missiles. The one required millions of semi-skilled soldiers, operating for the most part fairly simple machines, and millions of workers to supply them. The other required relatively small but highly skilled military and civilian work-forces developing highly complex and sophisticated weapon systems. The former implied mass mobilization, high military participation and militarization, the latter mass demobilization, a drastic decline in military (and wartime) participation and demilitarization. Within liberal democracies, the era of total war had heightened the relationship between military duty and social and political rights in citizenship. The era of nuclear war broke this connection – thus demilitarizing tendencies are not novel features of the post-Cold War years, but have their roots in the Cold War itself.

Britain was the first country to draw the logical military conclusion and abandon the conscription it had introduced during the Second World War and maintained in the early Cold War years. In 1957, the Conservative government decided to phase out national service (it ended in 1963) and rely chiefly on nuclear weapons for the country's defence. Britain had, of course, unlike most Continental states, no historic tradition of universal male military service. But in the 1970s, the USA followed suit and switched to 'all-volunteer' forces. By the 1980s, all the major Western states 'offshore' from continental Eurasia – including Japan, Canada and Australia – had non-conscript militaries. All the Continental states – Western and neutral as well as communist – retained conscription. Nevertheless, even in these states conscripts declined in importance compared to professional soldiers and weapons systems (van Doorn, 1975; Shaw, 1991, Chapter 3).

The democratic implication of this military change was profound, if not widely understood. States which no longer required their citizenry's military participation no longer needed to concede such substantial economic and social participation. Nowhere was the transformation more dramatic than in Britain, where the equation of rights and military duty was peculiarly the product of the Second World War. Within Conservative politics, which had incorporated this formula only under the exceptional circumstances of war, the shift to the nuclear-armed state undermined the rationale for the social-democratic settlement of 1945. From the 1960s onwards, Conservative politicians struggled to escape from it, but only achieved significant movement after Margaret Thatcher's election in 1979. 'Thatcherism' ruptured the linkages between the military and social sides of the settlement, attempting to replace the latter by the market. Although in the Falklands War of 1982, Thatcherite rhetoric imitated British Second World War ideology, the substantive link between military participation and democracy was missing (Shaw, 1987). The war was fought by small professional forces and its revived patriotism was quickly harnessed for anti-democratic purposes against the 'enemy within' (notably, the miners' union in the strike of 1984–85).

Elsewhere, the shift was more gradual, but none the less pronounced. Since the military-democratic connection was in many cases an old one, hallowed by national traditions, it was not until the 1980s that the challenge to it became explicit, and it was only after the end of the Cold War that the first states in Continental Europe – Belgium, the Netherlands and France – actually abandoned conscription (Shaw, 1991, Chapter 5). But even where conscription remains in Western states its significance has been greatly reduced. Conscientious objection has been secularized and made much easier: more than one third of young German men opt for *Zivildienst* ('civilian service') although this form of national service lasts longer than military service (Chambers and Moskos, 1993). Conscripts are generally no longer sent into combat situations.

Outside the West, the duty of military service has hardly been identified with democratic citizenship: modern authoritarian regimes, like classic totalitarianisms, have often relied on conscript armies. In the old Soviet Union and Eastern Europe, universal military service was identified with the communist state, and the movement to liberal democracy and the nation-state initially brought a challenge to the system. Young men, especially in nationally oppressed regions like the Baltic states, refused to serve in the Red Army. Even in post-communist states, military service remains highly unpopular, and although it is often argued that these states cannot afford professional militaries, Boris Yeltsin decreed the abolition of conscription during his 1996 re-election campaign (although it remains to be seen if and how this change will be implemented). Only in zones of war, such as former Yugoslavia, has the conscript system actually been reinforced, but with considerable resistance from many young men. Although states like Serbia and Croatia go through the motions of representative democracy, they (and their statelets in Bosnia) have offered caricatures of the classical military-democratic nation-state.

─────────────── *Summary of Section 2.2* ───────────────

- In the post-1945 world, the connection between military participation and liberal democracy has been eroded.

- The growth of a global economy and society, within the framework of Western military unity in the Cold War, transformed the nation-state context of liberal democracy and especially its 'military-democratic' form.

- The shift towards nuclear weapons and other military high-technology involved social demilitarization, the progressive abandonment of universal male military service and undermining of the 'military-democratic' consensus.

2.3 Implications for liberal democracy

The end of the Cold War has brought out four major sets of questions about liberal democracy which were implicit in the developments of the last half century, but which were difficult to pose directly while the Cold War lasted. First, there is the issue of how to re-found liberal democracy when the old national equations of military duty and political (and social) rights no longer work. Second, there is the question of how to redefine the relationship between military power and liberal democracy in the new global context of relations between states. Third, there is the issue of democratization of the armed forces themselves. Finally, there is the democratization of security politics. I shall look at each of these issues in turn. These questions are raised principally in the Western context, but they have some relevance to other world-regions.

Liberal democracy in a context of global pacification

It may seem strange to talk about the post-Cold War era as one of peace: since 1989 Europe and the former Soviet area have seen their first major wars since 1945, while in the Middle East, Africa, Asia and Central America wars continue as they have done throughout the last half century. The defining characteristic of the new period, however, is that major wars between major powers, which have become increasingly unlikely ever since nuclear weapons first implied mutual destruction, are now virtually excluded by international consensus. Whatever the outcomes of the ongoing political crises in Russia and China in the 1990s, these states' weakness compared to the West are manifest facts. It seems likely – although it is not certain – that their rulers will continue to seek some sort of accommodation with the Western-dominated systems of global economic and political power rather than to revive overt military confrontation.

The consequence of this situation is extensive demilitarization in the North (although not in Asia-Pacific). In most Northern states military expenditures have declined as proportions of total government expenditures and on a world scale there has actually been an absolute decline in military spending. Military production has also declined, although there is a sharp competitive struggle for markets in most kinds of weaponry. Armies throughout the North, already reduced during the Cold War, are being radically 'downsized'.

Mass conscript armies are unlikely to be needed again in the North – indeed even the nuclear arsenals which partially replaced them during the Cold War are also largely redundant. Military duty can no longer be conceptualized as a major component of citizenship. The majority of male citizens in the West will never serve in the armed forces, although in the former communist states conscript armies remain as the costs of going all-professional are too high. Women, who were second-class citizens as long as military service was of central importance, are now demanding full equality, but it would be anachronistic to incorporate them into military service systems. Recognizing this fact, however, undermines the remaining claims of compulsory military systems: in an age of sex equality, why should men serve if women don't?

To remove national military duty from the classical Western definition of citizenship leaves only the 'rights' side. From many sides comes a critique of an individualistic society in which people are only concerned with entitlements, at the expense of the contributions which they can make. The question arises of whether anything positive can be salvaged from the declining force of national military service, to reconceptualize individuals' duties to society? The German system of *Zivildienst* effectively supports a large part of the social work system, but this is an unintended consequence of the growth of conscientious objection to military service. The situation remains anomalous in that civilian service is not treated equally to military service, and even more that it applies only to men.

In the USA, military sociologists have been in the forefront of advocating a system of voluntary civilian national service, a variant of which was introduced by the Clinton administration (Moskos, 1988). Such schemes only begin to address the problem of the individual's obligation to society and how it should be conceptualized. The new US scheme – like the Peace Corps of the Kennedy era – includes options for overseas service, and so raises the issue of to what level of society, in an era of globalization, individuals should contribute. Social duties have been so identified with national duties that it is difficult to reconceptualize them.

A large pacified space has opened up at the centre of the global system, including not only North America, Western Europe, Japan and Australasia but also (albeit more problematically) parts of Central Europe, Latin America and Asia, and South Africa. Russia and other post Soviet states also aspire to participation. Especially within the Western core, older conceptions of democracy and citizenship linked to the nation-state are being challenged (Held, 1995). Increasingly global systems of economy, communication and culture make it easier to perceive a global society coming into existence. The collapse of the armed barriers, first between nation states and then between Cold War blocs, is one of the most potent signs of this new global society. Individuals' identities are no longer marked overwhelmingly by nationality, as in the late nineteenth and early twentieth centuries. Instead the nation appears as only one, if still in many cases the most important, community to which people belong. Increasingly people, especially in the advanced West, feel their membership of other communities – defined by sex, class, profession and lifestyle as well as ethnicity and religion – to be as important as, or even more important than, their state-defined nationality. These communities are local, transnational and global as well as national and international.

In the past, the nation as a political community was underpinned by the nation as a social and cultural community – even if nations were riven by divisions such as those of class. The changing context in which communities are now conceived raises the question of whether new political communities – local and regional as well as continental and global – can supersede the nation-state. In many parts of the world, global changes are reinforcing nationalism, but in the West especially, people are becoming accustomed to seeing themselves as part of larger political communities. People in Western Europe see themselves increasingly – if still problematically – as citizens of the European Union and more nebulously of 'the West' as a whole, institutionalized in the Atlantic alliance, and of the 'international community', organized however imperfectly around the United Nations. They face the issues of what 'democracy' means in these multiple contexts which have replaced the simple unity of the liberal-democratic nation-state.

What this discussion has tried to emphasize is that these transformations, which are discussed more fully elsewhere in Part I of this book, result partly from the changes in the world military situation since 1945 and, especially, 1989. However much they can be explained by wider socio-economic changes, transformations of the conditions of liberal democracy have depended crucially on the military context. The abolition of war, first between Western states and then between the USSR and the West, is a critical factor in the decline of the nation-state and the globalization of the problems of citizenship and democracy. Developing and institutionalizing global democracy demand, in return, that we look at the problems of developing and institutionalizing peace, and at the relations between liberal democracy and military power in the new era.

Institutionalizing a global democratic peace

The peace brought about by the Cold War and the nuclear stalemate was a peace of the superpower elites. Two highly centralized blocs and power systems faced each other with high-technology weapons systems. As Mills argued, this left a limited political role for wider democratic publics, just as it left a smaller role for the military contribution of the majority of society.

With the unravelling of the Cold War, the relationship between liberal democracy and the structure of military power is once again changing. The end of the Cold War has marked the 'triumph' of liberal democracy, as post-communist state elites have been forced to institutionalize electoral democracy and some Western-style freedoms. In Latin America, Asia, the Middle East and Africa, too, democratization has gained momentum; with the end of the Cold War, the USA and Russia have no longer had the same incentive to back authoritarian regimes for geopolitical reasons. (A sign of the change is that in Haiti in 1995 President Clinton intervened to remove a military junta and restore a democratically elected government, in contrast to

US interventions in Latin America during the Cold War which often supported military regimes against democracy.)

The first issue raised by these developments is whether the peaceful relations established among Western nation-states during the Cold War period, and extended to many former Eastern-bloc states with the end of the Cold War, can become a global norm. This is partly a question about how the state system develops and whether the institutionalization of inter-state relations will inhibit wars between states outside the West: we cannot yet answer this conclusively. It is also a question about whether state-fragmentation (in Africa as well as the former communist states), and the 'privatization of violence' to ethnic-nationalist movements and gangs, can be managed and contained. This seems, in the mid 1990s, to be the most intractable problem.

Western states have worked towards a new consensus of resolving international disputes by political rather than military means. Except with Iraq, they have emphasized war-management, negotiation, etc., in an attempt to bring international conflict within 'normal' political processes. But they have put few resources behind this policy, except in one or two situations, and have failed to develop the internationally legitimate institutions needed to enforce it as a general rule.

Moreover, the generalization that liberal democracies do not fight each other has not applied to the new would-be 'democracies' in the ex-Soviet and ex-Yugoslav regions. Leaders in countries like Serbia and Croatia have used nationalism and militarism to win elections and hold on to power and have exploited transnational links with diasporas in Western democracies to finance genocidal expansion. The wars which have broken out have revived older more 'democratic' forms of warfare, based more on manpower and artillery than high technology. These wars have sharply challenged the emergent pacific, globalizing, liberal-democratic post-Cold War consensus.

These problems have underlined the proposition that an effective global democratic order must effectively limit violence. There can be no transnational democracy without pacification. On the one hand, global and regional structures must offer democratic means through which states, groups and national representatives can raise and resolve grievances and disputes without resorting to war. On the other, legitimate global and regional authorities must possess effective means to prevent and control violence.

The experience of the early post-Cold War years is that the world is far from this situation. Global institutions are weak, dominated by the Western powers who nevertheless refuse to resource them adequately, and low in legitimacy among both non-Western states and the people of the world. The United Nations and regional institutions generally lack either the developed political systems to manage conflict short of war, or the military policy and forces necessary to limit wars once they have broken out.

Democratizing military institutions

Despite these failures of world political and military institutions, the role of military power has undergone a major change between the nuclear arms race and the war-management or peace-enforcement agenda which has dominated in the 1990s. Inevitably, the nature of military power has also changed, as armed forces have adapted to new roles. In the context of a democratizing world order, are militaries themselves undergoing democratization? Is there any evidence, in the development of armed forces, that the tension between military power and liberal democracy, which I noted at the beginning of this chapter, is being resolved?

Western forces are still used in classic war situations, and indeed most weaponry and training is devoted to preparing for these even if they are relatively rare. The Gulf War (1991) is a recent example of high-technology firepower used in a fairly conventional inter-state war, to force Iraqi troops out of Kuwait. More common are operations in which armed forces played very limited military roles, protecting convoys, monitoring combatants, and carrying out 'peacekeeping' or 'peace enforcement'. In ex-Yugoslavia, and virtually everywhere else that Western and UN troops have been deployed in the 1990s, activity has been of this limited kind. Air power has been used occasionally against Serbian forces in Bosnia, but with strictly limited objectives, avoiding sustained confrontation. Within the peacekeeping agenda, Western and UN military power has partly moved away from the high-technology fix which characterized the Gulf War.

There are, therefore, processes of transformation at work, even if Western armed forces are still predominantly designed for classic war (and many non-Western forces are still willing to use military power brutally against civilian populations). Military action and organization are increasingly about controlling civilian populations and restricting the actions of combatant groups. Western and UN militaries intervene as mediators in conflicts and operate under the gaze of media, placing a premium on political, management and presentational rather than war-fighting skills.

A multi-national group of UN Military Observers plan patrols in Croatia as part of the UN Protection Force (UNPROFOR), August 1992; UNPROFOR largely failed, however, to protect the civilian population

The mediation of conflict by mass communications creates particular pressures. Although reporting of atrocities against civilians generates demands for intervention, reporting of casualties to the intervening forces (as with the Americans in Vietnam) is widely held to be a grave political danger to Western governments. In a war situation, like the Gulf, this pressure has led to the use of high-technology weapons with minimal exposure of troops on the ground. In war-management situations, like the UN and NATO interventions in Yugoslavia, it has also led to the preference for demonstrative air-strikes; and where troops are exposed on the ground, to negotiation and manoeuvre rather than confrontation.

Whether these changes can be described as a democratization of military power is of course questionable. The concern for Western soldiers', and to some extent for civilian, lives contrasts with the treatment of soldiers as cannon fodder and the callousness towards civilians in the world wars. When the mothers of nine British 'friendly fire' victims – killed by mistake by American pilots in the Gulf – took court action, this was an attempt to make the military accountable for the lives of its personnel in the same way as other employers would be. But this concern for human life barely extends to enemy soldiers – Iraqi troops were massacred during the Gulf War – and only partially to civilians – while serious efforts were made to avoid direct civilian casualties in Iraq, indirect casualties through the targeting of the economic infrastructure were large.

The institution of an international war crimes tribunal, to try cases of genocide in Bosnia and Rwanda, is another, rather different attempt to make political and military authorities and personnel accountable for their actions in war. The tribunal, based in the Hague, goes beyond the Nuremberg precedent, since it is not based on 'victors' justice'. Nevertheless, it appears at the time of writing to have limited prospects of trying any of the leaders responsible for crimes against humanity or war crimes. Whether it will become the basis of a permanent institution is also uncertain.

It is clear, therefore, that the democratization of military power is in its early stages. Armed forces remain highly centralized institutions, to which internal democracy, in the sense of discussion, debate and accountability (let alone election of officers) mostly remain anathema. Militaries are being subjected, slowly, to the changing norms of society at large in areas like gender equality (including even acceptance of minority sexual orientations). But these changes relate more to the exercise of individual rights than to the mode of collective operation of armed forces as institutions.

The nub of the changes is where these two intersect. If armed forces came to be chiefly instruments of globally legitimate authority, used to protect civilians against genocide, it is possible to conceive of a different mode of military organization prevailing. If militaries were transformed into peace-making rather than war-fighting institutions, tools of a more democratic global order, then a more democratic internal structure would be appropriate.

The problem of utilizing national forces for international interventions, which means that these forces are subject to national political pressures and media coverage, could be partially overcome by following the proposal made by the UN Secretary General – but so far ignored by the great powers –

for a permanent UN armed force (Boutros Ghali, 1992). If individuals or military units from national armed forces volunteered for service with the UN, or even for a particular intervention, a greater commitment to its goals would be likely, and media and politicians would be less able to whip up opposition to UN operations by raising the danger to soldiers' lives.

Democratizing security politics

The interrelated changes in military power and liberal democracy have been accompanied by important shifts in how people think about security. During the Cold War, 'security' was identified with national security, which meant the security of the state, and was understood in an overwhelmingly military sense. 'National' security was of course an anachronism even in its own terms – except that in the USA it expressed American world dominance – because military state security had been internationalized during the Cold War. So theorists of security began to talk also about 'international security', the security of the state system as a whole, and 'security communities', the collectivities of interdependent states which had pooled their security concerns (Buzan, 1991).

Security has also come to be understood in less exclusively military terms. The 'issue agenda' of security has been transformed: with the disappearance of the Soviet threat to Western societies, mainstream international thinkers started to be concerned with economic, environmental and social dimensions of security. In part this was a 'securitization' of non-military areas of politics, reflecting a search for new 'threats' and a new role on the part of militaries and 'security intellectuals'.

Migration, for example, was often theorized as a security problem for Western states 'threatened' by influxes of poorer East Europeans, North Africans or Mexicans. Clearly this was at most an administrative or policing problem for states, not an issue for militaries, and not a serious threat to state security. And the posing of migration as a security issue often ignored the real insecurity, that of the migrants themselves, and the need for international policies to address that. To pose the issue in this way is, however, to upturn and democratize the statist agenda of orthodox security thinking. This is precisely what has happened, in the wider debate which has begun.

Thus more radical thinkers have argued that the individual should be the main 'referent' of security, rather than the state. According to Booth (1991), 'individual' security should have priority over state concerns, and indeed the state should not be defined as a provider of security to individuals: states may be threats to individuals as well as sources of protection for them. The individualist security agenda gives priority to human rights and sees close links between security and emancipation.

Others have argued, however, that individualism as such is not an adequate basis for rethinking, which requires us to understand how security is risked and produced in social relations. Feminists, for example, see security as highly gendered: women face particular threats from male violence in society at large and also in war (e.g. rape as an instrument of war). Giddens (1992) has presented a more general sociological theory of security. He argues that modernity generates knowledge-based systems which enable people to control the traditional risks and insecurities generated by their relationships with nature. Modern systems, however, generate new risks and security problems, and managing these 'risk environments', increasingly globalized in the late twentieth century, is a central task of modern politics.

In these terms, the global military system represents one environment in which risks are generated and individuals and social groups attempt to produce and manage their security. One attempt to think about these issues, which partially moves away from classic 'state-centred' thinking, is the proposal of Waever *et al.* (1993) to examine 'societal security', i.e. the security of societies. By defining 'societies' as ethnic-national-religious wholes, however, Waever ignores the ways in which such units can conflict with the democratic, pluralist and transnational values which are growing in importance with globalization. In Bosnia, for example, the security policies of ethnically defined parties were in conflict with the security, and even survival, of plural, multi-ethnic urban communities like Sarajevo, with the security of a democratic state in the country, and of course with the security of many individuals and families. The problems of this concept illustrate, however, the difficulties of rethinking security in an increasingly globalized world. Security, it can be argued, needs to be based on a plural, democratic concept of social change (Shaw, 1994).

The democratization of security politics is reflected in the emergence of new, often transnational, groups and institutions concerned with security. Some groups, like ethnic-nationalist parties which organize across state boundaries, base themselves on a distorted, exclusivist concept of democracy. Others, like humanitarian non governmental organizations and international movements for democracy, peace and human rights, raise the global democratic agenda which is not yet strongly supported by state leaders.

--------------------- ***Summary of Section 2.3*** ---------------------

- The pacification and unification of the West has meant that democracy and citizenship are understood in a way which is beginning to transcend the nation-state; the issue is whether this process can be extended to the world as a whole.

- Global democracy depends on global peace, and needs to be institutionalized; but current global institutions are weak and inadequate, dominated by Western states who are reluctant to allow them greater authority and resources.

- Military institutions are beginning to be subject to democratic accountability, but expanding this process depends on deepening the shift from war-fighting to peace-making; radical reforms of world military institutions and their roles are needed before we can talk confidently of democratization.

- There is a democratization of security thinking, which makes the security of people rather than states the centre of debate. This new security debate needs to centre on how the security of democratic, plural and transnational social communities, as well as of individuals, can be sustained.

Conclusion

This chapter opened by showing how, despite what appears to be an intrinsic opposition between military power and democracy, the two had been reconciled in the liberal-democratic nation-state. I noted that the explanation for this paradox was the convention which separated inter- and intra-state politics.

In the section which followed, I developed a historical discussion of the ways in which inter-state conflict – in the world wars of the twentieth century – had deepened this paradox. War had led to mass mobilization and wartime participation, out of which the understanding of democracy in liberal states had been widened to include social and economic dimensions of citizenship. I argued that the connection between political rights and military duties, which had been essential to Continental European definitions of democracy, became generalized to all Western liberal states and broadened to include economic and social rights as well.

Section 2.2 then looked at how the mid-century, post-Second World War democratic settlement has been transformed. I discussed how changes to the state system during the Cold War had weakened the role of individual nation-states. Western military unity had opened up a broad economic, social and political space in which the national context of democracy was weakened. I then argued that at the same time, reliance on nuclear weapons led to the decline of military participation, on which much of the broadening of democracy had depended. I linked liberal-democratic states' gradual abandonment of universal male military service with the movement away from the Keynesian welfare-state consensus of the early post-1945 period.

Finally, Section 2.3 looked at the implications for liberal democracy of the changes in military power. This section brought out four main issues. The first was the 'post-military' definition of democratic rights and, especially, duties: how do we define democratic citizenship in an era of increasingly global society, in which military service is no longer a majority experience? The discussion examined proposals for non-military national service and the ideas of global citizenship and global responsibility. The second issue was the role of military power in a global democratic order: the discussion emphasized the need for global pacification alongside democratization. The third issue was the nature of military institutions: the discussion tried to evaluate how far a process of democratization of the military is under way. I concluded that movements to a more democratic global order, a more peaceful global order, a more peaceful mode of operation for armed forces and a more democratic character for armed forces, must all be closely interrelated. Finally, I looked at the new security politics, and argued that the protection of individuals and plural, democratic communities needed to be at its centre.

In this chapter, I have tried to explore the sometimes paradoxical linkages between liberal democracy and military power which lie behind the apparent separation of democracy within nation-states and a war-regulated inter-national order. The development of a more global society is beginning to transform these relationships, although changes in the state system have not yet fully reflected the increasing globalization of economic, social and cultural life. The old idea of a world parcelled up into sovereign nation-states which are (or should be) internally democratic but which relate externally through military anarchy, is increasingly anachronistic. The development of transnational and global state structures, institutionalizing co-operation between nation-states as well as within society, raises the new agenda of global democracy with which this book is concerned. The central lesson of this chapter, however, is that the development of global democracy must first complete the settling of accounts with military power.

References

Addison, P. (1975) *The Road to 1945: British Politics and the Second World War,* London, Cape.

Andreski, S. (1954) *Military Organization and Society,* London, Routledge.

Booth, K. (1991) 'Security and emancipation', *Review of International Studies,* vol.17, no.4, October.

Boutros Ghali, B. (1992) *Agenda for Peace,* New York, United Nations.

Buzan, B. (1991) *People, States and Fear: an Agenda for International Security Studies in the Post-Cold War Era,* Hemel Hempstead, Harvester-Wheatsheaf.

Chambers, J.W. II and Moskos, C. (1993) *The New Conscientious Objection: From Sacred to Secular Resistance,* New York, Oxford University Press.

Clausewitz, K. von (1831) *On War,* Howard, M. and Paret, P. (eds), Princeton, Princeton University Press (1976 edn).

Giddens, A. (1985) *The Nation-State and Violence,* Cambridge, Polity Press.

Giddens, A. (1992) *Modernity and Self Identity,* Cambridge, Polity Press.

Held, D. (1995) *Democracy and Global Order,* Cambridge, Polity Press.

Hobsbawm, E. and Ranger, T. (1983) *The Invention of Tradition,* Cambridge, Cambridge University Press.

Lenin, V.I. (1917) *The State and Revolution,* London, Martin Lawrence (1933 edn).

MacKenzie, J.M. (1984) *Propaganda and Empire: the Manipulation of British Public Opinion 1880–1960,* Manchester, Manchester University Press.

MacNeill, W.H. (1982) *The Pursuit of Power,* Oxford, Blackwell.

Mann, M. (1988) *States, War and Capitalism,* Oxford, Blackwell.

Mann, M. (1993) *The Sources of Social Power, Vol.II,* Cambridge, Cambridge University Press.

Marwick, A. (1974) *War and Social Change,* London, Macmillan.

Mills, C.W. (1956) *The Power Elite,* New York, Oxford University Press.

Mills, C.W. (1959) *The Causes of World War III,* London, Secker and Warburg.

Moskos, C. (1988) *A Call to Civic Service,* New York, Free Press.

Shaw, M. (1987) 'The rise and fall of the military-democratic state, Britain 1940–85' in Creighton, C. and Shaw, M. (eds) *The Sociology of War and Peace,* London, Macmillan.

Shaw, M. (1988) *Dialectics of War: an Essay on the Social Theory of War and Peace,* London, Pluto.

Shaw, M. (1991) *Post-Military Society: Demilitarisation, Militarism and War at the End of the Twentieth Century*, Cambridge, Polity Press.

Shaw, M. (1994) *Global Society and International Relations*, Cambridge, Polity Press.

van Doorn, J. (1975) *The Soldier and Social Change*, London, Sage.

Vasillopolus, C. (1995) 'The nature of Athenian hoplite democracy', *Armed Forces and Society*, vol.22, no.1, pp.49–63.

Waever, O., *et al.* (1993) *Migration and the New Security Agenda in Europe*, London, Pinter.

Sweezy, P.M. (1968) *The Theory of Capitalist Development*, London, Monthly Review Press.

Further reading

Giddens, A. (1985) *The Nation-State and Violence*, Cambridge, Polity Press.

Held, D. (1995) *Democracy and Global Order*, Cambridge, Polity Press.

Mills, C.W. (1956) *The Power Elite*, New York, Oxford University Press.

Shaw, M. (1991) *Post-Military Society: Demilitarisation, Militarism and War at the End of the Twentieth Century*, Cambridge, Polity Press.

van Doorn, J. (1975) *The Soldier and Social Change*, London, Sage.

CHAPTER 3

Democracy in hard times: economic globalization and the limits to liberal democracy

Robert Cox

Introduction

During the 1980s and 1990s, the word 'globalization' has come to express the perception of a dominant trend in world political economy. In its broadest and most general meaning, globalization signifies growing connectedness and interdependence on a world scale. It is multidimensional: connectedness in politics and the organization of security, in economics and welfare, in culture, in ecology, in values of all kinds. No one area of human activity is isolated; and within each area, no one is untouched by the condition and activities of others.

It can, of course, be argued that this has always been the case but that it has been hidden from us by our mental habits of fragmenting and isolating domains of knowledge. Yet hitherto the assumption of *ceteris paribus* did seem plausibly to allow us to ignore the range of global forces that circumscribed particular situations. We could apparently deal with housing policy in Birmingham without having to think about migratory movements in Africa.

The difference now is that awareness of the crowding of the planet plus the intensity of communications makes it less and less plausible to ignore the pressures of global forces on particular situations. We have all become globalized even though we may be only dimly aware of how this affects us.

This chapter examines how economic globalization affects the prospects and possibilities for democracy – for what kind of democracy and for how much. Liberal democracy is usually understood to have a territorial site: the territory of a state with its population. Democratization – the process of becoming democratic – can also be applied to other non-territorial institutions or social entities: industrial enterprises, churches, trade unions, clubs, international institutions, and to social relations in community and family life.

Broadly, two directions of influences interact in shaping democracy: those from the top down and those from the bottom up. The top-down influences come from the established centres of power in the state and the interstate system, from national corporate and world economic and financial forces, from dominant forms of knowledge and the dominant ideologies which shape the way people think. The bottom-up pressures, which are those that may press for more democratization, arise from an awareness by people of negative effects on their welfare from some of the top-down pressures and a determination to counteract them: to avoid, ignore, or react against established political and economic power, to criticize conventional forms of knowledge, and to develop alternative visions of the world. These bottom-up and top-down pressures interact within a third category of forces: existing patterns of human habitation and the constraints imposed by ecology.

The space for democracy thus develops dialectically. Dominant forces, internal or external to the territorial or social setting in question, constitute the initial limits of the possible. These stimulate and configure a critical response. The response changes the power relations that once circumscribed what was thought possible. These changed power relations in turn create new limits and new challenges. This sequence is logical, but not necessarily temporal. The opposed forces, bottom-up and top-down, often act simultaneously. The sequential logical order is just a way of reasoning about the process of change.

There is a more specific meaning of economic globalization which led to the generalized use of the term and to academic exploration of its ramifications. That meaning of economic globalization is associated first with the internationalizing of production by multinational corporations (MNCs) and then with the establishment of unregulated global financial markets. This economic globalization opened the door to study of the broader ramifications. These developments from the late 1970s to the 1990s pose problems for democracy on the threshold of the twenty-first century and constitute the starting point for our enquiry.

Economic globalization has made competitiveness in world markets the primary goal and criterion of state policies. The set of measures pursuant to this goal include deregulation of economic and financial controls, privatization of public sector enterprises, fiscal constraint and public debt reduction notably through cuts in social expenditures. These measures mark a complete reversal of the set of policies that moved advanced capitalist countries towards welfare states in the post-war decades and nourished a hope for development in the Third World. The decade of the 1970s marks the threshold of this shift in the direction of public policies. The crisis of the 1970s was not confined to capitalist and Third World countries. It also marked the limits of viability of 'real socialism' (the term used to characterize societies organized under Communist Party leadership), which succumbed in its economic and political dimensions in the following decade.

The social consequences of this U-turn in public policies are clear:

–   social polarization in advanced capitalist countries undoing the work of social democracy and the welfare state, with higher unemployment and cuts in social expenditures;

–   even greater polarization and unemployment in countries that abandoned 'real socialism', accompanied by ineffective economic management and a rapid growth of organized crime;

–   imposition of austerity ('structural adjustment') on poor countries by world-economy authorities, the burden of which is disproportionately borne by the poorest people and especially by women.

These social consequences make for the 'hard times' that challenge the possibility of democratic development. Political structures are no stronger than the social base upon which they rest and this base has been shaped by 'globalization' in its late twentieth century meaning. This leads to three questions: 'Is economic globalization transforming the conditions under which liberal democracies operate?' 'What kind of democracy is compatible with this globalization?' 'Is economic globalization an uncontrollable, inflexible force to which liberal democracy is inevitably subordinate?'

3.1 Economy and democracy

To begin to answer these questions, we first should try to grasp the specific nature of contemporary economic globalization. One school of thought, taking the longest-term view, considers there is nothing fundamentally new about the global reach of capitalism. World-system theory initially argued that capitalism, emergent in Europe, became a world system in the sixteenth century and has continued as such since then, undergoing several changes of phase but remaining essentially the same (Wallerstein, 1974a, 1974b). A more recent revision of world-system theory perceives a 'perennial economy' existing from the 'worlds' of the ancient empires until today (Gills and Frank, 1992). So what is new?

Even if we restrict the sweep of history to the last two centuries, the *Pax Britannica* of the nineteenth century underwrote a world-wide capitalist economy. True, in the 1930s tendencies towards protectionist blocs fragmented this world economy, but the norm was re-established in the post-Second World War settlement, guaranteed by the *Pax Americana* of the mid to late twentieth century.

Looking at change in the world economy over a time-span shorter than millennia or even centuries allows for a heightened sense of variation. Perhaps there are certain perennial features of capitalism (or of world economies, since 'capitalism' is a recent name), but people's life chances may be very different under different historical variations of economic organization. The medium term marks the significant changes in opportunities and constraints that occur during the lifetimes of individuals or groups.

To think about the practical implications of economic globalization we have to move from the contemplation of a perennial economy to a frame of thought that focuses upon the distinctiveness of real historical time-bound and space-bound economies and the processes of their transformations. Karl Polanyi, an economic historian and anthropologist, gave his attention to such 'substantive' economies, in *The Great Transformation* (1944), where he analysed the relationship between economic organization, social structures, and politics.

The 'double movement'

A refugee from Vienna after the Nazi take-over of Austria, Polanyi sought to explain the breakdown of humanistic values and democratic structures in the Europe of the 1930s. He found the explanation in the attempt during the mid-nineteenth century to institutionalize a self-regulating economy separated from society and dominant over society. This he saw as unique in history, because in former eras and other civilizations the economy had never been conceived of as a separate realm of human action but was always 'embedded' in society – indeed, the very concept of 'economy' as a distinct sphere of human activity did not exist. It was only with the industrial revolution that the idea of an economy, self-regulating and independent from society, came to be accepted. The social consequences of this novel concept of economy were not long in arousing abhorrence and apprehensions. They were portrayed in literature by Dickens as social and moral breakdown and by Disraeli as the fracturing of society into 'two nations'.

The self-regulating market did not come about naturally or spontaneously. It was the creation of the state. The state was the guardian of the market's independence, of the rules of contract and of the value of money as the medium of exchange. New police powers within the country and sea power internationally were its instruments. As Polanyi said, the free market was *planned*. Politically, in Britain, it was brought about through a compromise worked out in the 1840s that allowed the landed ruling class to govern in the interests of the rising industrial-commercial bourgeoisie while restraining the potential for explosion of urban and rural rebellion. The self-regulating market required a strong state and cautious control over the extension of democracy. The unleashing of market forces was repeated in the France of the Second Empire (1851–71) and with greater controls in the Germany of Bismark. The strong state was the common feature. Political structures differed, though all manifested a prudent suspicion of extending liberal democracy (Hobsbawm, 1975).

The new market could not remain long in this condition of unregulated power over society because of the way it was destroying the old bonds of community and generating class struggle. Polanyi saw the historical process as a dialectic he called the 'double movement'. The first phase of liberating the market from social control undermined social cohesion and produced conflict. In a second phase, society, bit by bit, reasserted control over the economy, attempting to moderate the socially disruptive effects of the market and to bring the economy back under social control. The medium for doing this was politics, in which there came about a measure of agreement between traditionalist conservatives and social reformers against the 'extreme middle' of pure market liberals. The movement began with regulation of factory conditions, continued with social insurance and the institutionalizing of labour–employer bargaining and the rise of socialist and social democratic political parties, to culminate during the mid twentieth century in welfare states and the acceptance of full employment as a primary goal of state policy. This second phase of the double movement went hand in hand with the extension of the vote to all adults and with the expansion of the state's scope to cover most issues of concern to people. Liberal democracy acquired a social dimension and social ills became a primary concern of politics.

The democratic potential of the second phase of the double movement was challenged during the 1930s by fascism and Stalinism, leading to the Second World War. In retrospect, these developments signalled that the second phase of Polanyi's double movement was testing its limits. Fascism was nourished by the impoverishment of the middle classes of central Europe in the economic reversals of the interwar period; Stalinism force-marched a whole population in an effort towards rapid industrialization and militarization in a poor country at the margin of the world economy. Elsewhere in western Europe and North America, economies and societies were foundering with dismal but less dramatic effects during the Great Depression.

The post-war settlement re-established the second phase strategy and it endured successfully for three decades. The ability of capitalist states to manage their national economies and to maintain liberal democratic practice were made more secure by the institution of an international regulatory mechanism symbolized by the Bretton Woods institutions. This mechanism was designed to enable individual states, in capitalist countries, to regulate their internal economies so as to maintain a high level of employment and social services while sustaining international economic relations from which all countries could benefit. Funds were to be available to help avoid a conflict between national welfare and international co-operation by allowing countries time to make necessary and internationally agreed adjustments in national economic policies. The system was predicated upon national management of national economies plus co-operation among countries in the international economy.

The crisis of the 1970s: the coming of hard times

The Bretton Woods system reached its limits in the mid 1970s. The symptoms in the economy were higher rates of inflation accompanied by widespread unemployment in the core capitalist countries, a drying up of investment in less developed countries (indeed a reverse flow of capital from these countries), and growing rigidification in countries of 'real socialism' with an erosion of their social services. These symptoms can be traced to a common set of factors. Inflation spread internationally from US financing from abroad of its payments deficit, brought about notably by the Vietnam War. The dramatic increase in the price of oil achieved by OPEC (the Organization of Petroleum Exporting Countries) added to the volume of dollars in international financial circuits. The arms race between the USA and the Soviet Union not only added to the US payments deficit but put an intolerable burden upon the Soviet economy. Much of the accumulated supply of dollars was recycled at steep interest rates in loans to countries like Mexico, Brazil and Argentina and to a much lesser extent African countries. These countries had counted on being able to service their debt by exports to richer countries, but the world recession cut back their markets and thus their earnings.

These economic consequences were but the manifestation of a deeper change in social structures. It had been conventional wisdom in the major capitalist countries that governments should ensure conditions for capital accumulation while at the same time legitimating it by maintaining a satisfactory level of employment and adequate social services. This took the form of a social contract in which organized workers participated with employers and government in the management of the economy. The social contract involved some inflation, as public expenditures and negotiated wage levels rose, but as long as the economy was expanding this was quite

Box 3.1 *Institutions of the world economy*

Conceived at the Bretton Woods, New Hampshire, conference in 1944, the International Monetary Fund (IMF) was established as a fund to which member governments contributed gold and their own currencies to create a source of credit for countries in balance of payments deficit. The aim was to allow time for such countries to adjust their national economic policies so as to avoid the drastic social consequences of unemployment and welfare cuts that would otherwise result from an attempt to correct payments deficits by a sharp currency devaluation and budget cuts. The IMF rules provided for convertibility of currencies, fixed exchange rates and a fixed price for gold. This was part of an overall plan to introduce stability into post-war international economic relations. Voting power in the IMF is in relation to countries' contributions, so decisions are controlled by the rich countries and especially by the USA.

Subsequently in the 1970s, from being the principal world creditor, the USA moved towards becoming the largest debtor, and through unilateral action abrogated the fixed price for gold and promoted floating exchange rates, thus demolishing two of the basic principles of the Bretton Woods system.

Since the late 1970s, the IMF has functioned primarily in relation to Third World countries and, from the late 1980s, towards the ex-Soviet bloc and China. It has used its leverage as a provider of credit to influence economic policies in these countries to integrate them into a global capitalist economy functioning according to rules and practices shaped by the rich countries.

While IMF resources were intended to deal with balance-of-payments disequilibria, the World Bank, the other Bretton Woods institution, was set up to provide or underwrite loans to governments. It has functioned mainly in relation to Third World countries. Like the IMF, its voting system gives control to the rich countries and it raises the capital it lends in the principal financial markets. The Bank's lending strategy has also been consistent with the IMF's promotion of economic globalization.

A third institution to deal with international trade was envisaged at Bretton Woods, but the International Trade Organization never came into being. A negotiating forum for trade, the General Agreement on Tariffs and Trade (GATT) took its place. The richer capitalist countries with the biggest markets wielded the greatest influence in the GATT. In the 1990s, the World Trade Organization (WTO), a more permanent and comprehensive body, was set up with US backing.

tolerable. By the mid 1970s this was no longer the case. Business was no longer willing to invest in growth unless inflation and wage increases were blocked; and it was able to pursuade governments that these conditions would have to be met if business were to relaunch growth. In these conditions, governments were inclined to support business, to help break the power of unions and cut back social expenditures. The social contract of the second phase of the double movement was on the way to being dismantled (Cox, 1987).

With regard to countries of the Third World, the post-war decades put an international focus on development assistance. The rich countries discussed targets for transfer of a small proportion (less than 1 per cent) of their gross product to stimulate economic growth in poorer countries. In the early 1970s, the poorer countries organized themselves into an international pressure group demanding a New International Economic Order (NIEO) which would restructure international economic relations to their advantage. The crisis of the 1970s eliminated these projects. Third World debt became the dominant consideration in North–South relations. Public funds would not flow to developing countries; their capital needs would have to be met by offering conditions to attract multinational corporations (MNCs) or by borrowing from foreign banks. Policies for internally directed development had to be abandoned in favour of export-oriented development that could help to service foreign debt. The poorer countries had to cut what social services they had and reduce imports; the export orientation benefited a few local capitalists while the burden of the crisis fell upon the mass of the population.

The countries of 'real socialism' also had a kind of social contract. They were called 'workers' states' although the workers had no direct access to power. Their social contract was a *quid pro quo* in which workers acquiesced in the political power of the party leadership who in turn maintained full employment, prices at which people could buy a basic subsistence, and a relatively leisurely pace of work. By the 1970s, however, stagnating economic growth (which had been high in the post-war decades), deteriorating public services, lack of innovation in industry, and a grossly disproportionate emphasis on military expenditure led the leadership to reverse policies under the banner of *perestroika* (the new economic strategy proclaimed in 1985 by Mikhail Gorbachev) which shattered the social contract of 'real socialism' even more dramatically than had happened to that of Western capitalism (Cox, 1991).

The crisis of the 1970s thus demolished the social basis of states and international relations of the post-war decades. It posed the challenge of reconstructing a new basis for social and political authority in all parts of the world.

Some economists, by the late 1970s, perceived a distinction between the international economy with which classical economic theory had concerned itself, i.e. movements in trade, investments and payments across national frontiers; and a world economy or global economy, in which production and finance were being organized in cross-border networks by MNCs and which had given birth to 24-hour-a-day securities and currency trading (Madeuf and Michalet, 1978). The international economy had been the object of the regulatory systems built up nationally and internationally in the post-war years. The global economy was a very largely unregulated (and many would argue unregulatable) domain. This global economy was the matrix of 'globalization' as a late twentieth century phenomenon.

Alongside the economic dimension called 'globalization' and interacting with it, two other important factors shaped the conditions in which the challenge to reconstruct a social basis for authority was to be confronted. One was global ecology. The other was the impact of the Cold War in institutionalizing covert transborder activities.

An ecological perspective on the world emerged during the 1970s in which the economic growth of the post-war years was perceived as reaching a limit defined by the ability of the biosphere to sustain a continuation of existing levels of population growth, resource depletion and pollution (Club of Rome, 1972). This holistic ecological perspective can be called 'globalism' in contradistinction to economic globalization. There is an implicit contradiction between economic globalization and ecological globalism. Economic globalization envisages a continuing expansion of economic practices unregulated by political authority. Ecological globalism leads logically to a call for regulation and limitation of economic practices and social behaviour in the interest of equilibrium in the biosphere. Both take off from views of the world as a whole, transcending territorial and political subdivisions; and both have profound implications for the future of democracy.

As to the other factor affecting the prospects for democracy, the Cold War, in ideological terms, was a struggle between liberal democracy (identified for this purpose with market economics) and totalitarian communism. In practice, covert penetration by Cold War protagonists into the domestic politics of other countries (enemies, allies, and neutrals alike) played a large part in the struggle. A covert world developed in which intelligence services, terrorist groups, arms dealers, rogue banks and organized crime interacted, sometimes conflicting, sometimes collaborating. This opaque stratum penetrated corporate management, the media, and state agencies to the highest levels of government. This institutionalization of a covert world could only be detrimental to the authentic expression of people's will. When, in late 1990, the Cold War was officially declared to be over, the ideological face of it and the US–Soviet hostility subsided but the covert world remained in place, a continuing impediment to democratic development.

―――――――――――――― *Summary of Section 3.1* ――――――――――――――
From the crisis of the mid 1970s, several key points stand out:

- Economic power has, since the industrial revolution, sought to separate economics from politics as regards state intervention in market processes while at the same time demanding state enforcement of the rules of the market.

- Where such a separation of economics from politics has prevailed, society becomes polarized into extremes of rich and poor, protected and unprotected.

- Social forces respond to this polarization through political action demanding some control over market processes to moderate disparities in economic conditions among social groups and to secure enlarged access to political processes for all people, that is to say, greater democratization.

- In the 1970s, social forces were challenged but their response had yet to take coherent shape; the condition was analogous to the first phase of Polanyi's double movement, but this time on a world scale, not just a national one as in the early nineteenth century.

- The problem of a political response was complicated by awareness of ecological limits to economic growth and by the existence of a covert but powerful world-encompassing political stratum impervious to democratic control.

3.2   Economic globalization and its consequences

The transformation of production and social structure

The social conditions that result from economic globalization are being reshaped very largely by the restructuring of production which is often encapsulated in the notion of a transition from Fordism to post-Fordism.

Large-scale assembly-line mass production characterized the Fordist era. Big factories with large concentrations of workers favoured the development of powerful trade unions. Governments in the major capitalist countries encouraged labour–management bargaining and provided various forms of corporatist frameworks for economic management by government, business, and labour. Keynesian doctrine argued for the maintenance of full employment, a level of wages high enough for workers to be consumers of the products of industry, and a redistributive safety net for those who fell out of economic activity. A little inflation was able to lubricate the working of the system, reducing any tendency toward conflict without causing any serious damage. This was how the major capitalist countries enjoyed a relatively conflict-free passage in their societies during the expansive three post-war decades (Maier, 1977, 1978).

All this began to change in the 1970s. The economic jargon goes: economies of scale gave way to economies of flexibility. The combination of heightened international competition for market shares in a non-expanding world economy with the existence of surplus capacity oriented new investment towards cutting production costs. This took two directions: the introduction of automation, robotics, and analogous methods of displacing labour by equipment, and the more systematic use of cheap labour. Large-scale mass production no longer fitted well with markets that became more differentiated, where production had to be scaled to more diversified and more changeable demand. Production technology for complex consumer durables, e.g. automobiles, shifted from the assembly line producing standardized products by means of fixed special-purpose machinery to smaller groups servicing numerically controlled instruments and robots. The employment pattern became one of a limited number of technicians and skilled workers closely integrated with capital and a larger number of peripheral, more precariously employed workers in supporting tasks. This peripheral category constitutes a cushion that can be compressed or expanded according to the level of demand. It consists of downgraded skilled workers, temporary and part-time employees, workers in out-sourcing enterprises, and workers in globally dispersed production units located in areas offering special cost advantages to a multinational enterprise. The workers in this peripheral sector of global production organization are segmented by gender, ethnicity and geographical location. All of this weakens their potential for trade union organization. At the same time that production in consumer durables was being reorganized in this 'post-Fordist' manner, Fordist methods expanded in labour-intensive industries like fast foods, sales work in department stores and in those phases of global production off-loaded to less-developed countries.

As a consequence of these changes, the social structure of the world, as shaped by economic globalization, has taken the form of a three-part hierarchy. At the top are those people who are integrated into the global economy. They include everyone from the global economy managers down to the relatively privileged workers who serve global production and finance in reasonably stable jobs.

The second level in the hierarchy includes those who serve the global economy in more precarious employment – an expanding category segmented by race, religion and gender as a result of the restructuring of production by post-Fordism.

The bottom level includes those excluded from the global economy, superfluous labour and people living, in what one former commissioner of the European Union (EU) called 'useless countries' – useless, certainly, by the criteria of economic globalization. These people have been victims of drought and famine not unconnected with the engrossment of fertile lands for export agriculture and also with military conflicts for territorial control. They become a concern of the global economy as a potential destablilizing force, and through television they arouse the sympathy and concern of the public in richer countries.

So we have three categories: the integrated, the precariously linked, and the excluded.

To cope with the excluded and potentially disruptive, the institutions of global governance have devised instruments of global poor relief and riot control. Humanitarian assistance (the poor relief component) has become a top priority of the United Nations and a major activity of a vast range of non-governmental agencies. Where poor relief is inadequate to prevent political destabilization, then military force (the riot control component) is evoked by the international community. Together, they help to sustain the emerging social structure of the world by minimizing the risk of chaos in the bottom layer.

Global finance

If the internationalizing of production, one aspect of economic globalization, is producing this hierarchical social structure, another aspect, global finance, limits the power of governments to carry out policies that might moderate social disparities and maintain the kinds of social services that were developed in the richer capitalist countries during the post-war decades. Controls over the transnational movements of capital, which were part of the Bretton Woods system, were very largely removed by states following the crisis of the 1970s (Helleiner, 1994). The motivation was to encourage a business climate attractive to foreign capital and to match deregulatory moves by other countries in a competitive international financial environment.

As a consequence, when a government introduces policies that involve increased public expenditure for social services or employment creation, and raises taxes to pay for them, it may precipitate a flight of capital. When increased public expenditures require an increase in state borrowing, the interest rate a government must pay on new debt will rise, meaning that debt-ridden states will have to forego these ameliorative policies. Since governments have been borrowing increasingly from foreigners through the international financial market, it means their ability to borrow and the cost of borrowing is determined in the global financial market. Bond-rating agencies, mainly located in New York, have a determining influence over state budgets (Sinclair, 1994). Gone are the days when it could be said of the public debt that 'we owe it to ourselves' in the sense that it was a purely domestic matter. Now the global financial market rates government policies by the criterion of how far they are conducive to a business-friendly climate; and social policy ranks low by this standard. Global capital has gained an effective veto over state policies. Governments have in this sense become more accountable to the impersonal commands of the bond market than to their own electorates.

The internationalizing of the state

This leads to a third effect of economic globalization: the internationalizing of the state. The loss of effective sovereignty by states in economic policy is matched by the development of very complex transnational mechanisms for the development of what can loosely be called public policy guidelines. Since the crisis of the 1970s, all the advanced capitalist states, of whatever political colour, have come to accept as necessary and inevitable the same broad lines of economic policy – priority to reducing inflation over combating unemployment, carrying out deregulation and privatization, compressing social services in the interest of debt reduction, and obstructing the power of trade unions so as to keep wages and prices low enough to be competitive in world markets. This policy litany, the subtext of economic globalization, is pervasive.

There are, of course, variations in the severity with which it is applied, variations influenced by national traditions or concepts of civilization, and by the balance of power of social forces. The conflict within the EU between those forces seeking to enforce an Anglo-American concept of neo-liberal capitalism and those favouring the more traditional social market or social democratic form (Margaret Thatcher versus Jacques Delors) is perhaps the most significant instance of rival views of civilization (Albert, 1991). A parallel case can be seen in the different approaches by the governments of Ontario and Quebec in Canada, both confronted by a problem of indebtedness that was eating increasingly into public resources: a right-wing Ontario government took a confrontational stand by cutting welfare for the poor and challenging public sector unions, while the Quebec government convened a conference of business, unions and government to work out a consensus on how to deal with the problem.

If, for a time, one government might deviate from the new orthodoxy, as did the first government under the presidency of François Mitterand in France (1981–83), capital flight and a drop in the rates for the French franc brought state policy back to the common pattern. Nominally socialist governments as well as conservative ones have conformed to the same course.

Global governance

To whom, then, or to what, are national economic decision makers accountable, if not to their electorates? There is no clearly definable institutional structure in place that governs the global economy. One of the main tasks of political-economic analysis today should be to clarify how global economic governance actually works. Elsewhere, I have called this appearance of global governance a *nébuleuse*, a loose elite network of influentials and agencies, sharing a common set of ideas, that collectively perform the governance function (Cox, 1992). Policy and doctrine is developed and diffused through unofficial conclaves (e.g. the Trilateral Commission, Bilderberg conferences, the annual world economic meetings in Davos, Switzerland, and so forth) and by intergovernmental and 'expert' bodies: Organization for Economic Co-operation and Development (OECD) committees, the Basle central bankers meetings, and meetings of the IMF and World Bank. Private bond-rating agencies play their role as noted above in influencing the shape of state budgets. At the summit, the G7 governments of the principal economic world powers and the 'sherpas' or government advisers that prepare their agendas formulate what can be agreed and translated into state policy. In other words, there is no formal

Japanese Prime Minister Ryutaro Hashimoto and French President Jacques Chirac beg each other to take the lead through a path as other G–7 leaders follow during a meeting in Lyon in June 1996

decision-making process; but there is a complex set of interrelated networks that evolve a common economic ideology and inject this consensual outcome into national processes of decision making.

The *nébuleuse* is both external and internal to states. It is external in so far as various elements of it appear to be 'international', for instance in the Basle Bank for International Settlements or the OECD or the IMF. It is transnational, insofar as unofficial conclaves, like the Trilateral Commission or the Davos World Economic Conferences, play a role. It is internal insofar as powerful economic forces in the richest societies are parties to, and shapers of, the transnational consensus.

Both externally and internally, the *nébuleuse* is capable of shaping state policy and is very largely unobstructed by democratic control or accountability. Awareness of this has led various citizens groups to mobilize unofficial conferences of critics alongside meetings of the G7, the IMF, and the World Bank to dramatize alternative policies and to make the operations in the *nébuleuse* a little more transparent. The *nébuleuse* no longer goes unchallenged. Organized groups and scholarly thinking are endeavouring to demonstrate that there are, indeed, alternatives that could bring global finance under social control.

——————————— *Summary of Section 3.2* ———————————

The constraints upon democratic development that have evolved from the crisis of the 1970s can be summarized in the following points:

- The internationalizing of production is generating a global social hierarchy of: (1) a relatively affluent sector integrated into the global economy; (2) a more socially and economically dependent precarious sector sustaining the integrated group; and (3) an excluded group that plays no effective part in global production and is regarded by the management of the global economy as a potential object of poor relief and riot control.

- Global finance disciplines governments to make their economic policies conform to global-economy growth which involves as side-effects reduction of social protection and risks to the biosphere.

- A mystified structure of global governance (the *nébuleuse)* escapes democratic accountability and challenges civil society to make global finance and the other processes of globalization more transparent and to propose alternatives.

3.3 Can the socially polarizing consequences of economic globalization be reversed?

Let us consider how this trilogy of economic globalization, ecological globalism and the covert world has transformed the potential for democratic development. The context which links these three factors for good or for ill is civil society. Civil society is the realm of autonomous groups of people articulating different interests and convictions that exists outside of state institutions. Civil society is an intermediate layer between the state and the individual citizen. Within a healthy civil society human groups learn to adapt to each other's existence, working out a modus vivendi upon which state authority may rest.

The ideology associated with economic globalization, by separating the economic realm from the political and making competitiveness in the global economy the determining factor, denies the possibility for civil society consciously to shape human welfare. Ecological globalism threatens civil society with the deprivation of resources needed to sustain life if ecological degradation were allowed to continue unabated. The covert world fills the gap that a weakening and apathetic civil society leaves open for the control of political and economic activity. Together these tendencies undermine democratic accountability and people's ability to shape their own future.

It follows that to reverse these tendencies so that people gain control over their future, economic globalization must be brought under some form of social control and regulation nationally and internationally; people will have to devise new ways of producing and consuming consistent with sustaining the biosphere; and societies, from the lowest units to the highest, from the household to the world, will have to become actively participant – the concept of citizenship, with its rights and responsibilities as they exist for real political subjects, will have to be realized throughout the world. These are formidable objectives but they underscore the necessary conditions for achieving a substantive democracy. (I contrast substantive democracy or participatory democracy with liberal democracy that allows for a separation of the economic from the political sphere.)

What then are the prospects for movement in this direction?

Limited democracy

There is a body of doctrine linked to globalization theory which argues that the problem in the decades preceding the crisis of the 1970s was an 'excess of democracy': too much public demand upon political systems that led to inflation and indebtedness and had begun to make liberal democracies 'ungovernable' (Crozier *et al.*, 1975). Those who held to this thesis argued that a 'democratic surge' during the 1960s, manifested in the student–worker contestation in Europe of 1968–69 and the Civil Rights movement in the USA, had put an overload of demands upon the state while at the same time undermining public confidence in governments. The economic conse-quences were inflation and deepening public debt. The inference drawn from this thesis was that for states to become 'governable' and economically viable, a degree of demobilization of the public was desirable. The fact that this thesis was articulated by ideologues of the Trilateral Commission, close to the economic and political elites of the Western (and Japanese) world, suggests what kind of liberal democracy would be acceptable to them.

The limited kind of democracy compatible with economic globalization was bound to lose appeal amongst those who were disadvantaged by the market. Awareness that the formal political process is incapable of dealing with the real problems that face many people leads them either to apathy, shown for example by low voter turnouts, or to extra-parliamentary and sometimes formally illegal activities of protest. Public confidence in the democratic process is thus undermined.

Nevertheless, the number of countries that have adopted a liberal democratic form of government has increased in recent years (Potter *et al.,* 1997). This process of democratization has been encouraged by the major capitalist states. The policy articulated by the latter is promotion of 'democracy and market reform', i.e. the building in formerly non-democratic countries of state structures that will sustain the processes of economic globalization. Encouragement takes the forms of facilitating access to international lending and making loans conditional upon adoption of both liberal democratic practices (specifically electoral politics and the mitigation of human rights abuses) and observance of financial orthodoxy. In extreme cases, it may depend upon military intervention as in Haiti and Bosnia (but there is no guarantee in such cases that the reforms will endure). Of the tandem democracy/market, external forces have been inclined to be satisfied with formalism in democracy while pressing for substantive conformity in market matters (Robinson, 1996).

Much of the movement towards democracy noted in recent years must, however, be considered to be what Antonio Gramsci called 'passive revolution', i.e. the importing of democratic forms encouraged by external pressures that are embraced by a leading portion of the local population but without the authentic participation of the rest of the population. Gramsci's further analysis pointed to the tendency of passive revolution towards 'caesarism' or the recourse to a leadership that will try to hold the opposed parts of society together without being able to resolve their problems or create a consensually-based state (Gramsci, 1971) Thus much of the democratizing movement saluted in recent years is fragile, lacking a secure base in a participant, articulated civil society.

There are also more extreme cases where people are turning their backs on states and international institutions which appear to them as enemies trying to enforce austerity in the guise of 'structural adjustment' for the benefit of foreigners and the wealthy. This has happened in some of the poorest communities where people seek their salvation in local forms of self-help avoiding state control. Women are prominent as initiators of these local movements. This situation can be found in Somalia and some other countries of Africa. An Ethiopian economist has called it the 'silent revolution in Africa' because it is going on despite official state and international policies (Cheru, 1989). The key question for the future in these cases is whether an authentic democratic political culture capable of sustaining a new political authority can be built up from the base of society.

A consequence of economic globalization, which diminishes the control governments have over national economies, has been to transform politics at the national level into *management.* Politics, in the sense of choice between rival projects of society, no longer seems to be conceivable in the framework of economic globalization thinking. Margaret Thatcher's celebrated aphorism 'There is no alternative' becomes accepted realism. Once the logic of the global economy has been made into the unchangeable framework of state policy, the role of government is reduced to managing things as well as possible within that framework. All politicians move to the centre to compete on the basis of personality and of who is best able to manage the

Box 3.2 Structural adjustment

Structural adjustment programmes (SAPs), introduced in indebted Third World countries under the aegis of the IMF, have become the principal method for promoting economic globalization in these countries. They have emphasized reduction of trade barriers to expose local producers to foreign competition; elimination of government subsidies; removal of controls on capital movements; privatization of state-owned companies; encouragement of foreign investment by removing controls; and minimization of state intervention in the economy and in provision of social services. They have resulted generally in placing a heavy burden on the economically weaker elements of society by raising prices, generating higher unemployment, and reducing public services.

adjustments in economy and society necessary to sustain competitiveness in the global market. The words socialism, liberalism, and conservatism become no more than symbolic banners for competing groups of politicians who all claim they can do what is necessary better than the others. The concept of a possible alternative economy and society is excluded. A French academic and diplomat has written that this signifies the death of the citizen as a subject of politics, thus the death of the polity as the forum of active citizens, and by implication the end of democracy (Guéhenno, 1993).

Correspondingly, people become more cynical about politics as politicians seem to be incapable of solving the basic problems – unemployment, decline of public services, corruption. Democratic practices apply to those decisions that seem to have least importance to people, while those that most affect their daily lives are in the untouchable domain of the economy, the domain of inevitability. In the richer capitalist countries, there is evidence of public scepticism about traditional party politics. Various anti-party alternatives offer themselves as the answer. In the USA, the Texas billionaire Ross Perot personally financed and organized a political movement to run for the presidency in 1992 and 1996. He won about one-fifth of the popular vote in 1992 but only around 10 per cent in 1996. In Italy, the media magnate Silvio Berlusconi moved into the void created by the disintegration of the former majority party coalition, decimated by corruption investigations, to rally a large part of the then leaderless right-wing vote and become prime minister for a short period (until he in turn became the object of corruption investigation). But these non-party phenomena do not seem to have staying power. They are symptoms of the weakening of liberal democracy rather than promising alternative avenues of democratization.

There is more and more evidence that community groups outside of party political alignments are attempting both to organize self-help reacting to the erosion of public services, and to mobilize opinion on issues of public policy. One example, was the extensive non-party mobilization in Canada, the USA and Mexico against the North American Free Trade Area (NAFTA) and protests in Canada against the erosion of public health care. As neo-liberal economic policies consistent with globalization are translated into cuts in social services, more people are deprived of state support while enduring unemployment. Their recourse can only be to a revival of reciprocity outside of the exchange economy – mutual exchange of services on a local basis. In some cases, this has taken the sophisticated form of local units of exchange to replace money – the embryo of an alternative co-operative economy (Helleiner, 1995, 1996).

Apart from such strategies of opting out of the global economy, there have been some prominent instances of conscious popular revolt against economic globalization. The first to resonate in the global news media came from the Mayan Indians in the southern Mexican state of Chiapas. An armed revolt led by the Zapatistas Revolutionary Front (named from the leader of the southern peasant revolt, Emiliano Zapata, in the Mexican revolution of 1910) broke out symbolically on the day that the NAFTA came into force. It was a revolt by poor peasants against the way in which they were impoverished by globalization in its regional form (NAFTA), and against the landowners who obstructed their access to land and the corrupt political system which sustained the landowners' power. The revolt was sustained and did have an impact on the weakened political power structure of the Mexican ruling party (the PRI) which has rigged elections and controlled government office for decades.

Another revolt came about with the strikes which paralysed Paris and much of France in December 1995. Impressively, at a time when labour movements everywhere, including in France, have been weakened by the restructuring of national economies in consequence of globalization and have lost much of the public sympathy they once had, this strike was highly effective and was sustained with widespread public support. It was clearly directed against *mondialization*, the French equivalent for globalization.

Public sector workers march through Paris to protest against a freeze on their wages in 1995

One ominous factor accompanying the decline of public confidence in traditional political authority in the major capitalist countries is a resurgence of right-wing extremism. It has an appeal among young men alienated from the state, blocked by unemployment, and feeling threatened both by a more self-confident and assertive role of women in society and by immigration that can be imagined as a cause of the young men's joblessness. It has appealed also to workers who have lost jobs or who feel threatened by the restructuring of production on a global scale through which once well-paying jobs are being exported to areas of cheaper labour and lesser environmental controls. The National Front led by Jean-Marie Le Pen in France now has a primarily working-class constituency; and the economic nationalist Pat Buchanan made a significant impact in the US Republican presidential primaries in 1995 with his anti-immigrant and economic nationalist appeal. Right-wing extremism, often with racist and fascist overtones, must also be seen as stimulated by economic globalization.

The frailty of civil society

A counterpart of the apparent loss of power and credibility by states is a widespread but uneven tendency towards fragmentation of civil society. This has been encouraged by the global restructuring of production which fragments a labour force, formerly unified through comprehensive collective bargaining and class consciousness. The new production organization uses distinct pockets of workers often non-union, separated by ethnicity and gender, and as nationals and immigrants.

A weakening civil society also tends to alienate people from their political institutions. People lose confidence in politicians not only from evidence of widespread corruption and arrogance but also (and more specifically linked to the globalization effect) from a conviction that politicians do not understand and cannot resolve the major problems confronting their societies such as unemployment and the decline of public services.

The old civil society was formed in large part around interest groups like industrial and professional associations and trade unions, and also around co-operatives and charitable or self-help associations. More recently, these older components of civil society have been diluted by a greater emphasis on 'identities' defined by religion, ethnicity, and gender; and also on 'locality' rather than wider political authorities. 'Locality' here can be seen as a product of 'globality' in so far as globalization has undermined the authority of conventional political structures and accentuated the fragmentation of societies.

Economic globalization delivers a political challenge: whether from these fragments a revivified civil society and a new basis for political authority can be constructed. The decomposition and recomposition of civil society is the process that conditions democratic development in poor countries, ex-communist countries, and rich capitalist countries. Everywhere, though in different ways, the process is affected by economic globalization. Today decomposition is most evident. What are the conditions for, and chances of, recomposition?

The erosion of the old civil society and the psychic gap between people and their political institutions keeps a space open for the activities of the covert world. Some politicians have learned to rely on the support in money and influence (including the threat of violence) of this ramification of intelligence and organized crime networks. Cynicism and depoliticization leaves the field between the top positions in government and a weakened civil society free for the activities of occult actors, from organized crime to intelligence agencies, that are uncontrolled by accountable public authority. Only a strongly developed and self-conscious civil society can provide the healthy alternative base for political authority.

New social movements which exist on both a local and a transnational basis are candidates to help build this alternative (Camilleri and Falk, 1992). Feminist movements, the greens and peace movements are prominent. They all have some affinity for movements of indigenous peoples. There is, however, a problem of coherence among these various groups. Rich country and poor country feminists do not always define the gender problem in the same way. The greens are divided on priorities and even on basic ontological questions of the place of humanity in the biosphere and on their own relationship to capitalism. The relationship between the 'new' movements and the trade unions is ambiguous. Political thinking in the new movements is often suspicious of any attempt to achieve a broad coherence; yet their fragmentation spells weakness in confronting the coherence and aggregation of forces behind economic globalization.

Among the new movements, special mention must be made of the greens. Chapter 4 of this book deals with the question of the environment, but it is pertinent here to note the link between economic globalization, ecology and democracy. Only recently have we begun to understand the ways in which the biosphere has become an actor in the human drama. Taking this seriously will involve revision of our mental frameworks. In formal economics, nature, represented by land, has been subordinated to market logic. Nature, however, has its own logic, a logic based on the interdependence of different forms of life, human and non-human. So long as economic logic did not lead to a destabilization of nature, so long as there was enough slack in nature for the consequences of economic logic to be tolerated, this subordination of nature to the market went unnoticed.

Now, however, the limits to nature's tolerance are being tested. Global warming, the hole in the ozone layer, desertification and deforestation, the loss of biodiversity, the depletion of fish stocks, and so forth, all articulate nature's protest. The implication is a need to rethink economics in a subordinate relationship to a science of nature. This is more than an intellectual task. It implies a revision of our ways of producing and our model of consumption – our ways of life and work.

More than this, it raises the ultimate challenge to the ideology of economic globalization and also, in a way, questions the compatibility of ecological globalism with liberal democracy, in a curious parallel to the concerns globalization ideologues have concerning the 'ungovernability' of democracy as mentioned above. Consumption is the motor of capitalism and the motivation of consumer demand is indispensable to capitalism's continuing expansion. It would seem that a radical change in patterns of consumption will become essential to maintenance of the biosphere. When in preparation for the Earth Summit in Rio de Janeiro in June 1992, then US

President George Bush said 'Our lifestyle is not open to negotiation', he was implicitly acknowledging that a change of lifestyle may be necessary to biospheric survival and at the same time acknowledging that political survival in modern liberal democracies makes it highly risky for politicians to advocate. Eastern Europeans after the fall of the Berlin Wall, Chinese in the era of Deng, the populations of the newly industrialized countries and, more distantly, those of the lagging countries of the Third World, seem to have as the goal of their desires the consumption model of the USA and Western Europe. Any change in this model would have to be set by the pattern makers. Difficulty in imagining how this could come about leaves us with the troubling questions: Is biospheric survival incompatible with liberal democracy? Will democratic politics continue to press for maximizing consumerism? Or may people persuade themselves to refashion their aspirations so as to make them compatible with biospheric survival? This may be the most difficult challenge to civil society.

─────────────────── *Summary of Section 3.3* ───────────────────

Some of the tendencies noted here are not very propitious for substantive democracy. These include:

- Opinion among global elites has favoured a limited form of democracy with at least a partial demobilizing of public demand upon governments.

- In the Third World and the former Soviet sphere, the richer capitalist countries have encouraged liberal democracy and observance of individual human rights but have given priority to 'market reform', i.e. conformity to economic globalization, as a condition for financial and political support.

- There are some tendencies towards depoliticization, apathy towards formal political processes, a conviction of powerlessness to effect change, and scepticism about the integrity and competency of politicians.

- In consequence, a political space remains open to the manipulations of the covert world.

- Preference for authoritarian solutions and mystification of problems in extreme nationalist, racist and fascist discourses also invade this open political space.

On the other hand, there is some evidence of resilience in civil society, though not apparently in any effectively coherent form. This includes:

- A growth of community self-help on a local basis.

- Organized collective opposition to the adverse social effects of economic globalization in both rich and poor societies.

- Transnational social movements such as those concerned with feminism, peace, ecology, and indigenous peoples which are committed to the search for alternative ways of producing and consuming and an alternative world view that would combine social equity and biospheric sustainability with a more substantively participatory democracy.

3.4 Conditions for substantive democracy

This leads us to face up to a problem of intellectual and moral reform. In the realm of intellectual reform, a longer time perspective would be conducive to the kinds of changes that would make possible the development of alternatives to economic globalization and would be more conducive to biospheric survival. Our age is characterized by 'present-mindedness', an attitude of mind that is encouraged by the media with its emphasis on the instantaneous and the ephemeral. The perspective of time is necessary to an understanding of the threat of biospheric collapse and the development of alternative ways of living and working that could prevent it. Intellectual reform in this fundamental sense would have to become a task of resurgent civil society if a democratic choice for a sustainable world were to become possible.

Moral reform need not be discussed, in the first instance, in terms of 'values' (traditional values, family values, and so forth). The primary question, which arises prior to a debate about specific values, concerns the existence or absence of a sense of community, mutual responsibility, or collective solidarity, that is to say, the shared sentiment upon which political authority can rest.

A market economy is based in principle on individualism; but can a democratic polity be based on individualism alone? Does the very idea of democracy not presuppose an organic solidarity of community? Is not the central problem of liberal democracy the problem of loss of community, the atomization of populations into agglomerations of disconnected individuals? Of course, these cannot be just one big community. The sense of affinity and solidarity has to be built up on the basis of living local communities. These would be the substance of a resuscitated civil society capable of sustaining political authority and generating a common will to live in harmony with nature.

There is, of course, a danger to democracy in rejecting individualism altogether, not only in the more extreme forms this rejection can take, such as religious integralism and fascist idolatry of the state, but also in the more subtle discouragement of critical thought and innovation.

All we can say today is that a democratic movement which would transcend the limited formal kind to embrace a social dimension would have to be based upon a socially cohesive revivified civil society, and this will have to be generated from within. It would not be democratic if it were to be dependent upon infusion by well-meaning but intrusive foreigners. This is crucial to a politics that would work to sustain the biosphere, and to make social equity the goal of public policy. Such a movement would presage an alternative meaning of 'globalization'.

One well-publicized view of the present condition of the world is that with the end of the Cold War and the collapse of 'real socialism' human history, the history of conflict over the way in which societies should be organized, has come to an end. In this view, the only remaining historically valid form of polity and society is both liberal-democratic and capitalist. Since history has been about the struggle among different forms of society and polity, what this ultimate solution to the struggle brings us to is the 'end of history' (Fukuyama, 1992). Within this political-economic framework there are, of course, still problems to be resolved but these are in the nature of technical problems that do not call the overall framework into question. This view is consistent with the ideology of economic globalization. It is congenial to those who are the beneficiaries of the present economic and social order, living in what a critical US political economist has called the 'culture of contentment' (Galbraith, 1992).

The analysis presented in this chapter derives from other sources. It tries to look at the world from the perspective of those who cannot be content with things as they are – the view from below. It rejects the notion that the dialectic of history can reach finality. The dominant tendencies of one era, including very definitely our own, benefit some and disadvantage others. World history is a never-ending struggle to expand social equity and to overcome relations of dominance and subordination which are continually taking new forms.

The above passages constitute an attempt to define the obstacles to substantive democracy that result from economic globalization; and to show how they relate to ecological degradation and the decomposition of civil society. They also aim to suggest a strategy towards reversing these degenerative tendencies through a recomposition of civil society, at all levels from the household to the world, that could bring the economy within its control and provide the basis for a participative democracy. The suggestions are in the briefest outline. They will be elaborated less through intellectual concentration than by reflection upon the experience of an active citizenship.

References

Albert, M. (1991) *Capitalism Econtre Capitalisme*, Paris, Seuil.

Camilleri, J.A. and Falk, J. (1992) *The End of Sovereignty?: the Politics of a Shrinking and Fragmenting World*, Aldershot, Edward Elgar.

Cheru, F. (1989) *The Silent Revolution in Africa: Debt, Development and Democracy*, London, Zed Books.

Club of Rome (1972) *The Limits to Growth*, Meadows, D. *et al.* (eds), New York, Universe Books.

Cox, R.W. (1987) *Production, Power, the World Order: Social Forces in the Making of History,* New York, Columbia University Press.

Cox, R.W. (1991) 'Real socialism in historical perspective' in Miliband, R. and Panitch, L.; *The Socialist Register, 1991*, London, Merlin Press.

Cox, R.W. (1992) 'Global perestroika' in Miliband, R. and Panitch, L., *The Socialist Register 1992*, London, Merlin Press.

Crozier, M., Huntington, S.P. and Watanuki, S. (1975) *The Crisis of Democracy*. Report on the governability of democracies to the Trilateral Commission. New York, New York University Press.

Fukuyama, F. (1992) *The End of History and the Last Man,* New York, Avon Books.

Galbraith, K. (1992) *The Culture of Contentment*, Boston, Houghton Mifflin.

Gills, B. and Frank, A.G. (1992) 'World-system cycles, crises and hegemonial shifts, 1700 B.C. to 1700 A.D.', *Review* XV, vol.4, pp.621–716.

Gramsci, A. (1971) *Selections from the Prison Notebooks*, edited and translated by Hoare, Q. and Nowell Smith, G., New York, International Publishers.

Guéhenno, J.-M. (1993) *La Fin de la Démocratie*, Paris, Flammarion.

Helleiner, E. (1994) *States and the Reemergence of Global Finance. From Bretton Woods to the 1990s,* Ithaca, Cornell University Press.

Helleiner, E. (1995) 'Great transformations: a Polanyian perspective on the contemporary global financial order', *Studies in Political Economy*, no.48, pp.149–64.

Helleiner, E. (1996) 'International political economy and the greens', *New Political Economy*, vol.1, no.1.

Hobsbawm, E.J. (1975) *The Age of Capital 1848–1875*, London, Weidenfeld and Nicholson.

Madeuf, B. and Michalet, C.A. (1978), 'A new approach to international economics', *International Social Science Journal*, vol.XXX, no.2, pp.253–83.

Maier, C.S. (1977) 'The politics of productivity: foundations of American international economic policy after World War II', *International Organization*, vol.31, no.4, pp.607–34.

Maier, C.S. (1978) 'The politics of inflation in the twentieth century' in Hirsch, F. and Goldthorpe, J.H. (eds) *The Political Economy of Inflation*, Oxford, Martin Robertson.

Polanyi, K. (1944) *The Great Transformation. The Political and Economic Origins of our Time*, Boston, Beacon Press.

Potter, D., Goldblatt, D., Kiloh, M. and Lewis, P. (eds) (1997) *Democratization*, Cambridge, Polity Press.

Robinson, W.I. (1996) *Promoting Polyarchy: Globalization, US Intervention, and Hegemony*, Cambridge, Cambridge University Press.

Sinclair, T.J. (1994) 'Passing judgement: credit rating processes as regulatory mechanisms of governance in the emerging world order', *Review of International Political Economy*, vol.1, no.1.

UNRISD (1995) *States of Disarray: the Social Effects of Globalization*, London, United Nations Research Institute for Social Development.

Wallerstein, I. (1974a) *The Modern World-System. Capitalist Agriculture and the Origins of the European World-Economy in the Sixteenth Century*, New York, Academic Press.

Wallerstein, I. (1974b) 'The rise and future demise of the world capitalist system: concepts for comparative analysis', *Comparative Studies in Society and History*, vol.16, no.4, pp.378–415.

Further reading

Camilleri, J.A., and Falk, J. (1992) *The End of Sovereignty? The Politics of a Shrinking and Fragmenting World*, Aldershot, Edward Elgar.

Held, D. *Democracy and the Global Order: From the Modern State to Cosmopolitan Governance*, Stanford, California, Stanford University Press.

Helleiner, E. (1996) 'International political economy and the greens', *New Political Economy*, 1 (1).

Hettne, B. (1995) *Development Theory and the Three Worlds* (2nd edn), London, Longman.

Sakamoto, Y. (ed.) (1994) *Global Transformation: Challenges to the State System*, Tokyo, United Nations University Press.

UNRISD (1995) *States of Disarray. The Social Effects of Globalization*, London, United Nations Research Institute for Social Development.

CHAPTER 4

Liberal democracy and the globalization of environmental risks

David Goldblatt

Introduction

Across the world societies are currently experiencing and looking forward to historically unprecedented levels of environmental degradation that pose dangers to human health, ecosystem survival and increasingly threaten economic development and social stability. This is because the toxicity and complexity of pollution has increased and the sheer volume of people, consumption and production has risen exponentially. Environmental degradation, like demographic expansion, is a cumulative phenomena. We are all facing the toxic pay-back for the North's industrial revolutions – both capitalist and socialist. We are all beginning to reap the consequences of the explosive pace of industrialization and population increase in the South. Not all states or societies are affected equally, similarly or in proportion to the environmental degradation that they are collectively responsible for. Nor do all social groups in all societies experience similar environmental threats or accord a similar priority to curtailing environmental degradation. None the less, no polity, democratic or otherwise, has been left untouched by these epochal transformations. In this chapter I focus on the impact of these shifts on liberal democratic states.

In Section 4.1 I examine the implications of environmental degradation for democratic politics within nation-states. I argue that liberal democracy's capacity to respond to environmental degradation is limited and that its existing representative and parliamentary institutions do not allow for effective democratic control over environmental policy matters. Because of the causal origins of environmental degradation, states are forced to try and regulate areas of social life that have previously been ignored. Causally, environmental degradation is immensely complex – its origins can be traced to economic, demographic, political and cultural factors. For example, cars are too cheap to drive, too many people are driving them, politicians will not make it more expensive for them. In any case, we all love the car, don't we? In general, we seem capable of generating immense new technologies without stopping to consider their likely environmental consequences. States, democratic or otherwise, are called upon by the exigencies of environmental degradation to try and regulate the previously unpoliticized and apparently benign dynamic of technological change.

The political impact of environmental degradation is also complicated by its spatial character. Environmental degradation, actual and possible, is becoming increasingly *globalized* in its origins and consequences; knitting together states and societies in complex webs of mutual interdependence and international regulation and interaction. As such, it is not only the representative character of liberal democratic states that is problematized by environmental degradation, but also their territorial form as autonomous or sovereign nation-states. In Section 4.2 I review the concept of the *globalization of environmental problems*. This will allow us to determine the *transformations of the conditions of liberal democracy* that *global* environmental problems in particular, rather than environmental problems in general, set in motion. Finally, I examine the *democratic challenges* these changes pose for liberal democratic states.

In Sections 4.3 and 4.4 I examine two case studies of serious global environmental problems: ozone depletion and global warming. I review the character and causes of environmental degradation, the threats they pose, and the ways in which states have tried internationally and domestically to respond to these problems. I ask how the political peculiarities of environmental degradation in general, and global environmental degradation in particular, affect or prevent the nature of democratic responses to these issues. In Section 4.5 I ask whether, on balance, global environmental degradation is undermining the legitimacy and efficacy of liberal democratic states. Against this I examine the argument that new democratic practices, locally, nationally and globally are emerging which both preserve the democratic credentials of liberal democratic states and generate new spaces for democratic politics.

4.1   Environmental degradation and the limits to liberal democratic politics

In the 1950s environmental issues formed a small and insignificant part of public debate and political agendas in liberal democratic societies. On the margins the worst excesses of air pollution became the subject of legislation and regulation, land and species conservation legislation began to develop and the creation of national parks got underway. However, these hardly constituted the mainstream of politics. By the 1980s and 1990s, although environmental issues had not displaced more traditional concerns, they had acquired an enduring place on the political agendas of liberal democracies. It has been impossible for governments to avoid engagement with global warming, ozone depletion, acid rain and toxic waste issues. Nearly all liberal democratic states now possess a larger and more stringent body of environmental legislation; they have acquired permanent, environmental ministries and environmental protection agencies (Weale, 1992). While the fortunes of Green parties vary – from successes in Germany to the enduring irrelevance of the British Greens – and the power, income and membership of environmental pressure groups fluctuate, there has been a secular rise in their importance, their impact on mainstream parties of both left and right (all of whom must now profess, at least, to be environmentally concerned), their incorporation into the policy process and a shift in the terms and character of political debate (Robinson, 1992). None of this appears problematic for liberal democratic politics. Indeed, it is an example of democracy at work. A combination of protest, persuasion and electoral success has dragged environmental issues and interests into the political arena. However, a series of arguments also exists which suggests that the nature of environmental degradation and the rise of environmental politics pose a range of problems for liberal democracies.

Invisibility, uncertainty and the long term

Three physical characteristics of environmental degradation set particular constraints upon environmental politics: the *invisibility* of pollution; the *uncertainty* of its impacts; and the *enduring and cumulative* character of its consequences. Some of the consequences of environmental degradation may be visible to the naked eye and to the uncritical observer – dead fish in a river are difficult to miss. But, many of the physical and biochemical processes which generate environmental problems are socially invisible. No one can see heavy metals leaching into the soil from a waste dump, no one can sense radioactive isotopes in the atmosphere. More often than not, the occurrence of environmental degradation and its physical and biological causes can only be revealed by specialized technologies, scientific discourse and rigorous analysis. Having established the existence of some form of environmental degradation it remains open as to the extent of environmental change, its social origins and its significance for human health or ecosystem stability. Even then the answers suggested by scientific and sociological research are highly contestable. What is pollution?, what causes pollution?, what will its consequences be, for whom and when? are questions necessarily suspended in an open-ended debate.

In almost no other area of public policy is the accuracy of scientific argument more keenly debated and its epistemological status so critically examined. The complexities and uncertainties of environmental science, and the range of differing opinions on almost every issue demonstrate with great clarity what philosophers of science have been arguing for some time. Science as a practice does not generate clear, unassailable descriptions of the world or accurate predictions about the future. Yet the outcome of these scientific debates will have enormous environmental, economic and political implications. Therefore, access to scientific knowledge, the skills to engage with the technical debate, the resources to fund and interpret research and disseminate argument have all become critical sources of political power. If you cannot demonstrate that a factory is producing pollutants, or that those pollutants are finding their way into people's bodies, and once in those bodies have toxic effects, then it is almost impossible to successfully argue for the environmental control of that factory. If someone makes that claim and you can mobilize research which disproves it or throws doubt upon its findings, then the case for control is fatally weakened. Science becomes a powerful political tool and the scientific community plays an important role in environmental politics (see Haas, 1990; Beck, 1992, 1995; Rowlands, 1994).

Liberal democracies are unfamiliar with the politicization of these kinds of debate. Their capacity to deal with them may not simply be a case of learning new skills, there may be structural obstacles to making these debates and this form of power democratically accountable. Practically – given a politics dominated by definitions and technical decisions – can representative institutions function as effective or legitimate organs of decision making? The accuracy of scientific argument is not easily debated in the context of parliaments where neither expertise nor time is readily available. While the outcome of these debates is intensely political, the dividing lines between different positions does not sit meaningfully with the lines of representation in most liberal democratic political systems. Differences of opinion and interpretation are most likely to occur between producers and consumers of environmentally problematic products, or between experts and the public – class, regional or denominational based parties hardly align with these cleavages. In any case, the majoritarian principles of representative institutions do not combine easily with the character of scientific disagreements. A vote in the House of Commons simply cannot determine the rightness of an environmental or toxicological argument. Normatively, it can be argued that access to and control over scientific knowledge is so asymmetrically distributed between state and civil society, producers and consumers, experts and publics that the determination of environmental public policy is systematically skewed towards the interests of polluters rather than the public.

The uncertainty of environmental change combines with its temporal character to introduce further problems for liberal democratic politics (Pearce, 1990; Jacobs, 1991). It has become clear that the impact of pollution outlasts its initial moment of creation. Nuclear wastes will be with us for some time to come. Similarly, it is well established that the impact of pollution is cumulative. Weakened ecosystems become less and less able to endure similar levels of pollution. Pollutants build up in concentration in the atmosphere, in the seas or in human bodies unable to excrete them. More recently, chaotic models of biological systems as well as observations of environmental change have suggested that cumulative change can give way to sudden, unexpected and extensive change – the progress of the ozone hole discussed in Section 4.3 demonstrates this. What are the implications of enduring environmental degradation and the possibility of sudden and enormous change for liberal democratic polities?

One way of looking at this is to argue that the future course of environmental degradation will fall on a spectrum of outcomes ranging from the catastrophic to no change or danger at all – the pessimistic and the optimistic scenarios. In turn we can take up a response on a spectrum ranging from caution and pre-emptive action to business as usual where we make no changes. If the pessimistic predications on global warming are correct – and they may not be – we are looking at a pretty bumpy ride in the twenty-first century: increasing average global temperatures, major changes in climatic patterns, rising sea levels, shrinking polar ice caps, major coastal flooding, population movements and social turmoil in some places, desertification in others. These outcomes are not certain, but they pose a significant set of risks. There is, therefore, a case for pre-emptive caution in environmental policy making; big changes now before we are forced to face catastrophic consequences. This in turn rests on the idea that the interests of future generations, those that will actually have to live through such a situation, must be included in the calculations of contemporary decision makers. If we did not know which generation we were going to be born into would we accept as legitimate a political system that discounts the future and passes risks on through the generations? Many environmentalists say we should not accept such a system as legitimate (Barry, 1991). However, liberal democracies may have difficulty in incorporating this demand. Electoral competition and electoral cycles mean that democratic politics is rarely able to generate policies which look forward further than the next election. In the absence of a solid society-wide consensus on the inclusion of future generations' interests in policy making, liberal democracies provide few political incentives for their interests to be given prominence. In a representative democracy who is going to represent the interests of those that have no vote?

Alternatively, political communities may choose to ignore the risk, continue with business as usual and opt to deal with environmental problems if and when they show up. If that is the outcome of a democratic decision-making process then the cautious will just have to lump it, and if the pessimistic predictions are wrong then all well and good. However, if the pessimistic predictions are right we will be in trouble. Many environmentalists argue that the only adequate response to this threat is wholesale transformation of industrialized economies: affecting energy production, transport, agriculture, a shift to renewable resources and a generalized reduction in unnecessary consumption. Is it possible for liberal democracies to radically transform patterns of consumption and investment? Is it possible to divert sufficient capital into investments whose pay-off – if it comes at all – will only come 40 or 50 years hence? The question is whether the decision-making process in liberal democracies makes a cautious choice politically feasible or does the character of liberal democracy actually preclude some outcomes? It is taken for granted that democracies should institutionally preclude their own dissolution and the emergence of authoritarianism. Beyond this, their legitimacy has rested on the idea that they make space possible for a variety of different political projects to be pursued subject only to popular support and constitutional propriety. The risk of environmental catastrophe and the political options it presents us with may sharply challenge this aspect of liberal democratic politics.

Summary of Section 4.1

- The origins and consequences of environmental degradation are only made politically 'visible' through access to specialized knowledge. This key political resource is so asymmetrically distributed that democratic political resolutions to environmental questions may be a chimera. Parliamentary institutions may be a poor forum for democratically debating these issues.

- Liberal democracies may generate structural obstacles to the articulation and representation of future interests and the implementation of precautionary economic and political change.

- Technological development has important consequences for the scale and scope of environmental degradation. The regulation and development of technology has been constructed as non-political. States have proved poor advocates for environmental interests while key decision-making realms remain democratically unaccountable.

4.2 The globalization of environmental problems

What is environmental globalization?

There are three forms of environmental globalization – *transboundary pollution, environmental interdependence*, and the *degradation of the environmental commons*. Clearly, pollution and environmental degradation are neither impeded by nor acknowledge the existence and impermeability of any political and territorial jurisdiction – acid rain, a form of *transboundary pollution*, is a good example. Sulphur dioxides, generated in one place from the exhaust fumes of motor vehicles and the emissions from coal- and oil-based electricity plants, pass upwards into the atmosphere, are converted to sulphuric acids by their interaction with water in the atmosphere and then, as clouds and rain, are transported from their point of origin to wherever wind and climate take them. In the case of acid rain in Western Europe there are multiple national sites of pollution production and a multiplicity of destinations. Sweden, for example, receives acid depositions from Western and Eastern Europe, from its direct Scandinavian neighbours as well as Germany, the UK and the Baltic states. Thus, transboundary atmospheric pollution problems are often *regional* in their geographical form. It is only when they become inter-regional or transcontinental in their extent that we can consider them to be a form of globalization (see Chapter 1, Section 1.2).

The separation of the place of creation of degradation and the impact of that degradation can be conceptualized as *environmental interdependence*. These kinds of interconnections are primarily biological in their form, although derived from social processes. A chain of causal, physical effects is set in motion in one place, transported physically to another place (e.g. acid rain through the air on the wind) or has its impact elsewhere through a long and complex chain of physio-chemical interactions (e.g. greenhouse emissions leading to altered climatic patterns).

We can add to this a sense of social and political interconnectedness best captured by conceiving of globalization as the *stretching and deepening of social relations*. Consider the global politics and implications of population expansion. All environmental problems have a demographic dimension, for all other things being equal, more people means more pollution and resource consumption. Almost all contemporary population growth is occurring in the South. The environmental consequences of this are primarily located in the actual states experiencing rapid demographic change. However, there is a tendency for the consequences of those changes to spill over into the politics of other nations. Rapid demographic growth is a key factor in explaining the increasing immiseration of sub-Saharan Africa and the processes of desertification and soil decline. This has already spilled over into the growing economic problems of the region and its mounting international debts. In the future the demographic and environmental squeeze on the South may contribute towards political instability and migration, both of which will affect a widening pool of other nations, internationally and domestically.

While environmental degradation can be wrought upon highly localized and purely national environmental resources and ecosystems, it can also affect shared resources and ecosystems. Indeed, the entire planet can be viewed as a single interrelated ecosystem. The *environmental commons*, thus described, are those elements of the environment that are simultaneously used, experienced and shared by more than one state and under the effective jurisdiction or sovereignty of no one – the application of a singular national political authority or a singular private property owner is impossible. The atmosphere is the best example of this type of commons. It is a resource, essential for life, that immerses and exceeds every state and society. It is inconceivable that any one can effectively own the atmosphere and no one can be excluded from its usage, yet the consequences of any single action can have impacts of a highly unpredictable and volatile nature all over the planet. The American predilection for the motor car and profligate energy use entails a very large release of greenhouse gases into the atmosphere and a significant contribution to global warming. Thus we can establish a complex chain of causation between US transport and energy policy, the changing agricultural fortunes of Bangladesh or sub-Saharan Africa and their internal politics. Decisions on public expenditure on sea defences and desertification measures are tied to and dependent upon decisions made elsewhere about road building and energy efficiency. Politics is in effect *stretched*. As we already know this kind of intersection between two sets of domestic political forces and social change is nothing new. However, what distinguishes contemporary problems of the environmental commons and makes the application of the idea of globalization useful is that it alerts us to both the depths to which such interrelations reach inside national polities and the increasing number of separate national polities and policy areas drawn into the expanding web of stretched relationships – the *deepening* of spatially separate social processes or the increasing *intensity* of global and regional interactions.

Globalization of the environment and the transformation of liberal democratic politics

Environmental problems and their spatial organization are closely interconnected with the causal forces at work in their creation and the attempts to modulate them. Thus there is a fourth sense in which we can connect environmental matters with the idea of globalization. This does not derive from the material extent, organization or form of environmental degradation and change but from the spatial characteristics of the social institutions that both generate environmental degradation and attempt to control or limit it. The origins and consequences of global and regional environmental problems intersect with global and regional economic, political and cultural institutions and processes. An example of each shows how the idea of globalization can be usefully brought to bear on the phenomena.

In the case of economics it can be argued that the steady diffusion of industrial mechanisms of production from North to South – a form of globalization – has led to a massive increase in the total capacity of the global economy to generate environmental pollutants and threaten global commons like the seas and atmosphere. In political terms it is clear enough that a range of institutions and treaties have been established over the last 20 years which encompass a very large number of countries, place significant limits on domestic political and economic practices and lock previously national centres of politics and administration, like departments or ministries of the environment, into global and regional networks of agenda building, policy formation and policy implementation. The recognition and estimation of environmental degradation is clearly linked to an expanding international network of scientists (or epistemic communities) and pressure groups whose arguments and analyses spread rapidly over the globe influencing purely domestic debates and environmental perspectives, as well as helping to forge a broader global or international consensus on the character, consequences and appropriate responses to shared environmental problems. To the extent that environmental degradation is caused by the intensification of global economic processes, recognized by transnational scientific or epistemic communities and controlled or modulated by international regimes or organizations, or regulated by international law, we can confidently talk of an increasing *globalization of environmental affairs.*

What are the likely impacts, normative and practical, of these processes of environmental globalization on liberal democratic polities? In what sense has there been a *transformation in the conditions* of liberal democratic politics? Liberal democracies are *territorial* democracies. It is assumed that citizens in a demarcated territory constitute a shared political community of fate. They elect national governments who are responsive to the electorate's interests and capable of delivering on their electoral promises. In theory national government is the only political institution that has the sovereign right to legitimately rule within a delimited territory and the actual political autonomy and capacity to do so. The globalization of environmental problems throws all of these assumptions into the air (see Chapter 1, Section 1.3). First, the existence of the global commons and its collective ecological decline has generated an environmental community of fate far bigger than any single nation-state. This point is enforced by the existence of transboundary pollution and environmental interdependence. Thus both the rightful scope of the democratic political community and the extent of reciprocal obligations, responsibilities, and rights can no longer be located exclusively at the level of a nation alone. Second, even if we restrict ourselves to national political communities, the geographical scope of ecosystems and environmental degradation easily evades the sovereign reach of the largest nation-state. No state has the autonomous capacity to control the quality of its atmosphere or to prevent pollution arriving on the wind. Third, the sovereign legal entitlement to rule in a given domain has been compromised by the web of commitments, treaties and international legal obligations that states have acceded to. Fourth, the capacity of a polity to pursue an autonomous public policy is constrained by its necessary involvement in international environmental regimes where it must bargain with other states. However, in the one domain where a meaningful political community of environmental fate can be represented – international institutions – democratic accountability is particularly difficult to achieve. I shall

explore these problems below in connection with the international response to ozone depletion and global warming.

─────────────── **Summary of Section 4.2** ───────────────

- The globalization of environmental problems takes three forms:
  transboundary pollution, environmental interdependence and
  degradation of the global commons.

- One consequence of this has been an increase in the number, density
  and geographical scope of international networks, political processes
  and legal frameworks concerned with environmental issues.

- Globalization of environmental problems transforms the conditions of
  democracy in the liberal democratic state because the environmental
  community of fate is much larger than any single nation. Nation-states
  are too small to be effective and the international institutions that have
  emerged are not democratically constituted.

4.3   Ozone depletion

Ozone chemistry: the basics

Ozone is a bluish gas with a sharp and pungent odour. Its name is derived
from the Greek for smell. Chemically it is a particular form of oxygen, made
up of three oxygen atoms. Most ozone is concentrated in the mid-ranges of
the stratosphere about 20–35 km above the earth's surface – the ozone layer –
where concentrations rise a hundred-fold. The key environmental role of the
ozone layer is its capacity to absorb ultraviolet (UV) light from the sun and
prevent it reaching the earth's surface where it can cause considerable
damage. At one time the science was hotly contested, but today it is thought
that increasing levels of UV radiation are connected to increasing rates of
human skin cancer, cataracts and immune system disorders. UV radiation also
appears to have a widespread and dangerous impact upon aquatic life and
terrestrial plant life.

Very little ozone is naturally produced on the earth's surface. Rather,
stratospheric ozone is the product of a complex series of chemical reactions
in the earth's atmosphere. The whole ensemble of reactions exist in a state of
dynamic equilibrium in which other gases in the stratosphere act as *catalysts*
of the reaction that breaks ozone down. Catalysts speed up chemical
reactions but are not consumed themselves in the process. Thus every
catalytic molecule can take part in the destruction of hundreds of thousands
of ozone molecules before it is destroyed. These catalytic trace gases are
naturally occurring and contain either hydrogen, nitrogen and chlorine, like
nitrogen oxides and methane. In fact, the chemistry of stratospheric ozone
consists of hundreds of interrelated reactions and reaction cycles. None the
less, even at low levels of ozone concentration the absorptive capacity of the
ozone layer has been sufficient to keep UV levels on the earth's surface
within tolerable limits.

CFCs: origins and consequences

This is where CFCs or chlorofluorocarbons enter the picture. CFCs are carbon-based molecules in which one or more of the atoms binding onto the carbon is a halide, i.e. chlorine or fluorine (Benedick, 1991; Miller, 1995; Parson, 1993; Rowlands, 1994). They were first patented in 1928 by Du Pont and General Motors who had been seeking a replacement for the highly volatile materials previously used in refrigeration. The chemical and physical properties of CFCs made them ideally suited to this and many other industrial uses. They are extremely stable, inert, reasonably easy to produce and non-toxic. CFCs came to be used in not only refrigeration but in air conditioning systems, as industrial solvents, as the propellant for aerosols, for blowing foam and use in fire extinguishers.

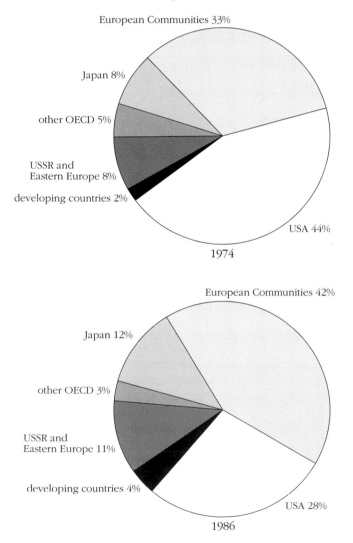

Figure 4.1   Global CFC production by region, 1974 and 1986
Source: Rowlands (1994, p.105)

Global production of CFCs doubled every five years through to the 1970s. Nearly half of global production was in the USA and half of that was Du Pont alone (see Figure 4.1). One or two significant producers were located in the UK, France, Germany, Italy and Japan with a smattering of smaller plants in the USSR, Greece and Spain. Over 50 per cent of output was consumed in aerosols. It was only in the early 1970s that these chemicals were first thought to be environmentally problematic. In a seminal paper by Rowland and Molina, the authors argued that very long-lived CFC molecules must, after use or disposal, find their way up into the stratosphere. Here they would release some of their fluorine and chlorine atoms which would act as very effective catalysts in the breakdown of ozone thus diminishing ozone concentrations. This in turn would increase the volume of dangerous UV light reaching the earth's surface, which would normally be absorbed by ozone breakdown reactions (Rowland and Molina, 1974). This triggered a series of national and international debates and political struggles over the production and use of CFCs.

Although significant early action was taken by the environmentally precautionary governments of Sweden, Norway and the Netherlands the political focus was in the USA, which was the biggest producer and consumer of CFCs. On one side the US environmental movement, concerned scientists and the Natural Resources Defence Council called for an immediate ban. Du Pont, the company with the biggest stake in their retention, argued that the scientific evidence was no more than hypothesis at that stage and should evidence be forthcoming they would cease production. It is important to note that at this stage the empirical evidence for levels of overall ozone depletion was lacking and no one had predicted or located the existence of ozone holes – areas of the stratosphere where ozone levels were peculiarly low. A turbulent and highly publicized conflict resulted in a US ban on CFC use for all except essential products. Moreover, US and Scandinavian pressure led to the first international meeting on ozone depletion, convened by the UNEP (United Nations Environment Programme) in Washington in 1977. This set up a permanent monitoring body, the CCOL (Coordinating Committee on the Ozone Layer), which acted as the international co-ordinator and clearing house of ozone chemistry and ozone depletion research for the next eight years.

From Vienna to Montreal

Progress remained slow for the following decade as the science remained uncertain and the lobbying powers of US and European CFC producers coalesced in the powerful Alliance for Responsible CFC Policy. In 1981, at the behest of the Swedish government, the UNEP called a further international convention on the ozone layer with a view to creating an international regulatory regime that would limit CFC use and production across the world. Meeting in 1982 and 1984 no agreement was possible between supporters of CFC control (small producer and consumer states with strong environmental movements like Sweden and the Netherlands) and opponents (large producer and consumer states). British, German, French and Japanese delegations were staffed, in part, by industrial representatives whose views dominated on technical and scientific committees. The leverage and presence of environmental non-governmental organizations was minimal and under Ronald Reagan's anti-environmentalist presidency the power of the EPA (US Environmental Protection Agency) to lead US negotiating positions was much diminished. A framework convention was signed in Vienna in 1985 only committing the parties to further research and action to identify the scale of the problem. What turned events around, primarily, was a decisive shift in the scientific debate.

Data on stratospheric concentrations of ozone had been recorded for a number of years by the British Antarctic Survey based at Halley Bay. In 1985 they released data which unequivocally demonstrated the existence of a seasonal ozone hole over the Antarctic ice sheets. While industrial representatives continued to dispute the evidence the balance of power began to shift away from the producers. The debate centred around two technical committees established by the UNEP after the Vienna convention. Meeting through 1985 and 1986 national governments began to adopt a different attitude to the CFC industry, environmental NGOs became more politically effective and the US delegation took a significant leading role in pushing negotiations forward. A split began to develop between US and European producers, with Du Pont accepting the case for controls on the growth of CFC production and investing heavily in CFC substitutes. Environmental NGOs and European Green parties also began to mount strong and very effective domestic campaigns against CFC use in key producer states like Britain and Germany. Thus by the time the Montreal convention had begun, in late 1987, a very significant weight of opinion had formed behind the creation of a much more stringent international regime that would combine binding legal commitments to action, processes of verification and timetables for implementation. Intensive negotiations produced the Montreal Protocol which required signatories to cut production of the five main CFCs by 50 per cent from 1986 production levels by the year

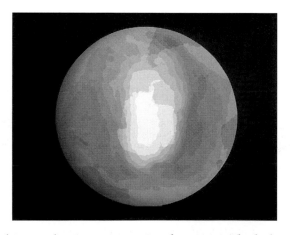

The 'ozone hole' over the Antarctic in October 1991. The hole is seen in white surrounded by increasingly darker areas representing increasing concentrations of ozone. The region of depleted ozone extends over the southern tip of South America at the top of the illustration

2000. In addition tight trade restrictions were placed on signatories preventing CFC imports. Further large cuts in production were planned for the early 1990s and a periodic review and updating procedure of the protocol established.

Montreal and London conventions: democratic implications

The Halley Bay observations stimulated and informed a NASA led scientific project through 1986 and 1987. The original Halley Bay observations were confirmed and a plausible mechanism for ozone depletion outlined. Previous work on ozone chemistry had been predominantly one-dimensional assuming an equivalence of conditions across the earth's surface, but results indicated a particularly intense level of Antarctic ozone depletion. Simply put, in the winter months a stable vortex of rotating air forms over the South Pole which keeps air trapped in the region. Within the vortex stratospheric temperatures are extremely low and encourage the formation of ice in the form of polar stratospheric crystals. These provide a surface on which catalytic ozone depletion is speeded even further while the vortex ensures that ozone-rich air from more temperate regions cannot flow in and replenish lost ozone. Thus ozone levels fall precipitously.

This evidence began to emerge soon after the Montreal meeting. It broke the stranglehold of the global chemical industries' scepticism and the willingness of governments to support them in international negotiations. By mid 1988 Du Pont was supporting a global phase-out of CFCs and it was joined by the European chemical industry in late 1988. By this time Du Pont had sunk over $40 million into the development of CFC substitutes. The UNEP re-convened international negotiations on updating Montreal. It was only at this point that developing nations began to be involved in the negotiations in any substantive way. By the late 1980s CFC production was beginning to expand in the South. China, India and other large southern states had to be incorporated because their potential CFC use was huge. However, these states feared that a CFC phase-out would leave their chemical and refrigeration industries dependent on Western corporations who controlled the CFC substitutes. The London Revision to the Montreal Protocol, signed in 1990, provided for a complete phase-out of CFC production by the year 2000 as well as more stringent controls on other ozone depleting chemicals. It provided for a permanent secretariat and the development of monitoring and non-compliance procedures. Its most innovative features were a commitment to North South technology transfer in CFC replacements and a financial instrument that would fund those transfers.

Ozone depletion is a clear example of the degradation of the global commons (although with an uneven geography of origins and conse-quences). It is a problem that exceeds the effective reach of any single state and generates an environmental community of fate that cuts across state borders. It has its roots in an earlier failure to predict the environmental consequences of a seemingly benign technology, consequences that seemed to suddenly shift towards the catastrophic. It is also worth noting that those areas most at risk from ozone depletion were Northern Europe and Australasia. However, CFC reduction, despite the continuing and unpredictable threat of ozone depletion, is a success story. Liberal democratic governments who were the main players in most of the international negotiations were able, in response to both scientific argument and considerable popular pressure, to co-ordinate national policies through an international regime for phasing out the production of CFCs. In so doing they were both responsive to the interests of current and future generations and able to circumvent the problems of national governments in a globalized political environment. The early stages of the struggle indicate the privileged position of producers and governments over consumers and publics in the creation, use and dissemination of scientific argument. Though as the NASA research shows when the evidence becomes more incontrovertible, industry's own commitment to the 'truth' of science acts against it. Du Pont was forced by its own rhetoric to abandon CFC production. The financial and technology transfer elements of the London convention show that it is possible for the interests of weaker states in the South to have some purchase in international institutions – for a global ban on production can be broken by the weakest link in the chain. However, these successes may not be repeatable. Only a very small number of chemicals, products, technologies, companies and jobs were at stake in only a few countries. The resource transfers required were small scale and thus the distribution of environmental and economic 'bads' were quite minimal. The science, for all its complexity, was focused enough that consensus was possible. None of these factors apply to the case of global warming considered in the next section.

─────────────────────── **Summary of Section 4.3** ───────────────────────

- CFC production has led to the creation of ozone holes at the poles creating significant increased risks of skin cancer and other environmental damage. This is an example of the *degradation of the environmental commons.*

- Scientific research stimulated national regulatory efforts in the West in the 1970s and international efforts in the 1980s.

- Slow progress and industrial resistance were broken by dramatic new scientific research and domestic, as well as international, campaigns by environmental NGOs.

- International agreement on the regulation of technology and production proved possible because: the science was reasonably clear, the number of losers from a phase-out small, and the costs of incorporating the developing world relatively low.

4.4 Global warming

Global warming: the basics

Global warming and the enhanced greenhouse effect are often used interchangeably (Legget, 1990; Nillson and Pitt, 1994; Rowlands, 1994; Young, 1994). In this chapter I use the greenhouse effect to refer to the physio-chemical processes by which the atmosphere retains heat and keeps the earth appreciably warmer than it would otherwise be. I use global warming to refer to the climatic consequences of transformations in the gaseous composition of the atmosphere produced by human action. The idea that the earth's atmosphere acted like the panes of glass in a greenhouse – letting sunlight in but not letting as much out, thereby heating the interior – was first proposed by Fourier in the early nineteenth century. The actual interaction of sunlight with the earth's surface and atmosphere is very complex, but the basic principles are simple. Sunlight that reaches the earth is a mixture of many different wavelengths, visible, infra-red and ultraviolet. Some of that light is reflected back out into space immediately, some is absorbed by the earth's surface and oceans and some is reflected back but in the form of infra-red light – this light and the energy it carries is trapped by gases in the earth's atmosphere and warms the planet. In the late nineteenth century the Swedish meteorologist Arhheius argued that the burning of fossil fuels released an increasing level of carbon dioxide into the earth's atmosphere. Carbon dioxide is the most important gaseous element of the greenhouse effect. Over time the accumulation of carbon dioxide in the atmosphere should lead to more heat being trapped and an overall rise in the ambient temperature of the atmosphere and the earth's surface. Moreover, it was obvious enough that should temperatures rise, then the earth's climate, patterns of cloud formation, rain fall, wind and sea currents would all change as well.

Despite the scientific pedigree of the argument it raised no political or environmental alarms for another 70 years. Indeed climatologists were arguing in the 1960s that the natural variations in the earth's climate due to the changing nature of the earth's orbit round the sun were more likely causes of major climatic change. None the less, concern amongst climatologists and international environmental organizations began to mount. The prospect of global warming was mooted at the first major UN sponsored international environmental conference at Stockholm in 1972 and was echoed, with greater scientific data, at the first world climate conference in 1979.

The road to Rio: global warming in the 1980s

Through the early 1980s scientific research demonstrated that the correlation between changing global temperatures in the past and atmospheric concentrations of carbon dioxide was closely linked. Energy researchers demonstrated not only that the rate of fossil fuel use was climbing but levels of carbon dioxide in the atmosphere had been on an exponential path since the end of the Second World War. They were approaching levels of atmospheric concentration that were quite off the scale of recent geological experience. These debates coalesced at a series of specialist seminars amongst increasingly politicized climatologists and atmospheric scientists and government agencies organized under the auspices of the UNEP in 1987. The growing body of evidence and a recognition of the profundity of ecological and social change that might be on the cards coincided with a series of more contingent meteorological and political events. 1987 and 1988 proved to be exceptionally hot years with seemingly freak weather patterns. Green parties in Europe and environmental NGOs in the UK and the USA were nearing a peak of influence and support while the increasingly successful Montreal Protocol on CFCs suggested a model of international political and scientific co-operation.

Given the complexity and uncertainty of the scientific debate the UNEP and WMO (World Meteorological Organization) took the initiative and established the IPCC (Inter-governmental Panel on Climate Change). This consisted of a global network of leading institutes and individuals in climatology, oceanography and the atmospheric sciences. It was divided into three working groups which were to investigate, assess and synthesize the evidence and arguments on the origins and character of the greenhouse effect, the potential risks and implications of global warming and policies and proposals for dealing with those risks.

The results of the IPCC's research were contested on every count but the strongest area of research, on which most consensus was achieved, was on the origins and existence of global warming. Temperature records suggest that a process of global warming is occurring. Estimates of the likely rate of change vary, but suggest something around 0.5°C per decade for the next 40 or 50 years. This, of course, is an average global temperature, some areas would experience much sharper rises, others less or none at all. Given the rate and scale of change the cause is unlikely to be due to slower natural forces or cycles. The greenhouse effect is the only plausible explanation available. Concurrent with global warming there has been a steady build-up of greenhouse gases in the earth's atmosphere. With only 15 per cent of the world's population, the West contributes about 80 per cent of global greenhouse emissions (OECD, 1993). This consists of carbon dioxide (CO_2) produced by burning fossil fuels for electricity production, industrial uses and transport – primarily motor vehicles – and the burning of rainforests. The decline in rainforests also diminishes the earth's capacity to absorb CO_2 for plant photosynthesis. Other contributors to the greenhouse effect include sulphur and nitrous dioxide which also cause acid rain, and methane – primarily released by decomposing waste and agriculture. Of all environmental problems uncertainty of impacts is, perhaps, greatest with global warming. Changes are likely to shift climate patterns, rainfall levels, and wind directions all of which interact with each other in complex and unpredictable ways. Increasing temperatures may melt the polar ice caps leading to rising sea levels and coastal flooding or a diversion of the main ocean currents. With an increase in area the sea may have an increased capacity to absorb carbon dioxide, slowing global warming – we still don't know.

As a consequence, to date there has only been limited political agreement on what measures should be taken, or whether measures should be taken at all, on the basis of the IPCC's work during 1989 and 1990. Preparatory discussions leading up to the Second World Climate Conference descended into arguments around the podium at Sundsvall in 1990. However, political paralysis was less to do with scientific disagreements and everything to do with the enormous differences between states depending on their economic interests and the perceived environmental risks. The Gulf oil states were implacable opponents of all restrictions and commitments to reduce emissions, not far behind came the USA. India and China were both cautious about restrictions, leading developing country pressure for the West to raise its environmental commitments and make financial transfers available to the

South in return for reducing or controlling emissions. The Association of Small Island States – those islands, mainly in the Pacific and Caribbean most immediately and perilously threatened by rising sea levels – pushed hardest for some kind of agreement. Indeed such were the differences that the climate conference's only important decision was to establish negotiations for creating an international convention on climate under the auspices of the General Assembly of the UN. These negotiations finally generated a Convention on Climate Change that was signed at the 1992 UN Conference on Environment and Development (UNCED) in Rio de Janeiro.

Opening speeches at the UNCED in Rio de Janeiro, 3 June 1992

The Framework Convention, as it is known, was signed by 155 states. If nothing else it established a permanent international secretariat for monitoring and disseminating research on global warming and provided for a regular series of Conferences of the Parties at which more substantive regulation could be established. It established the basic principle that the northern states needed to reduce their greenhouse emissions, though it only committed them to stabilization of existing emissions by 2000. It also established the principle that the control of emissions in the South would be tied to financial transfers from the North. However, given that the IPCC's conservative estimates suggested that to merely stabilize the current rate of change an immediate 60 per cent reduction in greenhouse emissions is required and that the increase of economic growth, electricity production, car use and thus greenhouse emissions is exponential in the industrializing areas of the South – the practical response was, at best, minimalist.

Beyond Rio: global warming and democratic politics

Since the 1992 conference in Rio de Janeiro the scientific debate on global warming has hardened. The most recent IPCC reports confirm and entrench earlier arguments and even the most recalcitrant of opponents – particularly the scientific lobby funded by the oil and motor industries in the USA – has been forced to tone down their scepticism. Political responses, however, have remained muted. Industrialization and growing emissions have proceeded apace in the South. In the North, attempts to stabilize emissions have been achieved or almost achieved as much by the run down in economic activity of the early 1990s as concerted government measures. Comprehensive proposals like carbon taxes have been defeated at both the national and European levels. US energy taxes have remained alarmingly low and the global electricity industry remains committed to increasing outputs rather than energy conservation. Everywhere attempts to control levels of car use are failing. Progress at an international level has been little better. In 1995 the parties to the Framework Convention met in Berlin in an attempt to firm up the commitments to emission stabilization and reduction. This resulted in over a week of procedural disputes before any new agreements could be established. The Berlin Mandate established a commitment by the parties to negotiate real reductions in emissions by 1997, based on agreement that current commitments were woefully inadequate.

What are the democratic implications of these events at the level of the nation-state and the international state system? Global warming presents polities with nearly all of the problems outlined in Sections 4.1 and 4.2. The existence and likely course of global warming has only been revealed by scientific work, the results of which are highly contested. Global warming presents us with a future in which there may be very considerable environmental 'bads': the process of economic growth becomes more problematic; established patterns of consumption and investment in the North require a radical change; and the South will only be able to achieve economic development without very damaging environmental consequences if it is able to pursue a mode of development radically different to that which the North took and with access to northern capital and technology. It is the global environmental problem par excellence, no state or group of states can resolve it alone, it effects almost everyone, everywhere.

So far, at the national level, no liberal democratic state has been able to commit itself to much more than stabilizing emissions. This suggests that there are structural problems associated with taking the 'cautious' policy option and including the interests of future generations. No mainstream political party has been electorally successful, or thinks it can be electorally successful, if it argues for the kinds of measures cuts in emissions would require. These are infinitely more complex and politically significant than the regulation or abolition of a single chemical, technology or industrial sector. They include, for example, increases in energy taxes and major measures to control car use which would impact on every economic sector and group of the population. At the international level, the question of democracy is problematized by the issue of efficacy. In international institutions where states are the key representatives and consensus is required for decisions to be taken the divergence of state's interests is so great (high and low energy users, creators and potential victims of global warming, states that have reached their peak energy use and those that are rapidly growing) that significant policy measures have been impossible to achieve. The absence of representatives of environmental and future interests makes such measures even less likely to achieve. The incapacity of institutions to generate effective policy programmes is unlikely to do much for their democratic legitimacy or institutional entrenchment.

――――――――――――― *Summary of Section 4.4* ―――――――――――――

- The enhanced greenhouse effect caused mainly by fossil fuel burning in the North is probably responsible for global warming which impacts on everyone everywhere, although in an uneven manner.

- Scientific research has consistently stimulated national and international political responses.

- This culminated in the Rio Framework Convention which has proved to date woefully inadequate in securing major policy changes at the national and international level.

- Dealing with global warming requires major precautionary measures, technological regulation and the distribution of environmental 'bads' at a global level. Liberal democracies may structurally impede this while international institutions seem incapable of either representing environmental interests or securing agreement.

4.5 Democratic conclusions

Drawing up a balance sheet that registers the impact of global environmental problems on democratic politics requires us to look at two different but interconnected sets of questions. The first set of questions looks at the impact at the level of individual nation-states. We need to ask, how effective have liberal democratic states been in generating solutions to environmental problems in general and global environmental problems in particular? To what extent are the successes and failures of this enterprise related to either the national or territorial character of these states or the democratic or representative qualities of these states? Have the *conditions* of politics been *transformed* so greatly that their democratic status is in question? As a coda to these questions we might also ask whether authoritarian polities have proved any more successful than democratic ones in dealing with these problems. The second set of questions looks at the international institutions that have emerged in response to the national-territorial limitations of nation-states – democratic or otherwise. We need to ask whether international environmental institutions have been more successful in generating environmental solutions than national institutions. Moreover, where they have done so, has that success been bought at the cost of centralizing power and circumventing democratic procedures? I deal with these two sets of questions in the following sections.

Liberal democratic nation-states: environmental efficacy and territorial limitations

In Section 4.1 I asked whether the liberal democratic component of liberal democratic nation-states generated problems in dealing with environmental degradation, for example, dealing with uncertainty. I argued that liberal democracies have structurally determined difficulties in generating and implementing suitable policy programmes. When faced with global problems that pose immense environmental risks two difficulties stand out. First, there are problems of the long term. Environmental degradation, whether states respond to it or not, implies a complex distribution of costs and benefits within and between generations. In representative systems there are few immediate requirements to take into account the interests of future generations. The electoral cycle of parliamentary government reinforces political short-termism while the absence of a society-wide consensus on environmental problems means that those who do seek to represent the interests of future generations are constantly undercut by electoral competition from those representing the interests of the present generation. Second, whether states respond to environmental problems now, never, or some time in the future, the scale and scope of those problems means that there will be very substantial costs and benefits to be politically apportioned. While the precise dimensions of a sustainable response to global warming are not finalized, we can be certain that it will entail a comprehensive restructuring of agriculture, energy and transport sectors, as well as aggregate patterns of production and consumption with significant changes in taxation, public expenditure and employment. Such a policy programme would create a significant number of short-term losers, while the main beneficiaries of such a transition would be absent. It is not clear at all whether liberal democracies will be capable of creating or sustaining the kinds of political support required to put this level of inter-generational distribution into action.

In Section 4.2 I looked at the ways in which the national component of liberal democratic nation-states made effective resolutions to environmental problems even more difficult. The existence of transboundary pollution, environmental interdependencies and the degradation of the global commons have meant that there are many environmental communities of fate who demographically and territorially encompass and cut across national political communities. As a consequence the legitimacy and efficacy of national liberal democratic states is directly challenged. Their efficacy is challenged because it is clear that the actions of individual states will rarely be sufficient to protect the environmental interests of their own citizens. Their legitimacy is challenged, for if the election of a national government cannot deliver on basic environmental security, then why vote?

For all of these deficits there are credits on the democratic balance sheet. First, liberal democracies have been sufficiently open to new currents of public concern that the wave of environmental degradation, and increasing concern over that degradation, has been channelled into new government machinery, legislation and funding for environmental protection. Second, liberal democracies have provided the organizational space for Green parties and a host of activist, informational, research and campaigning bodies to emerge and for some pressure to be placed on the environmental programmes of conventional political parties. In turn, this has forced a reassessment of the boundaries of previously depoliticized arenas – like technological development and medical research – opening them to democratic debate.

Perhaps the decisive entry on the balance sheet is not against the account of liberal democracy, but against the performance of authoritarian regimes. While both environmental legislation and environmental movements have emerged under authoritarian regimes of both left and right, it is incontrovertible that they have proved much more hostile territory for environmentalists. While the case for environmental protection and the interests of future generations is difficult to implement under liberal democratic polities, it is doubly difficult when environmental information is impossible to obtain, where no electoral pressure can be brought to bear on politicians, where the rule of law, environmental and other, is systematically bypassed and where environmental movements are harassed, controlled, censored or eradicated. In that regard, liberal democracies commend our attention for being the least worst environmental option.

International environmental institutions: environmental efficacy and democratic legitimacy

In response to the evident territorial and political limitations of the nation-state – be it liberal democratic or authoritarian – Section 4.2 argued that a plethora of international institutions have been created to provide collective solutions to environmental threats. Sections 4.3 and 4.4 examined two in particular – the array of ozone and CFC related protocols and the emerging cluster of institutions and regulations monitoring and governing global warming. Again, we need to ask whether these institutions can practically deal with environmental problems. Second, we need to ask whether they do so on a democratic basis. Normatively, if not practically, it is one thing to hand political power from national to international institutions. It is another to pass that power from democratic nation-states to undemocratic and unaccountable international institutions. At the very least we need to be clear about the trade-off involved.

As far as practicality and efficacy goes, the history of ozone depletion and CFC regulation lies on the positive side of the balance sheet. The successive negotiations and protocols of the 1980s and 1990s enabled a common international framework for negotiations to emerge and aided the establishment of a scientific consensus in the face of uncertainty. On the basis of this it proved politically possible to transform the production and consumption of CFCs, first in the West and then through new financial mechanisms in the South. However, the speed of negotiations when measured against the pace of environmental degradation looks alarmingly sluggish and the relative simplicity of the politics of ozone depletion (few producers, possible substitutes, many non-essential uses) are unlikely to be replicated in other situations.

The case of global warming illustrated some of the reasons why international environmental institutions have so far been unable to provide solutions to global environmental problems. In some ways these are the same problems encountered by nation-states. Agreement on the scope and scale of the environmental threat has been difficult to achieve. Similarly, there has been profound disagreement on who has been responsible for creating the problem and the extent to which past contributions to global warming should be included in future calculations of redress. The implications of global warming in terms of both environmental costs and the costs of transforming large economic sectors like energy, agriculture and transport are so large that agreement on the distribution of those costs becomes complex and difficult. Different states and different economic sectors within those states have radically different interests which are not at the moment amenable to negotiation. Even where agreement on costs and risks has been possible, the international institutions have neither the moral weight nor practical executive power to force compromises, extract significant concessions from participants or take independent action. On all these counts nation-states retain an effective veto through inaction and indecision should they choose to. No mechanism exists for forcing recalcitrant states into line.

The democratic status of these international institutions is debatable. Policy discussion and negotiations are invariably arcane and under-reported. Hidden within the vortex of international negotiations national governments are rarely under significant domestic pressure from political parties or environmental campaigns. The space for environmental NGOs within these institutions though opening out is still small. No meaningful mechanisms exist through which the opinions of national publics or the entire global community of environmental fate can be registered or tested.

Faced by both the impending threats of catastrophic environmental degradation and the intractable political problems of conducting an enlightened environmental policy in a democratic polity – be it national or international – some have speculated that environmental sustainability might require the creation of benign ecological dictatorships. Authoritarian polities and authoritarian international institutions would be able to force through the necessary but unpalatable changes required to bring national and international economic activity within the pale of environmental sustainability. This argument is raised more often by opponents of the environmental argument than by its supporters. None the less, if environmentalists cannot win, nationally or internationally, under demo-cratic auspices, is there a case for 'ecofascism'? It seems to me difficult to imagine the sociological composition of an authoritarian environmentalist coalition, all the usual supporters of authoritarianism – like the military, landowners, big business, state bureaucracies, etc. – would make extra-ordinary bedfellows for contemporary environmental coalitions. In any case, authoritarianism, however ecologically benign, is a form of regime deeply unsuited to tackling environmental questions. While it may be capable of enforcing unpalatable social and economic change it is unlikely to be able to deal with the uncertainties of environmental policy. This requires that institutions and elites remain reflexive, critical and sceptical, open to examination and argument. There is not, and cannot be, any monopoly of truth on assessing environmental threats and responding to them. The less one consults and the more one silences opposing voices, the more likely it is that bad decisions will be made, defended and entrenched. In terms of environmental degradation, such inflexibility becomes increasingly costly. I see no reason to trust in the benevolence or wisdom of democratic politicians on these questions, I see even less reason to entrust authoritarians of any hue.

It is clear that the territorial dimension of contemporary liberal democracy makes any kind of national response inadequate – democratic or not. Global and regional environmental problems require global and regional institutions and legal frameworks to resolve or mitigate them. Some from within the liberal and realist traditions (see Chapter 1) would argue that nation-states should cede a minimum of sovereign authority to them, using them predominantly as frameworks in which bargaining between national interests can be made more rational. I would argue that such a programme would make precautionary politics at a global level impossible to implement, and that it is no longer normatively justifiable for states – who have no autonomous capacity to meet these problems – to hang on to the fiction of sovereignty that precludes them from actively tackling these threats.

In terms of this book, global environmental problems require a cosmopolitan model of geo-governance to resolve them. Beyond the territorial dimension of democratic responses there is a need both nationally and internationally for more democracy and more substantive democracy. First, because the weight of numbers of those threatened by – rather than profiting from – environmental degradation can only overcome the massive economic and political capital of environmentally problematic interests through electoral and participatory measures. Second – and somewhat at odds to the first argument – because cutting the Gordian knot of environmental politics – persuading the powerful and the wealthy to trade both for the interests of the future and the poor – cannot be achieved on the basis of a politics of interests alone (Habermas, 1991; Goldblatt, 1996). At some point the politics of moral choice must intervene. The only possible context for making such a transformation is one in which political decision making is grounded in wide-ranging, open discussion in which all points of view are recognized, in which all interests are given equal standing and in which the inequitable distribution of other forms of power is laid to one side. Such a polity would indeed be democratic, radically democratic. Whether it would still be liberal democratic, what its institutional form would be and whether it can be created at a national or an international level are other matters entirely.

References

Barry, B. (1991) 'Justice between generations' in *Liberty and Justice: Essays in Political Theory 2*, Oxford, Oxford University Press.

Beck, U. (1992) *Risk Society: Towards a New Modernity*, London, Sage.

Beck, U. (1995) *Ecological Politics in an Age of Risk*, Cambridge, Polity Press.

Benedick, R. (1991) *Ozone Diplomacy: New Directions in Safeguarding the Planet*, Cambridge, Mass., Harvard University Press.

Goldblatt, D. (1996) *Social Theory and the Environment*, Cambridge, Polity Press.

Haas, E. (1990) *When Knowledge is Power*, Berkeley, University of California Press.

Habermas, J. (1991) 'What does socialism mean today?' in Blackburn, R. (ed.) *After the Fall*, London, Verso.

Jacobs, M. (1991) *The Green Economy*, London, Pluto.

Legget, J. (ed.) (1990) *Global Warming: the Greenpeace Report*, Oxford, Oxford University Press.

Miller, M. (1995) *The Third World in Global Environmental Politics*, Milton Keynes, Open University.

Nillson, S. and Pitt, D. (1994) *Protecting the Atmosphere: the Climate Change Convention and its Context*, London, Earthscan.

OECD (1993) *The State of the Environment*, Paris, Organisation for Economic Co-operation and Development.

Parson, E. (1993) 'Protecting the ozone layer' in Hass, P. *et al.* (eds) *Institutions for the Earth: Sources of Effective International Environmental Protection*, Cambridge, Mass., MIT Press.

Pearce, D. (1990) *Blueprint for a Green Economy*, London, Earthscan.

Robinson, M. (1992) *The Greening of British Party Politics*, Manchester, Manchester University Press.

Rowland, F. and Molina, M. (1974) 'Stratospheric sink for chloro-fluoromethanes: chlorine atom-catalyzed destruction of ozone', *Nature*, no.249.

Rowlands, I. (1994) *The International Politics of Atmospheric Change*, Manchester, Manchester University Press.

Weale, A. (1992) *The New Politics of Pollution*, Manchester, Manchester University Press.

Young, O. (1994) *International Governance: Protecting the Environment in a Stateless Society*, Ithaca, Cornell University Press.

Further reading

Beck, U. (1995) *Ecological Politics in an Age of Risk*, Cambridge, Polity Press.

Doherty, B. and de Geus, M. (eds) (1996) *Democracy and Green Political Thought*, London, Routledge.

Vogler, J. (1995) *The Global Commons: a Regime Analysis*, London, Wiley.

Wagner, P. (1996) *Environmental Activism and World Civic Politics*, New York, State University of New York Press.

Yearley, S. (1996) *Sociology, Environmentalism, Globalization*, London, Sage.

CHAPTER 5

Counting women in: globalization, democratization and the women's movement

Donna Dickenson

Introduction

> Feminism offers the only politics which can transform our world into a more humane place and deal with global issues like equality, development and peace, because it asks the right questions: about power, about the links between the personal and the political; and because it cuts through race and class.

> (Antrobus quoted in Bunch and Carillo, 1990, p.73)

This quotation from the Caribbean writer Peggy Antrobus introduces complex relationships between globalization, democratization and the women's movement. These are the concern of this chapter.

The feminist movement may seek democratization on a global scale, according to Antrobus, but women are still hampered by a 'democratic deficit' in terms of economic and political power. Even in the European heartlands of liberal democracy, democratic representation for women has only been fully achieved in the late twentieth century – as late as 1971 in Switzerland. In some parts of the world gains made earlier this century are being lost. Following the 1992 revolution in Afghanistan, for example, women lost their voting rights after a mere 27 years of the suffrage.

Even where they retain democratic rights, women still lack political and economic power, along with access to the sites of power (see Figure 5.1). As of 1993, women still owned only 1 per cent of the world's property (including land) and earned 10 per cent of the globe's income. They constituted a minuscule 4 per cent of heads of state, and 5 per cent of cabinet ministers. Their representation in national legislatures was only marginally better at 10 per cent overall. They held 6 per cent of senior posts in international governmental organizations and 5 per cent of high positions in national policy making (Peterson and Runyan, 1993, p.6). Women have not necessarily benefited from what is conventionally seen as the 'triumph' of liberal democracy and the process of global democratization since 1989 (see Figure 5.2).

But on the other hand, global feminist networks and new expanded forms of (non-territorial) political 'space' *do* appear to be increasing democratic participation for women. This, too, contradicts a conventional hypothesis: that the liberal democratic state's autonomy and political effectiveness are hampered by an increasingly interconnected global system

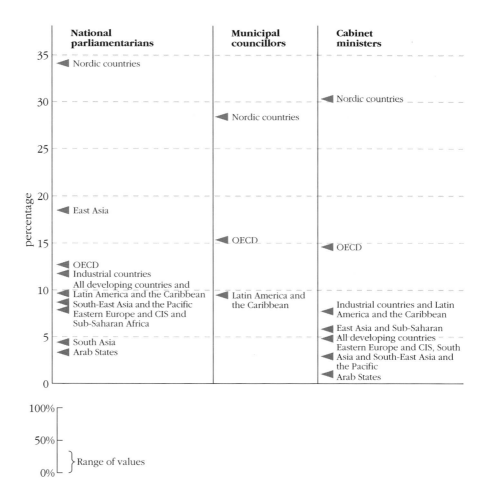

Figure 5.1   Women's political participation is low

Source: United Nations Development Programme (1995) *Human Development Report 1995*, New York, Oxford University Press, Inc.

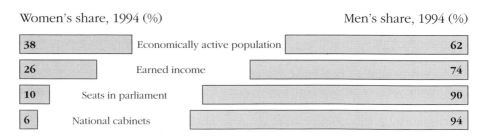

Figure 5.2   In most respects, it is still an unequal world

Source: Economically active population – UN forthcoming (*The World's Women*); earned income – calculated on the basis of the data from UN 1994i and ILO 1994b, consultant reports prepared for the 1994 and 1995 Human Development Reports, World Bank 1992 and UN forthcoming (*The World's Women*); parliament – IPU 1994; cabinets – data from UN 1994i, as analysed by the United Nations Division for the Advancement of Women (revised by the Human Development Report Office in 1995.

of power relations. This is the paradox which I want to explore in this chapter. I want to suggest that *globalization may finally make democracy real for women, in a way that the liberal 'democratic' nation-state never has.*

So this chapter focuses on the relationships between globalization, the women's movement, and the transformation of liberal democratic politics. This discussion is subdivided into three sections:

– How has globalization affected women's lives around the world? (Section 5.1)

– What form has women's response to globalization taken? In particular, what new forms of democratic participation and what new kinds of political space have resulted? A case study in Section 5.2 on the Fourth World Women's Conference, held in Beijing during August-September 1995, illustrates how the women's movement has transformed our nation-state-centred understanding of the democratic political arena into a global one. This leads into the final question:

– To what extent has the global women's movement transformed the nature of democratic politics?

Coming at the end of the first section of 'Global transformations', this chapter pulls together the discussion of the key domains of globalization introduced so far. The impact on women of economic globalization and global environmental degradation are discussed in Section 5.1 whilst democratization and militarization in a global context is examined in Section 5.3, where I argue that there has been a 'feminization of citizenship' in the nuclear and post-nuclear period, transforming the traditional link between military service and democratic participation.

Yet if the abstract parameters of citizenship have shifted, women's ability to participate is not necessarily any greater. At the Beijing Conference, economic, ecological and military factors affecting women were all on the agenda, but so were other issues barring women from fuller access to power: the globalization of religious fundamentalism, for example, discussed in Section 5.1. In Section 5.4, I conclude by evaluating the achievement of feminism and its impact on the transformation of (territorial) liberal democracy.

5.1   How has globalization affected women's lives?

At first glance it may well appear that the forces of globalization restrict, rather than increase, women's levels of democratic participation. This is particularly true of economic factors. Economic globalization, linked to modernization, was initially expected to improve women's condition world wide. But its effect has actually been far more complex than a naive model of linear progress would predict.

Economic globalization

Modernization and economic globalization may give women more extensive civil rights than under traditional regimes, but economically they often remain subordinate – frequently, increasingly disadvantaged. This is particularly true of the globalization of structural adjustment programmes (SAPs) (see Chapter 3), which have been called 'the most profound and serious political and economic issue affecting most of the world today' (Sparr, 1994, p.1). The Sri Lankan writer Swarna Jayaweera agrees, stressing the interplay between the sexual and global division of labour (Jayaweera, 1994, p.107). SAPs affect not only women but also men, not only poor people in the Third World but also middle- and low-income earners in those economies of the old 'First World' which have embraced neo-liberal economic policies. Yet it is women who bear the brunt of structural adjustment policies.

Women did not benefit greatly from the development loans which precipitated the global debt crisis of the 1970s and 1980s, bringing structural adjustment policies in their wake. Whereas women grow 70 per cent of the food in Third World nations as a whole, they receive only 5 per cent of the 5.8 million agricultural loans given by the multilateral development banks. Women in both Africa and Asia rarely own the land on which they work, and so they rarely benefit from the global loan schemes for land improvement through irrigation, fertilization and mechanization. But although they have rarely been the beneficiaries of international loans and global development projects, women have been the principal victims of the structural adjustment programmes which followed them. In 1991 a report by the UN International Fund for Agricultural Development showed that the number of Third World rural women living in poverty had *increased 50 per cent in the previous 20 years*, during the 'high tide' of structural adjustment policies (Peterson and Runyan, 1993, p.177).

Structural adjustment in the broadest sense involves 'a *conscious* change in the fundamental nature of economic relationships within a society' (Sparr, 1994, p.1). Political relationships are also affected: the core concerns of liberal democracy become more procedural, as governments draw back from assuring positive welfare entitlements to protecting negative rights such as freedom from government intervention (see Chapter 3). Typically SAPs entail the following government policies:

–   Acceptance of a *laissez-faire* 'free market' ideology.

–   Less government intervention, price control and/or subsidy, sometimes in an apparently contradictory pairing with wage restraint.

–   Production for export rather than local consumption (often in newly privatized firms or multinationals).

–   Raising interest rates, making loans to small businesses more expensive.

–   Cutbacks in government provision of welfare services.

Most of these measures have a gendered impact. For example, cutbacks in government activity mean redundancies for women, who are heavily represented in public sector employment in Ghana and other African countries, as in much of Europe and North America (Manuh, 1994). In Sri Lanka, government handicrafts programmes for local consumption, begun in the 1960s to increase female employment, were shut down in favour of concentrating on exports (Jayaweera, 1994). Higher interest rates hurt market women and small entrepreneurs in nations like Jamaica and Nigeria, because these women generally have less capital and collateral than their male counterparts (French, 1994). The reduction in welfare entitlements under structural adjustment programmes has left women with the burden of caregiving abandoned by governments. State entitlements which previously reduced women's reproductive labour, e.g. by providing care for the elderly, have been radically cut, but at the same time women have come under increased pressure to augment subsistence labour with low-paid jobs in the productive sector.

On the other hand, by entering paid work women can be seen to emerge into the public arena, even if their conditions are poor. In industrial work, the globalization of 'high-tech' information and service industries has combined with encouragement of production for export in tax-subsidized Export-Processing Zones (EPZs) to create a higher demand for female employment. Some Third World writers claim that EPZ work is liberating for women and that Western feminists have been ethnocentric and patronizing in condemning EPZs (Lim, 1989).

A woman worker prepares to spray a car in Accra, Ghana

What has been the overall impact of structural adjustment programmes on women's lives around the world? It is difficult to separate the effect of SAPs from the international debt crisis of the late 1970s and 1980s, the restructuring of the global economy to produce a new international division of labour, and the world-wide recession which had already reduced the export price of many commodities in the South. In addition, the direction of causation is unclear. It has been argued that gender inequality further contributes to global economic crises; at the same time that globalization produces or worsens structural gender inequality, inequality aggravates global crisis (Peterson and Runyan, 1993).

It is well-nigh impossible to come up with generalizations that fit all the world's women. For example, the introduction of charges for education under SAPs has reversed prior gains made in educating African girls: only 30 girls are educated, for every 100 boys. Yet girls' educational achievement rates now exceed those of boys in western Asia, Latin America and the

Caribbean, despite government cutbacks under SAPs (United Nations, 1995). In Britain government cutbacks in education have been more or less continuous since the 1970s. Yet although class divisions in education have widened, girls are now performing better than boys in examination results.

Nonetheless, we can say that generally the following changes, with particular implications for liberal democracy, have accompanied structural adjustment programmes:

–   There has been an *increase in female labour force participation* – documented by studies throughout the North, as well as in Turkey, the Caribbean, Southeast Asia and Latin America. Waged employment could give women opportunities for administration and decision making, skills which might enhance democratic participation. But where women are simultaneously underemployed and overworked, they have no time or inducement to take up these opportunities. In this sense SAPs are often said to *lessen* women's involvement in civil society (Manuh, 1994).

–   Yet the number of women wishing to be active in the labour force has often been coupled with *higher female than male unemployment* – exacerbated in countries such as Egypt by Islamic fundamentalist groups who have taken advantage of privatization to urge women back into the home. In Turkey, for example, there was an increase in female employment as a percentage of the overall labour force, but female unemployment has also consistently outstripped that of men.

–   *Widening male–female wage differentials* have been documented in many countries: for example, Egypt, Sri Lanka, and Argentina. Lack of gender-disaggregated income and poverty data for many other nations makes it hard to be sure whether this is actually a *global* trend, and whether it is caused by, or correlated with, SAPs (see Figure 5.3). But if

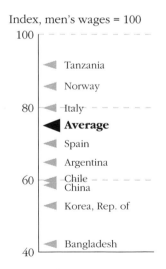

Index, men's wages = 100

Figure 5.3   Women's average wages languish below men's

Source: United Nations Development Programme (1995) *Human Development Report 1995*, New York, Oxford University Press, Inc.

the gap between men's and women's wages is not necessarily widening worldwide, neither is it shrinking. The expected reduction in the difference between men's and women's pay – the objective of the equal pay acts which many European nations enacted in the 1970s – has notably failed to materialize in the First World (Davidson and Cooper, 1993).

– *Substitution of women's unpaid work for welfare services by governments* (e.g. shorter school hours, cutbacks in public transport, and fewer clinics) means that women spend more time tending children, walking to work, or caring for the sick at home. It is not clear whether women's work time has increased overall or is being redistributed towards income generation, with daughters taking up mothers' reproductive work at the expense of their own schooling. But either way, there is less time available for women's political participation.

Global environmental degradation

The planners behind structural adjustment programmes thought that women were only responsible for subsistence and reproduction. Yet in a self-fulfilling prophecy, SAPs push women further in that very direction by making subsistence such a pressing concern. The global degradation of the environment has also made subsistence increasingly difficult, although it in turn has been exacerbated by both structural adjustment and development programmes. We would expect women to respond by turning more and more towards family concerns and away from political participation. However, the globalization of environmental issues has provided a political arena for some women activists, at both local and global levels.

The initial impact of SAPs on the environment was severe. Servicing debt and concentrating on exports encouraged farmers to abandon traditional farming methods in favour of intensive agriculture. Women are affected for two reasons: as subsistence farmers they rarely benefit from agriculture for profit, but the quality of land and water supplies declines. For example, the introduction of cotton as an export crop in Tanzania increased male farmers' incomes. Following the traditional East African man's preference for cattle as wealth, these farmers put their profits into cattle, which overgrazed the grasslands and sparked soil erosion that spread to women's smallholdings (Dasgupta, 1993, p.287).

Where the resource of water or fuel remains common, women must now spend up to half of their work time and energy collecting it from further and further away. Privatization, often a requirement of structural adjustment, also has a disproportionate effect on women. Common-property resources constitute 15–25 per cent of family income in India and are usually women's and children's entitlement, although local male elders often stand to profit from privatization (ibid., p.291).

Whilst poverty is generally viewed as the sole cause of under-nourishment, unequal bargaining power must also be considered. 'A family in abject poverty not only has to make do with little, it cannot even afford to share its poverty equally' (ibid., p.500). Men are given more food because their productivity is perceived to be higher, and more dependent on nutritional status. Yet intensively cultivated small family farms, where women play the greatest role, exceed the productivity of large farms in yield per hectare and production of staple food (Berry and Cline, 1979).

The most minimal effect of undernourishment is 'reproductive stress' for women, the worst is increased female mortality (Bantje, 1995). Whatever we might expect of progress in modern medicine, in some parts of the South women's life expectancy is either falling or failing to keep pace with improvements in male longevity. In India the ratio of females to males has fallen consistently throughout the twentieth century, from 0.97 in 1901 to 0.93 in 1981, with rates as low as 0.75 in some regions. The widening difference between male and female life expectancy in India is insufficiently explained by variables which exclude gender i.e. population pressure, investment in social services, or class inequality (Mazumdar and Sharma, 1994, p.189). Much of this growing disparity is explained by environmental degradation, mediated by discrimination against women and girls.

The political effect of global environmental degradation, like that of structural adjustment programmes, appears at first sight to be that hard-pressed women will have less and less time for political participation. But the other side of the coin is the political activism bred by environmental disaster. The 'tree-hugging' movement in northern India, in which women activists chained themselves to trees in order to prevent loggers from cutting local forests, is matched in the North by the Newbury bypass protest (1996) in which women were likewise active. Another sort of global environmental catastrophe – the devastation of East Africa by the HIV virus – has prompted the revival of traditional support networks among women and the development of new forms of political organization and collective action (Obbo, 1995).

The resistible rise of fundamentalism

Women's democratic deficit, in an era of 'triumph' for liberal democracy, is intimately linked with another form of globalization: that of religious fundamentalism. There are radically new connections between fundamentalist movements, which are frequently regional, and in other cases genuinely global. For example, archtheocratic regimes, such as those in power at the time of writing in Afghanistan and Iran, are partly funded by global oil revenues, either their own or those provided by financial aid packages from oil-rich states such as Saudi Arabia (Goodwin, 1994, p.82).

These links are not confined to the Islamic world. Saudi Arabia supplied arms and aid to the Afghan Resistance, which took power in 1992 as a fundamentalist regime; yet this aid was matched dollar by dollar, although indirectly, by the USA. That Afghan women should owe their political veiling, as it were, to both a fundamentalist Islamic regime and a pluralist Western one demonstrates just how complicated the connections are between globalization and women's political situation. But do such links indicate a genuine globalization of fundamentalism?

The 'globalization of fundamentalism' thesis is supported by Karen McCarthy Brown (1994), who holds that a close analysis of gender in American fundamentalism reveals a strong family likeness to Third World fundamentalisms. All are reactive attempts to reproduce order where it is most symbolic, in the family. However, Jay Harris (1994) asserts that to see fundamentalism this way is ethnocentric and simplistic ignoring the longevity and diversity of religious traditions to which it appeals.

There is a compelling likeness, I think, between the globalization of economic 'fundamentalism' under SAPs – the return to neo-classical 'basics' after the 'excesses' of Keynesianism – and that of religious fundamentalism. Neo-liberalism resembles other fundamentalisms in that it seeks a return to a supposed golden age of unfettered free market capitalism. It, too, defines itself through opposition – to the excesses of state intervention.

Fundamentalism generally seeks to return women to the private sphere, to a past golden age of traditional family values. This is a central plank on which a global miscellany of fundamentalist movements appear to agree. It is not so much that models of the family are universal – clearly they are not – as that woman as 'other' is universal. 'Embodying the other that is at once intimate and ubiquitous, women serve as a fine canvas on which to project feelings of general besetment' (Hawley, 1994, p.27).

What does this entail for women and democratization at the national level? In some nations there are clear links between structural adjustment, fundamentalism and diminished economic or political participation for women. This, too, contradicts the conventional hypothesis about the 'triumph of liberal democracy' across the globe.

In Egypt, for example, the acceptance of structural adjustment programmes and privatization has gone hand in hand with the demise of 'state feminism' – by which the Nasser regime had rewarded anti-colonial women's movements such as Bint al Nil (Daughters of the Nile). Independence in 1952 ushered in substantial rights for women, to distinguish the new state from the *ancien régime*. But the 1970s witnessed an unlikely alliance of the IMF and the World Bank, together with fundamentalist Muslim groups. State employment of women diminished or stagnated under privatization; in turn female unemployment was increased by employers' nervousness in the face of Islamic demands that women return home.

Whereas older fundamentalist groups like the Amish in Pennsylvania, the Mennonites in Belize and the Jewish Hasidim isolated themselves in separatist enclaves, modern fundamentalism typically battles to gain the high ground of politics. Often it aims to seize the modern nation-state itself, and to reinstate the alignment of church and state. The feminist movement has sought to outmanoeuvre this stratagem as much through global political activity as through campaigns bounded by the conventional nation-state – through the creation of new global political arenas. The most potent symbol of this trend is the Beijing Conference of 1995.

―――――――――――― *Summary of Section 5.1* ――――――――――――

- Women did not benefit proportionately from the 1970s development loans which resulted in the international debt crisis and ensuing structural adjustment policies, because their reproductive labour was undervalued and because they rarely owned land.

- However, they have suffered disproportionately from structural adjustment programmes, which have created a 'triple burden' of paid work in low-wage EPZs or the informal sector, plus the existing 'double shift' of subsistence labour and housework. In general we have witnessed a globalization of gender inequality, bringing even non-elites in the Third World into the ambit of a global division of labour.

- Although paid employment, which has increased under SAPs, may involve women in civil society, the 'triple shift' seems to leave them little time for democratic political participation.

- The forces of economic globalization have had a mixed impact on women's opportunities for political participation, and on the structures of the nation-state.

- Global environmental degradation, which hits rural women particularly hard, has often accompanied structural adjustment programmes and has sometimes been worsened by them.

- Although the immediate effect of environmental degradation is to increase women's workload still further, a subsidiary effect is sometimes the stirrings of political activism.

- Fundamentalism as a global reaction to modernization has attempted to take the centre ground of politics in many states, typically calling for women's removal from the political stage, along with other forms of regulating the key ideological space of the family.

- In addition to concrete financial links between fundamentalist groups throughout the world, there are ideological similarities which may justify the notion that fundamentalism has become globalized.

- But so has the women's movement – and in the process it has created new democratic political arenas and new kinds of political organization, symbolized by the Beijing Conference of 1995.

5.2   New 'communities of fate': women's democratic political initiatives above, below and across the nation-state

In this section I look at women's political response to economic globalization, international environmental degradation, and global fundamentalism. That response has been real and innovative, I argue here, despite the apparently overwhelming strikes against it. But because it does not necessarily follow conventional political routes, it is easily overlooked or downplayed. It is a form of *reinventing democratic politics*, entailing a new notion of the democratic political community – and therefore not easily recognizable in existing categories.

These conventional categories limit democratic development to the sheltering boundaries of the nation-state (e.g. Huntington, 1991, cited in Chapter 1). The liberal democratic state, it is usually argued, has proved very adaptable towards the demands of a variety of groups desiring further democratization. What this argument omits is the intransigence of liberal democracy towards women's demands for full citizenship. Indeed, even the notions in which the democratic debate was couched before the twentieth century – 'universal suffrage', for example, meaning male suffrage – failed to count women in (Dickenson, 1988).

Women's political participation was not conceded by the 'accommodating' liberal democratic state until two *global* crises in the twentieth century – the First and Second World Wars. It was not until the First World War that women in the USA and the UK obtained the vote for which they had been lobbying since the early nineteenth century; in France, where women first demanded the vote during the Revolution, true universal suffrage was not obtained until after the Second World War, 150 years later (Rendall, 1985). The economic mobilization demanded by total war required women's labour and support, which had to be recompensed. The sovereign nation-state has *not* been associated with democracy for women, I would argue (see also Pateman, 1988); only when its sovereignty is *threatened* has the nation-state interested itself in its female citizens.

Because female political participation has been circumscribed in most liberal democracies, it is not surprising that women have appealed to alternative models of association than the nation-state. Women's movements often tend to operate below the nation-state level; but they also organize across and above state boundaries (Peterson and Runyan 1993, p.113). A powerful recent example of this second, global tendency was the Fourth UN World Women's Conference, held in Beijing during August and September 1995.

The Beijing conference: a global political arena

Though trivialized in much of the Western press, the Beijing Women's Conference was an instance of women developing innovative political fora, including the newest global space, the Internet. Whether the conference's Platform for Action (PFA) will translate into measurable improvements for women is difficult to predict, and perhaps we should not be too optimistic in the face of the adverse factors which I detailed in Section 5.1. Nevertheless, there was a measurable difference in the political strategy of the women who attended the Fourth World Conference, compared with the three earlier meetings in Mexico City (1975), Copenhagen (1980) and Nairobi (1985). There was little sense of an international community of women at these earlier conferences; their concerns were coterminous with those of the governments involved. But the 'national community of fate' had become a global community for women by the time of the Beijing conference.

The very title of the First (Mexico City) Conference, 'Equality, development and peace', was dictated by Orwellian opposition among three power blocs – rather than by any local or global women's movement (Bunch and Carillo, 1990). 'Equality' was the catch-phrase required by the First World representatives, 'peace' by the Soviet bloc, and 'development' by the Third World. But the three slogans put together did not represent a coherently thought-out programme. Ideological disagreement between East and West, North and South, drastically weakened the conference.

The Second (Copenhagen) Conference, marking the midpoint of the UN Decade for Women, was dominated by the Palestine question. The conference's Programme of Action was rejected at the last moment because it condemned Zionism. US, Australian, Canadian and Israeli delegations voted

The Beijing International Convention Center, site of the Fourth UN World Women's Conference

in opposition, although the US delegation was riven in two by African-American members' support for the condemnation: race rather than gender was the salient divide for these women. Perhaps any expectation of consensus at Copenhagen was unrealistic, but then again perhaps *that* is to accept that *Realpolitik* has to dominate: that national loyalties must take precedence over gender identities (Ashworth, 1982). This is less a fact than an assumption, and feminists have challenged the presumption that the nation-state is *the* primary or exclusive political space (Peterson, 1992).

The Third Conference, held in Nairobi in 1985, did manage to achieve agreement at the eleventh hour, but at the price of failure to specify particular commitments. The only follow-up was a 1990 review of governments' implementation, to which only one-quarter of states bothered to reply. By contrast the 1995 Beijing conference did reach consensus on a Platform for Action which contains very specific commitments on women's sexual rights, unpaid work, property rights and resource allocation. Bella Abzug, co-chair of the Women's Economic Development Organization, described the result as 'the strongest consensus on women's equality, empowerment and justice ever produced by the world's governments' (Beijing Forum UK, 1995, p.4).

It is noteworthy that the world's governments did *not* achieve this consensus in their capacity as individual liberal democratic states acting in association, but rather through a global 'legislative' process by women delegates. Groundwork for the Beijing conference began two years ahead of time; it came to include five regional conferences, an international preparatory meeting in March 1995, and steering committees of experts on particular issues who met to consider sticking points. The regional women's delegations who were to attend the Fourth Conference spent months beforehand hammering out watertight agreements on the draft Platform for Action. They identified common concerns and strategic objectives for 1996–2001, with only a limited number of bracketed phrases remaining to be agreed at Beijing itself.

Besides paving the way for Beijing, these regional conferences also obtained important concessions from previously recalcitrant governments. For example, at a preparatory African workshop in July 1995, South African deputy president Thabo Mbeki committed his government to filling all future ministerial and deputy ministerial posts with women until gender balance was achieved.

Nor was the Beijing conference dominated by the national foreign policy concerns of individual nation-states, as at the Copenhagen conference. Although delegates to Beijing had feared that progress made on women's sexual rights would be undermined by the Vatican and some Islamic states in a concerted rearguard action the agreements worked out at the Conference on Population and Development in Cairo in 1994 were actually strengthened. When agreement on using controversial *terms* such as 'sexual rights' proved impossible, Beijing delegates simply got on with agreeing the practical *content* for those rights. In the end all 189 delegations endorsed the Platform for Action.

Much of the prior negotiation between women's delegations was done through the global electronic communication system, the Internet, raising the notion of a virtual political community. For example, 'Women's Net', a global community of women, activists and organizations using computer networks for information sharing, broadcast and collaboration with the intent of increasing women's rights, featured region and country listings for women's organizations in Africa, Asia/Pacific, and Latin America in addition to the First World. These electronic bulletin-boards remained in place after the conference, offering new political spaces for global organization, mobilization and enhancing the political accountability of governments.

The UN conferences, in addition to mobilizing women at the global level, require national member governments to submit sex-disaggregated data on basic indicators (health, education, productivity, and employment). If concrete targets and strategies based on those indicators are agreed at the conferences, individual states may be embarrassed into measuring up to their own failures, even though the Platform for Action is not legally binding and there is no formal enforcement mechanism. Already some governments have made concrete vows: a target of 30 per cent of women in key government posts in the Lebanon, a promise to increase women's education budgets to 6 per cent of GDP in India, a women's bank in Côte d'Ivoire, a six-year $1.5 billion initiative against domestic violence in the United States. Even within China itself, the conference acted as a catalyst: within a year of the gathering, 5,000 new women's education groups had been set up.

Beijing was not an unmitigated success. Geographical separation, imposed by the Chinese government, impaired communication between representatives of governmental and non-governmental organizations. The sheer number of NGOs – over 4,000 were accredited – made networking difficult. Experienced lobbyists had the upper hand, which 'effectively created a two-tier system, with only those on the inside likely to be directly involved in the negotiations' (Beijing Forum UK, 1995, p.3).

Another flaw is the uncritical acceptance of market economics throughout the Platform for Action. Although re-allocating and increasing resources to benefit women figure in the document, there is little analysis of the underlying causes of poverty or of the effect of SAPs on women. This is partly inevitable, given national governments' commitment to the market. UK non-governmental bodies which held discussions with the British government about implementing the PFA found far more receptive attitudes towards environmental, educational and health initiatives than to suggestions that economic efficiency should not be the be-all and end-all of development policy (Beijing Forum UK, 1996). Even though a debt moratorium was commonly forecast at the time of the Beijing conference, the PFA's language on the debt crisis and international aid is quite weak. However, the document is strong on commitments to measure and value women's reproductive labour. For the first time, governments are instructed to count women's unpaid reproductive work within national accounts.

One final point indicates that Beijing marked the emergence of a fully globalized women's movement. At previous conferences, the difficulties of organizing across national boundaries were exemplified by tension between Western and Third World feminists, even over practices which both condemned – such as polygamy, veiling, purdah, unilateral divorce, dowry, bridewealth, child marriage, and genital mutilation. Women in the South were angered both by these practices and by interference from feminists outside their own societies; the previous result was an impasse.

Some Western feminists (e.g. Morgan, 1984) had wrongly assumed that women's experiences are the same around the globe, and, most importantly, that women's experiences were effectively non-political. 'Universal sisterhood, defined as the transcendence of the "male" world, thus ... effectively erases material and ideological power differences within and among groups of women, especially between First and Third World women (and, paradoxically, removes us all as actors from history and politics). Ultimately in this reductive utopian vision, men *participate* in politics while women can only hope to *transcend* them' (Mohanty, 1991).

But the impasse was breached at Beijing. The Beijing Platform for Action deliberately eschews relativistic clauses which would 'count women out'. Delegates voted against allowing national governments to refuse reforms such as the abolition of female genital mutilation on the grounds of conflict with religious codes. Whereas the 1994 Cairo Conference on Population and Development declaration included the limiting phrase 'respecting cultural values and religious beliefs' in delineating the rights of women and girls, the Beijing text does not.

So perhaps we might say that human rights (see Chapter 6) were globalized, too, at Beijing. It is particularly appropriate that this development occurred in the section on parental rights and the rights of the child (paragraph 262 of the Platform for Action). A safely private, 'female' domain – motherhood and the family – had become a platform for public, political action.

I have presented the 1995 Beijing conference as a generally successful transformation of democratic political organization at the global rather than the national level: as a restructuring of conventional political space and as a challenge to the conventional assumption that 'global' is somehow less democratic than 'national'. But before closing this section, I want to emphasize that the Beijing delegates did not ignore democratic politics at the nation-state level: far from it. They returned to their home countries ready to continue lobbying for the PFA's implementation with their own governments. In Sierra Leone, one conference delegate is now Minister for Gender and Children; in the UK, the Beijing Forum – an umbrella organization of NGOs concerned with women's issues – was invited to help set policy at a senior level in the Overseas Development Administration.

Without a critical mass of women in key positions at the national level, however, women will continue to be 'counted out' of liberal democratic politics. The UN itself is often alleged to be one of the least representative international institutions in terms of women at a senior level. The Beijing Platform for Action includes a demand for a senior UN post of assistant secretary-general for women. Getting more women into democratic politics through proportional representation or quotas, in the UN, as in national governments, was an important goal at Beijing. But it is a necessary though not a sufficient condition, in the eyes of many women's activists, for a feminist-derived *transformation* of liberal democratic politics – 'ungendering' what is now an invisibly gendered international dimension.

Below the national level: new models of democratic participation

If the Beijing conference is seen as a global, feminist transformation of liberal democracy, it is also important to recognize how the women's movement has presided over the *downward* shift of political networks. This is consistent with my basic premise about women's democratic deficit at the level of the nation-state. The global political community of women has been one response; another has been the attempt to create 'communities of fate' below the nation-state level. The possibilities of self-determination, long denied at nation-state level, may be realized by circumventing the nation-state from above or below. This section concerns concrete initiatives taken by feminists working *below* the level of national democratic politics.

Just as the Platform for Action section on parental and child rights produced the most public, political statements at Beijing, so has the family been a potent political symbol for organizing below nation-state level. But whereas the democratic participation sought by women in the North has been seen in terms of alternative models of association to the family, women in the South have retained and built on the family and their reproductive role as a basis for citizenship. Both, however, challenge the liberal democratic assumption that the family is separate from political life; both see the personal as political.

At the Greenham Common anti-cruise missile encampment from 1981 onwards, women were deliberately making themselves homeless – and yet setting up an alternative form of 'home', the largely-autonomous Peace Camps at the several base gates. They saw themselves as abandoning the non-political space allotted to women, and as refusing male 'protection'. Because the traditional justification for the military's anomalous presence in a liberal democracy is the protection of the nation, this was a particularly sensitive area (see Chapter 2). Whether or not the Greenham women actually achieved the withdrawal of US cruise missiles, their symbolic importance was considerable (Rosenau, 1992). The Greenham women also used more conventional political channels for maximum advantage. For example, they launched a joint US/UK district court action against the Reagan administration for deploying missiles in Europe in violation of international and US constitutional law.

In contrast to the Greenham women, Third World women more frequently use an idealized extended family as a cornerstone for new political 'buildings'. For example, women's producer co-operatives in Zimbabwe, set up to combat the effects of SAPs, preserve African women's traditional responsibility for the domestic mode of production, but expand that role to supplying local markets with products ranging from foodstuffs to uniforms. Although these co-operatives have been successful on an international scale, it is doubtful that they represent a new mode of democratic organization; their governance is quite conventional in form. What is distinctive is their emphasis on female solidarity (Sylvester, 1994).

Below the state level, practical concerns like food shortages or lack of health care often develop into strategic gender interests, sometimes accompanied by a more global analysis of women's subordination and transformation (Molyneux, 1985). Many of the regional caucuses behind the Beijing conference evolved out of such campaigns. However, volunteer local interest groups, emerging out of women's domestic responsibility for the family, are often unpaid and undervalued, as is women's reproductive labour generally. Men generally dominate paid formal community leadership, within the framework of national politics (Moser, 1991). This division is perpetuated by international agencies: for example, a UNICEF (UN International Children's Emergency Fund) basic services programme in India was designed so as to give men paid employment in the organization but to require unpaid community work by women. Given women's double or even triple shifts (paid work, subsistence production and household work), there are limits to how far local organization as a form of democratic transformation can proceed.

Women in the South have also made use of notions such as positive discrimination, more commonly associated with Western feminists. In India, for example, a new positive-action statute requires that one-third of local council elders must be women. In both North and South, however, women have often abandoned conventional politics in order to combat other issues which seem more real, such as domestic violence. Women's rights organizations monitoring domestic violence around the world have called for an overhaul of the UN Universal Declaration of Human Rights to make it reflect the women's rights concerns raised by CEDAW (Convention on the Elimination of All Forms of Discrimination Against Women, adopted in 1979 and ratified by 110 nations as of 1991). Domestic violence was also a key concern in the Beijing Platform for Action.

Similarly, female genital mutilation is increasingly seen by African women as incompatible with the health of girls and the reproductive and sexual wellbeing of adult women. Campaigns centred on promoting family health have reduced rates of genital mutilation dramatically in a ten-year period in Burkina Faso. Whereas campaigns against female circumcision were once seen as neo-imperialist interference, or at best as a diversion from more pressing economic concerns, African women are spontaneously beginning to use the imagery of the ideal rather than the actual family to end this most intimate invasion of women's space.

Structural adjustment programmes have catalysed economic development researchers from the North into co-operation with local women-run grassroots movements in the South. One example is Women in Development, a global group set up by American development economists concerned that capitalist development models imposed on the Third World have increased inequality between the sexes. Women in Development worked with some success to influence United States Agency for International Development policies. It is an interesting example of a *trans*national phenomenon moving into the sphere of *inter*national relations through the inter*governmental* machinery of the UN (Newland, 1991).

_____ *Summary of Section 5.2* _____

- Beijing succeeded where earlier women's conferences had failed because it drew on previous groundwork through regional and global electronic networks; because it concentrated on practical targets rather than ideological sloganeering; and because it benefited from growing recognition of women's rights as universal human rights.

- The Beijing conference itself, the electronic virtual political community which preceded it and still continues, and ongoing global and regional networks of activist women – all represent new forms of political activity and space.

- In addition, previously intransigent nation-states have begun to meet some of the demands of the Beijing Platform for Action, indicating a trickle-down from the global to the national level. This stands in stark contrast to the conventional assumptions which see global forces as hampering democratic decision making at the national level. Where women are concerned, the global political arena is arguably more accommodating than the national arena.

- Women's movements in both North and South have countered the fundamentalist notion of returning to 'family values' by challenging what we understand by the family. Western groups such as the Greenham Peace Campers have tried to produce alternative models of the family; women in the Third World have more typically transformed existing models of the family without rejecting them outright.

- Campaigns of positive discrimination to bring more women into democratic politics are common to both North and South, as are feminist movements against domestic violence and female genital mutilation.

5.3   To what extent is the women's movement transforming the discourse and practices of liberal democratic politics?

In Section 5.2 I evaluated the extent to which democratic political space has been restructured through *concrete* initiatives above and below the nation-state level. In this section I also want to argue that the extent to which the women's movement has transformed liberal democratic politics should not be measured by operational indicators and concrete initiatives alone. This is to gauge its success only in terms of seizing *conventional political spaces* – whereas it has been equally or even more concerned with *changing the topography* of the political map. We should also look to *theoretical* reworkings of key democratic concepts.

I have already mentioned one small example: the recognition that 'universal suffrage' was a much misapplied term. But the theoretical contribution of the feminist movement goes well beyond that fairly obvious statement. Women activists and scholars have sought to reconceptualize *political identity*, question the *public–private* distinction central to liberal democratic thought, rethink the nature of *democratic citizenship*, and query taken-for-granted assumptions about who counts in the democratic *political community*. Indeed, *political community* can be seen as the overarching question here: citizenship, political identity and the boundaries of the public are all subsumed in that one concept. The key theoretical contributions of the feminist movement all involve a challenge to conventional notions of the democratic political community, transforming political discourse to count women in.

Some feminists argue that economic globalization, global ecological crises, and global militarism combine with our increasingly global citizenship to require that we rethink our political identities. For example, no nation-state can solve global ecological crises on its own (Peterson, 1992). Because women's public identity as full citizens has only been grudgingly granted by national governments, and because the women's movement has experimented with alternative identities, such as politicized forms of the family, the transformation to global identities and the de-emphasis on national security may well be led by the feminist movement, if such a transformation is to occur.

The gender-neutrality of much liberal democratic theorizing has been tellingly questioned by feminist political theorists (Pateman, 1988). In particular the family, with a male head, is, according to such critiques, central to the public/private distinction in liberal democratic theory and practice. Feminist reconceptualizing has also cast doubt on the legitimacy of the nation-state's authority, understood in Weberian terms as a monopoly of violence. Nationalism, too, is seen as gendered by many feminists.

Conventional accounts of how national identity is constructed seem to be based on masculinist notions of self-determination and sovereignty. This has implications for another commonly made linkage: that between military participation and the rights of citizenship (see Chapter 2). I want to argue that this amounts to the *feminization of citizenship* (cf. Douglas, 1977).

In Chapter 2, Shaw notes that the linkage between military participation and citizenship has been broken because the military in a nuclear age no longer requires mass conscript armies. This has an ambivalent effect for women. Earlier I accepted the common argument that it was mass mobilization for war which gave women democratic rights of citizenship in the twentieth century. What happens, then, when the state no longer requires the military efforts of its male or female citizens?

Although I accept the strategic importance of the two world wars to the suffrage movements, I think that in general the link between military duty and citizenship rights is far more tenuous than is conventionally argued. Women have been exhorted, rewarded, or compelled to bear sons who will be soldiers in regimes from ancient Sparta through Napoleonic France to Ceaucescu's Romania; yet this undoubted contribution to the military effort has not entitled them to political participation (Le Docuff, 1989). It is exactly such taken-for-granted notions as what constitutes service to the state which feminism is best at questioning. Counting women in means rethinking what counts as full membership in the democratic political community.

In classical Athens citizenship was defined in terms not only of militia duty, but primarily as ownership of the means of independent living, such as a small farm. Women were excluded from political life not because they could not bear arms – indeed, we have records of Greek female naval captains – but because Athenian women did not own the means of independent living. Nor, more importantly, did they own the property in their own persons: that belonged to their *kyrios* or lord, usually their husbands. Without autonomy over their own bodies and actions, they could not be given the right of political control over those who did own themselves, freeborn men. The liberal model of democracy, too, is rooted in a period when married women were effectively 'dead' at law, with no property or political rights. Similarly, except in Hobbes, women are not conceived as participating in the social contract which underlies liberal democracy (Pateman, 1988).

The models of democracy which we have inherited from Athens and seventeenth-century England rely on a linkage between *democratic citizenship* and *property in the person*. Other feminist writers have considered the troubled relationship between women and property in democratic political theory (Dickenson, 1997). Only recently have women begun to own their persons: the campaign against female genital mutilation shows that this struggle is ongoing. There is a stronger association between property ownership and citizenship, for women, than between military participation and democratic rights. Sweden and Switzerland both have a long-standing tradition of citizen conscript armies, needed to maintain their neutrality. One gave women the vote at the beginning of the century, well before the First World War; the other only towards the end, in 1971. By contrast, there is a consistent association between improvements in the property laws relating to married women and the extension of the franchise. The first precedes the second in most Western countries.

Yet the linkage between military duty and democratic citizenship has been broken *for men*, as Chapter 2 argues, and in that sense we have witnessed a *feminization of citizenship*. Men now participate in democratic politics on the same terms as women: as Shaw rightly says, primarily in terms of democratic entitlements rather than duties to the nation-state. And if there has been any democratization of military power, much of the impetus has come from the women's movement. The 'mothers of the Plaza de Mayo', whose adult children were among the 'disparicidos' under the military regimes in Chile and Argentina, challenged the authority of those regimes even while they were still in power. These women's private grief became the vehicle for public activism. It was mothers of the nine friendly-fire victims in the British forces during the Gulf War who took the American military to court. The unlawful dismissal of pregnant officers by the British army resulted in large court settlements and proof that the army had been consciously disobeying the law. And the Greenham Common women represented a symbolic challenge to the military.

Such rethinkings of quintessential political concepts are among the most far-reaching and exciting transformations of liberal democracy through the women's movement (Phillips, 1992). As these examples show, conceptual transformation is not 'merely' theoretical: it can affect practical politics. 'Counting women in' does not mean 'adding women' as a few token participants in government, but requiring the key concepts of liberal democracy – and membership of the democratic political community – to be *genuinely* universal.

─────────────── ***Summary of Section 5.3*** ───────────────

- Practical indicators such as levels of women's representation are important, but the feminist movement has also challenged existing ideologies and democratic concepts. The discourse of democratic political theory has been affected in four key areas:

  political identity; the public/private distinction; the nature of citizenship; political community, the overarching concept which embraces the other three as well.

- The feminization of citizenship results when men are no longer required to bear arms as a basis for citizenship in a post-military age, combined with the accession of women to political participation as they come to control their own bodies.

Conclusion

Feminism may be a global call for action; but to paraphrase Hotspur in Shakespeare's *Henry IV, Part I,* 'will action come when you do call for it?' I have argued that the democratic deficit at the nation-state level, despite the global spread of liberal democracy, has impelled women towards a global response. At the same time, women's organizations operating beneath the nation-state level have transformed the appearance of liberal democratic politics. Finally, at the theoretical rather than the practical level, the discourse and ideology of liberal democratic politics is itself a site of feminist discontent and attempted transformation.

But is this enough to prove my initial suggestion – that globalization may make democracy real for women in a way that the liberal democratic nation-state has failed to do? After all, global transformations such as structural adjustment and environmental degradation really press women towards concentrating on survival, not political activism. Successive UN reports have found that the situation of women is worsening all over the world. World economic crisis, shifting sorts of labour discrimination such as 'flexibility', transfer of inappropriate technology to developing countries – all reinforce women's dispossession and their exclusion from economic and political power. In those nations where fundamentalist movements threaten women's involvement outside the home, there are further reasons to doubt whether women can increase their engagement with politics.

The gradualist approach to women's integration is also outstripped by the proliferation of state and international financial bureaucratic machinery. Ill-funded women's groups simply cannot keep up. The Beijing conference may have approved the Platform for Action, but will implementing equality stumble on cost? At the same time, the backlash against affirmative action in the USA, the rise of movements determined to deny women's reproductive rights in Eastern Europe and the Islamic world as well as in the USA, and the dominance of neo-liberal economics almost everywhere threaten the implementation of those advances within the nation-state which have been agreed after lengthy political processes.

Not only are there increasing practical barriers to 'counting women in' as part of liberal democratic politics, on a theoretical level, many feminists doubt whether liberal democratic concepts as currently framed can admit women. Although some feminist theorists are attempting to rework existing concepts such as authority, community and citizenship, others despair of such key concepts, seeing them as excluding women finally and irredeemably. To those feminist theorists, there is no chance for reform in democratic political discourse: it is male-centred all the way down. But the corresponding risk is that feminist political theory will descend into navel-gazing introspection.

These are powerful arguments for pessimism about the extent to which the women's movement can transform democratic politics within the nation-state. But the arguments for optimism are also powerful, and in the course of writing this chapter I have become more convinced by them. The recognition of women's rights as universal human rights; increasing unwillingness to accept multi-cultural 'opt-out clauses' through which governments attempt to resist reform of abuses condemned by their own women as well as Western feminists; the casting of rights demands in terms of very concrete and universally agreed programmes of action at Beijing – all these argue against cynicism.

The Beijing conference also suggests that women now identify more strongly with other women as a constituency than at the time of the Mexico City, Copenhagen and Nairobi conferences. Delegates refused to let other concerns such as racism, imperialism and neo-colonialism dominate the Beijing agenda. This identity is both reinforced and served by international electronic networking, which was much in evidence before, at and after Beijing – itself a transformation of what counts as political space, and a new kind of 'virtual' democratic political community.

True, factors affecting women must be dealt with at a level above that of the nation-state, but the global women's movement is arguably better placed than any other international movement to demand change. And the very plasticity of the women's movement – its distrust of institutional structures and rigid concepts – may be an asset in an era of global unpredictability.

I have argued that the liberal democratic state has not been so adaptable as is generally supposed: that on the contrary, it has consistently been inflexible about 'counting women in'. It may only be the emergence of a *global civil society*, symbolized by the Beijing conference, which will finally force the full inclusion of women as part of the democratic political community at nation-state level.

References

Ashworth, G. (1982) 'International linkages in the women's movement' in Willets, P. (ed.) *Pressure Groups in the Global System*, London, Frances Pinter Publishers.

Bantje, H. (1995) 'Women's workload and reproductive stress' in Bryceson, D.F. (ed.) .

Beijing Forum UK (1995) *Newsletter*, no. 5, November.

Beijing Forum UK (1996) *A Beijing Forum UK report based on consultations between NGO representatives and the Overseas Development Administration in the light of the Fourth World Conference on Women*, London.

Berry, R.A. and Cline, R. (1979) *Agrarian Structure and Productivity in Developing Countries*, Baltimore, Johns Hopkins.

Brown, K.M. (1992) 'Fundamentalism and the control of women' in Hawley, J.S. (ed.).

Bryceson, D.F. (ed.) (1995) *Women Wielding the Hoe: Lessons from Rural Africa for Feminst Theory and Development Practice*, Oxford, Berg Publishers.

Bunch, C., and Carillo, R. (1990) 'Feminist perspectives on women in development' in Tinker, I. (ed.).

Dasgupta, P. (1993) *An Inquiry into Well-Being and Destitution*, Oxford, Clarendon Press.

Davidson, M.J., and Cooper, G.L. (1993) *European Women in Business and Management*. London, Paul Chapman Publishing.

Dickenson, D. (1988) 'Feminist critiques of democratic theory', Block 7, Option 1, D308 *Democratic Government and Politics*, Milton Keynes, The Open University.

Dickenson, D. (1997) *Property, Women and Politics: Subjects or Objects?* Cambridge, Polity Press.

Douglas, A. (1977) *The Feminization of American Culture*, New York, Alfred A. Knopf.

French, J. (1994) 'Hitting where it hurts most: Jamaican women's livelihoods in crisis' in Sparr, P. (ed.).

Goodwin, J. (1994) *Price of Honour: Muslim Women Lift the Veil of Silence on the Islamic World*, London, Little, Brown.

Gralnt, R. and Newland, K. (eds) (1991) *Gender and International Relations*, Milton Keynes, Open University Press.

Harris, J. (1992) 'Fundamentalism: objections from a modern Jewish historian' in Hawley, J.S. (ed.), *Fundamentalism and Gender*, Oxford, Oxford University Press, pp.137–74.

Hirschmann, N. J. (1992) *Rethinking Obligation: A Feminist Method for Political Theory*. Ithaca and London, Cornell University Press.

Jayaweera, S. (1994) 'Structural adjustment policies, industrial development and women in Sri Lanka' in Sparr, P. (ed.).

Le Doeuff, M. (1991) *Hipparchia's Choice: An Essay Concerning Women, Philosophy, Etc.* Tr. by T. Selous from *L'Etude et le Rouet* (1989). Oxford, Basil Blackwell.

Lim, L.Y.C., (1989) 'Women's work in export factories: the politics of a cause' in Tinker, I (ed.).

Manuh, T. (1994) 'Ghana: women in the public and informal sectors under the economic recovery programme' in Sparr, P. (ed.).

Mazumdar, V., and Sharma, K. (1994) 'Sexual division of labour and the subordination of women: a reappraisal from India' in Tinker, I. (ed.).

Mohanty, C.T. (1991) 'Introduction: cartographies of struggle: Third World women and the politics of feminism' in Talpade, C.T. *et al.* (eds), pp.1–47.

Moharty, C.T., Russo, A. and Torres, L (eds) (1991) *Third World Women and the Politics of Feminism*, Bloomington and Indianapolis, Indiana University Press.

Molyneux, M. (1985) 'Mobilization without emancipation? Women's interests, the state and revolution in Nicaragua', *Feminist Studies*, 11, summer, pp.227–54.

Morgan, R. (1984) *Sisterhood Is Global: The International Women's Movement Anthology*, New York, Anchor Press/Doubleday.

Moser, C.O.N. (1991) 'Gender planning in the Third World' in Grant, R. and Kathleen Newland (eds).

Newland, K. (1991) 'From transnational relationships to international relations: women in development and the international decade for women' in Grant, R. and Newland, K. (eds), pp.122–32.

Obbo, C. (1995) 'What women can do: AIDS crisis management in Uganda' in Bryceson, D.F. (ed.) pp.165–78.

Pateman, C. (1988) *The Sexual Contract*, Cambridge, Polity.

Peterson, V.S. (1992) (ed.) *Gendered States: Feminist (Re)Visions of International Relations Theory*, Boulder and London, Lynne Rienner Publishers.

Peterson, V.S. and Runyan, A.S. (1993) *Global Gender Issues*, Boulder, Westview Press.

Phillips, A. (1992) 'Universal pretensions in political thought' in Barrett, M. and Phillips, A. (eds) *Destabilizing Theory*, Cambridge, Polity, pp.10–30.

Rendall, J. (1985) *The Origins of Modern Feminism: Women in Britain, France and the United States, 1780–1860*, London, Macmillan.

Reynders, H.J.J. (1963) 'The geographical income of the Bantu areas in South Africa' in Samuels, L.H. (ed.), *African Studies in Income and Wealth*, London.

Rosenau, P. (1992) *Postmodernism and the Social Sciences: Insights, Inroads and Intrusions,* Princeton, Princeton University Press.

Sparr, P. (1994) 'Introduction', in Sparr, P. (ed.), pp.1–39.

Sparr, P. (ed.) (1994) *Mortgaging Women's Lives: Feminist Critiques of Structural Adjustment,* London, Zed Books.

Sylvester, C. (1994) *Feminist Theory and International Relations in a Postmodern Era,* Cambridge, Cambridge University Press.

Taylor, D. *et al.* (1985) *Women: A World Report,* London, *New Internationalist* and Methuen.

Tinker, I. (ed.) (1990) *Persistent Inequalities: Women and World Development,* Oxford, Oxford University Press.

United Nations (1995) *The World's Women 1995: Trends and Statistics,* New York, UN Publications Office.

Further Reading

Boserup, Ester (1990) 'Economic change and the roles of women' in Tinker, I. (ed.), *Persistent Inequalities: Women and World Development,* Oxford, Oxford University Press, pp.14–24.

Enloe, E. (1989) *Bananas, Beaches and Bases: Making Feminist Sense of International Politics,* London, Pandora.

Krause, J. (1995) 'The international dimension of gender inequality and feminist politics: a 'new direction' for international political economy?' in MacMillan, J. and Linklater, A. (eds) *Boundaries in Question: New Directions in International Relations,* London and New York, Pinter Publishers, pp.128–144.

UNDP (1995) *Human Development Report 1995 – Gender Inequality,* Oxford, Oxford University Press.

Waring, M. (1989) *If Women Counted: A New Feminist Economics,* introduction by Gloria Steinem, London, Macmillan.

PART II
Democratizing world order

Introduction

Anthony McGrew

The chapters in Part I suggest that the global and transnational scale of contemporary economic and social organization present a unique challenge to the liberal democratic state. On the one hand, globalization generates a 'democratic deficit', as transnational forces escape the reach of territorial democracy, whilst on the other hand, globalization also stimulates new political energies and forces which provide the impetus towards a more democratic world order. But the prospects for democratizing world order, to help redress the democratic deficit of territorial democracy, can only be properly assessed through a proper understanding of the obstacles which confront its realization. The chapters in Part II conduct a kind of democratic audit of the key structures of global and regional governance, including the UN, the EU and the multinational corporation, paying particular attention to the limits and possibilities for more democratic forms of global governance. But Part II begins with an examination of how far the globalization of human rights invites the prospect of a more democratic world order. All four chapters highlight the tensions which exist between the Westphalian model of world order and the emerging world order of states and peoples shaped by the forces of globalization. They also reflect upon the normative principles and designs which inform the struggle over the democratization of world order. Accordingly, all four chapters offer singular responses to two key questions :

1   How far are existing structures of global governance responsive to democratic control or reform?

2   What are the primary obstacles to the democratization of world order?

    The book's concluding chapter, Chapter 10, critically reviews the normative debates concerning the meaning of democracy and the prospects for the democratic project under conditions of contemporary globalization.

CHAPTER 6

Democratization and human rights

Tony Evans

Introduction

The 'idea' of universal human rights, or 'the rights everyone has, and everyone equally, by virtue of their very humanity' (Vincent, 1986, p.13), is a powerful image in late twentieth-century politics. Although the 'idea' is not new, the moral shock of Nazism provided the catalyst that propelled it into the imagination of all the world's peoples. As the full horror of the concentration camps, medical experimentation, forced labour and the holocaust emerged from the aftermath of the Second World War, people began to question previous assumptions about the nature of sovereignty and the right of states to treat their own citizens as they will. At the Nuremberg war crimes trials, for example, the court rejected the plea that the defendants had no case to answer because their actions were lawful under the legitimate law of Nazi Germany. Consequently, the rhetoric of post-war politics suggested that human rights were a legitimate concern for the whole of the international community, rather than the exclusive preserve of national government. The United Nations (UN) Charter recognized this important shift in the principles of international relations by placing the protection of human rights at the centre of the post-war order. When in 1948 the Universal Declaration of Human Rights was passed by resolution of the General Assembly, many thought the realization of the 'idea' was only a matter of time.

However, while the 'idea' of universal human rights has achieved considerable prominence in the rhetoric of international politics, it remains largely unfulfilled. Increased awareness of human rights seems not to have touched the traditional principles of international society. At both the national and international level, the state remains the highest authority for making and implementing rules and norms. According to Hedley Bull, sovereign states continue to aggregate to themselves the right to be the principle actors in world politics, and work collectively within the society of states to 'resist the claims of suprastate or substate groups to wrest these rights and competencies from them' (Bull, 1977, p.68). The fundamental principle of international relations is therefore sovereignty, which includes domestic jurisdiction, self-determination and non-intervention in the domestic affairs of other states. Universal principles, like human rights, are therefore a challenge to traditional 'realist' notions of international relations. As an appeal to a higher authority than the state, universal human rights threaten the principle of sovereignty and therefore all members of international society.

The tensions between universal claims and those of sovereignty remain an important barrier to achieving the realization of human rights. However, with the collapse of the Cold War, increasing globalization and the near universal acceptance of the idea of liberal democracy, some political practitioners and writers have suggested that the prospects for protecting human rights have never been better. Today, democracy and human rights are increasingly thought of as two sides of the same coin (Carothers, 1993, p.109).

Such assertions should, however, be treated with some caution for two reasons. The first concerns the question of whether national democracy is a sufficient condition to ensure the protection of universal human rights. While all theories of democracy include a concern for rights, these are not necessarily extended to all groups or individuals. Athenian democracy, for example, bestowed rights on all adult males born in Athens; women and slaves were excluded from political participation. Therefore, if a commitment to democracy does not necessarily mean a commitment to equal rights, it cannot necessarily imply a commitment to universal human rights. Indeed, any attempt to legitimate a set of universal human rights may be seen as a threat to a democratic community's claim to decide its own particular political, economic and social system.

Secondly, even if national democracy by itself could be relied upon to deliver human rights, states exist in a world characterized as 'globalized'. Although some authors have argued that growing economic interdependence brings with it a parallel growth in 'moral interdependence', global society shows few signs of democratizing itself as a solution to the potential failure of national governments to deliver rights (Donnelly, 1986, p.618). One of the consequences of globalization is that it is no longer possible – if it ever was – to understand development, security, environmental degradation or human rights as exclusively national problems. And if they are not exclusively national problems then the institutions of national democracy alone cannot be expected to provide a framework for the people to participate in seeking solutions. Therefore, if we are serious about protecting human rights it will not be enough to enhance the institutions and practices of liberal democracy at the national level. While democracy must be supported by strengthening national institutions, ensuring that deprived, marginalized or forgotten groups can exercise their right to participate, this will achieve little unless global society itself is democratized (Sakamoto, 1991).

In this respect the United Nations is often thought of as the first step in democratizing global politics. The UN's role in the field of human rights is, however, paradoxical. On the one hand, the impressive amount of international law on human rights generated by the UN has stimulated extensive debate in a wide range of national and international forums. This has kept the 'idea' of human rights at the centre of global politics and engaged the interest of a growing number of non-governmental organizations (NGOs) devoted to securing justice and the protection of rights throughout the world. It has also prompted a shift in the international normative order, if only because the addition of human rights to the international political agenda 'alters the day-to-day conduct of international relations', with human rights demanding more attention, and of a different kind, than in the past (Ruggie, 1983, p.100). In this way, the UN has contributed to the global reach of the 'idea' of human rights. On the other hand, as an organization based upon sovereign equality and non-intervention, the UN cannot respond to the demand for human rights it has itself engendered. This is reflected in the often-heard claim that the UN is good at setting standards but poor at implementing them. In short, the UN remains responsive to the demands of states, not to peoples and their demand for rights.

This chapter will take a critical look at the claim that universal human rights represent part of a process to democratize world order. It will begin by looking at the distinction between human rights and other types of rights. Following this is an examination of the formal arrangements designed to protect human rights at both the global and regional levels. A further section will discuss several issues that present barriers to developing a system for protecting human rights as part of a process of democratizing world order. The chapter will conclude by raising some questions about the future of universal human rights under conditions of globalization.

Summary

- When thinking about human rights it is important to distinguish between the 'idea' and the implementation of rights.

- The relationship between democracy and human rights is not self-evident. As a universal principle, human rights offer a challenge to national democracy that many states find hard to accommodate.

- While liberal democracy at the national level is necessary for the protection of human rights, it is not sufficient. Given the conditions of globalization, the democratization of world order is a further requirement.

6.1   Rights as universal human rights

Before taking a brief look at the existing international machinery for protecting human rights, it is important to distinguish human rights from other types of rights. The language of rights is now so much part of our everyday speech that we rarely stop to think that 'rights' is not a singular word. Imagine you are visiting a friend who is receiving hospital treatment following an attempt to save a child from drowning. During your conversation the word 'right' might arise in three different ways. In the first your friend might simply respond 'I'm all right' to your concern over their health. In the second your friend might be concerned with whether he or she used the 'right' technique for the rescue, raising questions about alternatives that might have produced a better outcome. Lastly, your friend might want to talk about the 'right' of the drowning child to be rescued. The first two uses of 'right' suggest a state of being and acting respectively, while the third raises more complex moral questions to do with the obligations, duties and responsibilities we assume in our relationships with others (Vincent, 1986, pp.7–8). Rights in this sense can be thought of as the possessions of individuals as members of society.

The possession of a right, however, does not always make it a universal claim. A person may have a legal right to something, supported by the law of the land in which he or she lives. Such claims could arise from general legal norms, like the right to free health care, or from particular contractual agreements made between two or more parties. While such laws may reflect the dominant moral view of a society, the legitimacy of law may be challenged by those who hold alternative views. For example, in a country where abortion is legal, a woman may make a legitimate contract with a surgeon to abort a foetus. However, while the surgeon and woman involved can claim legal rights derived from the law of the land, and special rights derived from the contract, many questions still arise over the moral right of the surgeon to perform the operation, the moral right of the woman to seek such an operation and the rights of the unborn child. These questions understand rights as moral possessions that stand above the law which provide anti-abortionists with the political space to call for legal change. Rights in this sense are moral possessions of a special kind that are 'essentially extra-legal: their principle aim is to challenge or change existing institutions, practices, and norms' (Donnelly, 1989, p.14). Consequently, universal human rights offer a legitimate basis for challenging accepted social and political norms, even in democratic, law-governed societies.

However, not all moral possessions are universal human rights. After all, ideas of morality may vary according to culture. For a right to be a universal human right it must be a claim that any person can make by virtue of their membership of the human race. The moral community upon which the claim is made is the global community of humankind. It cannot be confined to a particular national or local community, not even a democratic one. In any hierarchy of rights, human rights are therefore at the top. In a sense they 'trump' all other claims (Dworkin, 1987, p.90). While a logging company operating in the rainforests of South America may claim a right to fell the trees on land it claims proprietorship over, the human rights of indigenous peoples living in the forest should take precedence over all other claims. In this example, threatening the habitat of a tribal people threatens their human right to life.

Finally, human rights, like all rights, are claims against someone. Someone has a duty to respond to your rights claim and ensure your rights are protected. In some cases, like the right to life and liberty, finding a duty holder is unproblematic, because all members of society have a duty of forbearance. That is to say, the protection of your life and liberty is dependent on you accepting a duty not to violate the life and liberty of others. These are often called 'negative' rights because they require nothing more of us than restraint. However, the claim for economic and social rights is less clear. Economic rights are 'positive' rights because claiming them requires the participation of a duty holder. If there is a right to food then someone has to fulfil it. Throughout the history of rights the duty holder for economic claims has been understood as the state in which the claimant lives. While this view may have had some force in the past, the global organization of finance and production, including agriculture, weakens this argument. As Johan Galtung has argued forcefully, poverty, violations of human rights and loss of human dignity are among the social costs of globalization (Galtung, 1994).

─────────────── *Summary of Section 6.1* ───────────────

- Human rights can be thought of as the moral possessions owned by all human beings. They are at the top of any hierarchy of rights and are often used to challenge other rights claims.

- The distinction between 'positive' and 'negative' rights is important when thinking about duty holders.

───

6.2   The globalization of human rights

In the post-war period the idea of human rights has been globalized through the creation and institutionalization of human rights regimes. The concept of 'international regimes' has become a common approach to understanding international society and world order. Regimes are understood as sets of principles, norms, rules and decision-making procedures that states agree to in a given issue-area of international relations (Evans and Wilson, 1992). Regimes operate at either the global or regional level. Although most regimes are concerned with regulating economic relationships (trade, money, shipping, energy, etc.) the internationally recognized rules and norms regulating behaviour in other aspects of international politics, including human rights, have also been described as regimes (Onuf and Peterson, 1984; Donnelly, 1986; Evans, 1996). Indeed, since norms are so central to international regimes, and human rights are a normative issue, the regime approach seems entirely appropriate.

The global human rights regime

Although recognizing the principle of universal human rights, in an age of globalization, states continue to guard their right to domestic jurisdiction and have consistently resisted strong implementational procedures for the protection of human rights that imply intervention, even of the weakest kind. This is reflected in the global human rights regime, which focuses on the activities of the UN, an organization itself based on the principle of sovereignty. As Jack Donnelly has noted, the weakness of the global regime 'is the result of conscious political decisions' that safeguard sovereignty by keeping human rights to the level of rhetoric (Donnelly, 1989). We must therefore keep in mind that the formal 'paper norms' of the regime may tell us nothing about the 'real norms' associated with actual behaviour (Watson, 1979, p.210).

It is generally accepted that the norms of all human rights regimes are based on the thirty articles of the Universal Declaration of Human Rights. The Declaration expresses a broad range of rights, including the right to life (Article 3), the right to be free from slavery and torture (Articles 4 and 5), the right to be treated equally before the law (Articles 6-10), the right to own property (Article 17), the right to freedom of thought and religion (Articles 18 and 19) and the right to work and fair pay (Article 23). Articles 3 to 21 are concerned with civil and political rights, while Articles 22 to 27 set out economic, social and cultural rights. The Declaration is the outcome of a political struggle during the early years of the UN but the norms it articulates are widely accepted as having a strong Western, liberal bias (Evans, 1996). When the Declaration was passed by resolution of the General Assembly on 10 December 1948, UN membership stood at 56 states, 30 of which represented the political culture of white, Western, industrialized countries. The Assembly today has 191 members, with Western representation remaining at 30. Consequently, the Declaration is criticized increasingly for emphasizing norms that do not satisfy the political, social and cultural demands of many countries (Kausikan, 1993).

The rules of the global human rights regime are found in the various conventions, covenants and protocols of international law. The most important of these are the Covenant on Civil and Political Rights (CCPR) and the Covenant on Economic, Social and Cultural Rights (CESCR), both of which were open to ratification in 1966 and came into force in 1976. Other important pieces of international law include a Covenant on Racial Discrimination (1966), another on the Elimination of Discrimination Against Women (1979) and a Convention Against Genocide (1948). The rules of the global regime are based on the norms found in the Declaration, but differ in that they place specific duties and responsibilities on states and set up systems of monitoring progress towards reducing violations.

Implementation represents the decision-making element of the global regime (see Figure 6.1). Keeping in mind the tensions between sovereignty and universal claims, the most favoured method for implementation is a system requiring state parties to a covenant to present periodic reports to a body of experts or a committee. The Human Rights Committee (HRC) performs this role under the terms of the CCPR, while a committee set up by the UN Economic and Social Council receives reports under the CESCR. Although self-reporting systems have resulted in some minor alterations to domestic human rights practices, those that require an extensive overhaul remain relatively untouched. The HRC has no powers to force compliance with the Covenant. Self-reporting is also open to considerable abuse. For example, although it was widely reported in the 1990s that Sikhs were suffering gross violations of rights in India, the HRC had to make four requests before the Indian government submitted its report. When the report was finally received, it hardly mentioned the Sikh situation. Even when reports are received they often prove inadequate, sometimes claiming that citizens had no need to invoke the Covenant because national legislation is at a more advanced level (Guinea, 1985), or simply stating that all Covenant rights are enshrined in national law (Bulgaria, 1979).

Two further methods of implementation under the CCPR should be mentioned. First, under Article 41 a state party to the covenant may complain about another state party, provided both have declared the Committee competent to receive such complaints. This procedure has never been invoked and is likely to remain unused in the foreseeable future. Second, the HRC also receives communications under an Optional Protocol, which provides for complaints by individuals once all domestic avenues have been exhausted. This is a major departure from the traditional view of international law and suggests an important weakening of sovereignty. By 1991 the HRC had found 472 submissions concerning 36 states admissible, and offered a view on 125 cases. This should be seen against the reported 35,000

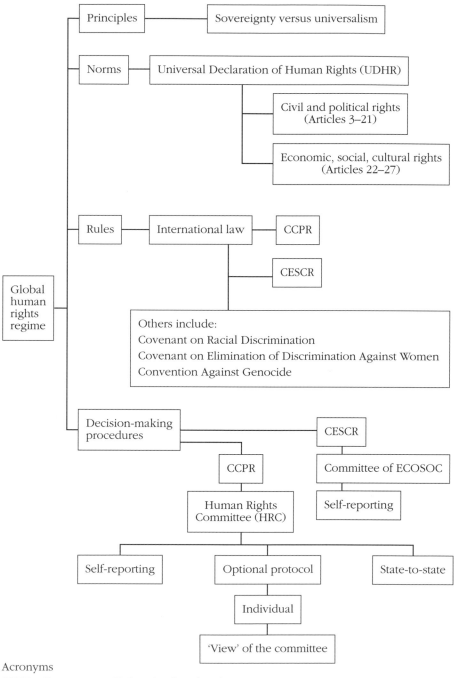

Acronyms
CCPR – Covenant on Civil and Political Rights
CESCR – Covenant on Economic, Social and Cultural Rights
ECOSOC – UN Economic and Social Council

Figure 6.1   The global human rights regime

communications received by the HRC annually. Although many of these are considered frivolous or inadmissible for technical reasons, this figure puts the achievements of the Optional Protocol in perspective. In the final analysis, the implementational procedures adopted by the United Nations can be fairly described as 'more than a whimper' but 'less than a roar' (Farer, 1987).

The European regime

The European Convention for the Protection of Human Rights and Fundamental Freedoms was adopted in November 1951, some 25 years before the two UN Conventions. It is recognized as the most advanced of all the regional regimes. The European regime represents an attempt to list human rights and to create machinery for their protection. All the rights listed are of a civil and political nature, including the rights to life, to a fair trial, to property and to freedom of association. According to Robertson, the list of rights found in the European Convention is limited to those rights 'necessary in a democratic society' (quoted in Vincent, 1986, p.96). The Convention establishes a Commission (the European Commission on Human Rights) and a Court (the European Court of Human Rights). The Commission reviews complaints received from groups, non-governmental organizations and states. A state party can also recognize the competence of the Commission to receive complaints from individuals. If 'friendly settlement' cannot be achieved following a Commission report, the case can be sent to the Court for adjudication. Neither the Commission nor the Court has the power to enforce a decision.

The importance of allowing non-state actors and individuals the right to petition the Commission cannot be overemphasized because it tentatively accepts that the protection of human rights takes precedence over sovereignty. Although the parties to the European Convention are states, the mechanism for individual complaints suggests the emergence of some form of transnational, cosmopolitan or supranational law, as opposed to international or interstate law. Perhaps this is unsurprising in the European

The European Court of Human Rights in session

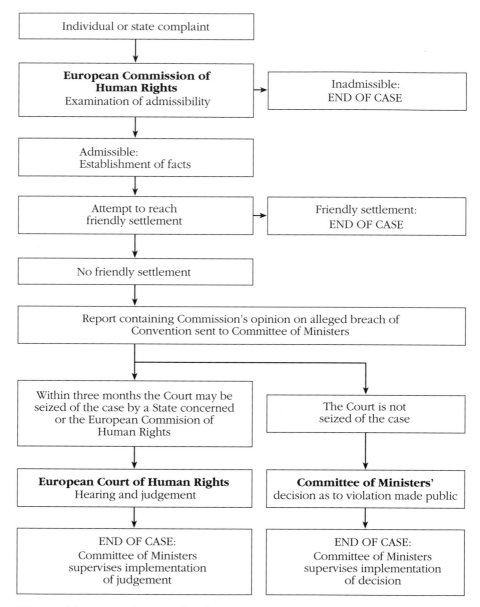

Figure 6.2   Procedure under the European Convention on Human Rights

context, where all the signatories share a political culture that features respect for civil and political rights. In this respect, the achievements of the European Convention might be regarded as 'less a cause than a reflection of the regime's strength' (Donnelly, 1989, p.214). However, if this phenomenon was pursued to its full potential on a global scale the traditional definition of sovereignty, and the concept of the national democratic community, would be strained.

    In addition to the formal regime is the work of the Organization for Security and Co-operation in Europe (OSCE). This is important in that the membership includes both the old Western European democracies and the newly independent states of Eastern Europe. In particular, the OSCE has been very involved in helping the new eastern European states to draft constitutions that include provisions for human rights.

The American regime

The American Convention of Human Rights (1969) – covering all the states within the Americas – also allows petitions for individuals, groups and non-governmental organizations, suggesting that transnational law on human rights is not limited to Europe. The list of rights supported by the American Convention is all within the category of civil and political rights. Both a Commission (Inter-American Commission on Human Rights) and a Court (Inter-American Court of Human Rights) are provided for. However, while the Convention created the Court, the powers and responsibilities of the Commission are conferred upon an existing organ, the Organization of American States (OAS). In contrast to the European regime, the Commission can make decisions on particular cases, though these are often ignored by signatories.

The political and cultural consensus reflected in the European Convention does not exist between members of the American regime. Any compliance with the rules of the regime may therefore have more to do with the United States, which 'has often used its hegemonic power to support the Inter-American regime' by persuading 'reluctant, even recalcitrant, governments of the wisdom of co-operating with the investigations of the commission' (Donnelly, 1989, p.216)

The African regime

The African Charter of Human and People's Rights (1981), sometimes known as the Banjul Charter, differs from the European and American regimes in two important respects. First, while the African Charter accepts the importance of individual rights, it also includes an emphasis on the collective rights of peoples. Important among peoples' rights are the right for a people to dispose of their wealth and natural resources, the right to economic, social and cultural development, and the right to peace and security. Second, the African Charter also sets out in general terms the duties of the individual. These include service to the national community, a duty to foster a sense of social and national solidarity, to promote African unity and to preserve and strengthen positive African cultural values.

The Charter also established an African Commission on Human and People's Rights. Although the African Charter provides for communications and complaints from individual and non-governmental organizations, no authoritative mechanisms are set up to deal with them. With no common political culture to cement the regime together, and no hegemonic power to support human rights, the African regime seems unlikely to gain in strength in the future.

Although widely discussed, so far no formal Asian regime has yet emerged.

Non-governmental organizations (NGOs) and human rights

The link between the formal regimes and the demand for human rights is most visible in the activities of NGOs. The increasing number of domestic and transnational NGOs devoted to human rights, suggests the growth of global civil society and the potential for a more democratic world order. In other words, the idea of human rights accentuates the similarities between all the world's peoples, helping to strengthen transnational ties that then seek expression in institutions beyond and across states. While the formal regimes on human rights display very weak implementational machinery, the globalization of a complex network of communications has enabled NGOs to exercise the 'power to embarrass' (Bergeson, 1982). Although not always successful, NGOs can influence public opinion to the extent that populations take action independently of their state. An example of this is the anti-apartheid campaign conducted against South Africa during the late 1980s. While many countries were reluctant to impose sanctions on South Africa, including Britain and the United States of America, unofficial sanctions were encouraged by NGOs. By activating the world's media, NGOs placed pressure on important economic interests (Salim, 1993). This pressure culminated in the Ford Motor Company withdrawing its interests in South Africa following declining sales in the USA. Furthermore, public opinion was instrumental in encouraging institutions to disinvest in South Africa. In Britain, the National Students' Union followed a policy of boycotting Barclays Bank, and persuaded many tens of thousands of students to open accounts elsewhere. Although denying any connection, Barclays' share of accounts held by the future generation of high-income graduates was so threatened that the bank sold its interests in South Africa.

NGOs have limited resources at their disposal, but many have shown considerable imagination in exploiting the norms and rules of the formal regimes. First, when an NGO has evidence of violations of rights, international law legitimates accusations against the perpetrators and offers a rallying point for public opinion. Second, NGOs act as conduits for transmitting reliable evidence of human rights violations to the formal regimes. For example, during sittings of the HRC, NGOs are always on hand to brief members and to advise on the human rights records of all countries. Since the Committee has no powers to conduct its own investigations or research to confirm the accuracy of state reports, NGO advice is often sought unofficially, sometimes literally in the corridor outside the Committee room (Fischer, 1982). Third, many NGOs are engaged in direct action for securing the rights of individuals and groups. Direct action articulates the idea 'that people in high positions of authority are more likely to act properly when they know that their conduct is under public scrutiny' (Vincent, 1986, p.98). Perhaps the most widely known example of this type of action is Amnesty International's letter-writing campaigns designed to embarrass political leaders into releasing prisoners of conscience. Other examples include peaceful demonstrations and marches and direct confrontation with government, sometimes leading to revolution.

Representatives of NGOs hold signs with the letter 'S' during speeches, protesting at the use of the phrase 'indigenous people' instead of 'peoples' in the final document of the UN World Conference on Human Rights, Vienna, 23 June 1993

The increase in the number of NGOs, and the kind of activities they pursue, offer some tentative indication of the link between the formal regime, the growing global demand for human rights and the growth of a global civil society. However, it should be noted that NGOs are not part of any formal democratic process. Indeed, most NGOs are far from democratic in their internal practices and procedures. NGO leaders and officials are rarely accountable to their supporters. This being said, rights campaigns receive considerable support both at the level of direct involvement, and from the wider public, indicating the place of human rights as an important social movement in the democratization of world order.

Summary of Section 6.2

- Human rights regimes operate both globally and regionally.
- All regimes are based on the set of rights found in the UN Declaration. However, economic rights are excluded from the European and American regimes.
- While all the regimes have added considerably to the task of standard-setting, only the European regime has made any progress in enforcement and implementation.
- Human rights NGOs symbolize the emergence of a global civil society and a step towards the democratization of world order.

6.3   The realization of universal human rights

This section will examine several issues that have historically frustrated the realization of universal human rights and the possibilities for a more democratic world order. These are: the role of power; cultural relativism; lists of rights; and limits to international law.

Power and human rights

An examination of democracy and human rights cannot avoid a consideration of power. Although the human rights debate is often conducted in the language of idealism, the global regime owes much of its form and character to a struggle between competing interests. The Western tradition of political philosophy has sought a foundation for rights in universal and timeless concepts like natural rights, a deity or self-evidence. However, rights should also be understood within a social and political context, including power and interests. This means that 'ideas and practices concerning human rights are *created* by people in particular historical, social and economic circumstances' (Stammers, 1995, p.488). While the Magna Carta or the American Bill of Rights are often explained in the language of reason, philosophy and democracy, rights claims have always represented a political challenge to the existing economic, political and social order. The current debate on human rights is also concerned with power. At the national level this is manifest in resistance or pro-democracy movements, while at the international level it is expressed in criticisms of globalization as a form of Westernization and cultural imperialism.

Two aspects of the role of power in the post-war human rights debate should be noted. First, in the past, rights claims signified a challenge to the dominant interests that supported an existing status quo order. For example, the American Declaration of Independence (1776) articulated rights claims opposed to continued British rule. In the post-war period, however, no clear status quo order existed. As the most powerful state to emerge from the war, the United States sought to establish an international order that included a liberal view of rights. Opposed to this order were less developed and socialist states whose interests lay in asserting a view of rights that supported their demand for self-determination and development, including a right to control their own natural resources. The post-war human rights debate was not therefore a challenge to an existing status quo, but rather part of a struggle over the character that the post-war world order should take. Consequently, the human rights regime must be understood within the context of the Cold War, characterized as an ideological struggle over values (Evans, 1995).

Second, less developed states have often accused powerful Western states of attempting to impose a set of values on them or forging new structures of colonial dominance. The emphasis given to civil and political rights by Western states derives from liberal principals that include freedom of individual action, non-interference by the state in economic and social matters and the important principle of *laissez-faire*. For Western states, particularly the United States, human rights can only be defined as that set of claims that require government abstention from acts that violate the freedom of the individual (Tetrault, 1988). Liberal ideology offers the individual the maximum freedom to innovate and to invest time, capital and resources in the processes of production and exchange. Applying the principle of *laissez-faire* to human rights suggests negative rather than positive rights. Importantly, negative rights are civil and political claims, which place a duty on governments to refrain from interfering in the private, social and economic world of their citizens.

Following the inhumanity of the Second World War, the West assumed that all the peoples of the world would accept the logic and virtue of observing liberal values based on the liberty and freedom of the individual. The global regime for human rights was therefore understood as a sign of 'arrival' (Raphael, 1987) – the acknowledgement that certain civil and political rights provided the essential foundation for a just and peaceful world. By contrast, the East European states saw human rights as a point of 'departure' towards a new world order that sought to deliver economic and social justice. Understanding human rights as a point of 'departure' reflected socialist states' view of history, which saw the world in transition from capitalism to socialism. The human rights regime, they argued, should therefore place an emphasis on a range of rights that reflected the norms of some future socialist utopia. Accordingly, the socialist states argued that human rights were neither natural nor inherent. Rather, they were determined by the forces of history that governed a people's level of economic and social development (Kudryartov, 1986). Thus the socialist states argued that their view of human rights was progressive, while that of the West clung conservatively to outmoded ideas and values,

Lin Hua Qui (right), head of the Chinese delegation, and the Chinese Ambassador to Switzerland (left), attend the opening ceremony of the UN World Conference on Human Rights, Vienna, 14 June 1993. Following pressure from the Chinese government, the UN decided to bar Tibet's Dalai Lama from speaking at the Conference.

The end of the Cold War, and the apparent universal acceptance of liberal, free market values, suggests that the struggle over human rights is over. While this view supports the argument that dominant groups attempt to keep control of the definition of rights as a basis for legitimating their own image of utopia, and in the process exercise the power to include or exclude lesser groups on grounds of morality, it is unlikely that the human rights debate is settled (Galtung, 1994, p.14). As Stammers has pointed out, alternative moral codes, including a view of rights, are a central feature of opposition to dominant groups (Stammers, 1993). NGOs are important in this respect, but so also are those countries who reject the Western view of rights. Among these are many Asian countries who object to the Western view of human rights and the value of liberal democracy (Kausikan, 1993).

While the demise of the Cold War has brought to an end the ideological struggle over rights, the cultural struggle is only now beginning.

Cultural relativism

Central to the rights debate for over two centuries has been the argument that human rights are moral values derived from a particular culture, which is tied to time and place, and cannot therefore be the rights of all human beings universally. If one accepts this view of rights, any attempt to promote a particular set of moral values could be defined as cultural imperialism. In recent times, less developed states have sought to pursue this argument in protesting against Westernization. At the 1993 World Conference on Human Rights in Vienna, Asian countries claimed that human rights were not universal, but the product of a Western culture based on industrialization and economic development. The West, it was argued, 'sought to use human rights as a stalking horse, to achieve global economic dominance over the developing and poorer world' (Boyle, 1995, p.84). Such arguments, which go by the name of cultural relativism, are often used to maintain the traditional realist view of international politics that rights are an exclusively domestic issue.

Several alternatives exist between the two extremes represented by 'radical universalism', which asserts that all human values are universal, and 'radical relativism', which sees rights as the product of particular cultural contexts. Closer to the radical relativist end of the scale is the argument that, although human rights exist, they can only be defined for particular societies. It argues that human values are 'principally, but not entirely, determined by culture or other circumstances' (Donnelly, 1993, p.36). For example, while human rights might express a view of human dignity particular to Western thought, other traditions of thought such as Islam or Confucianism are equally valid within their own social and cultural context. Universal claims, insofar as they exist at all, serve only as a check on the excessive demands made by cultural values. The idea of human rights is something that all societies recognize, but every community defines them in terms of their own culture. Your identity is defined by your membership of a particular culture, not by some abstract notion of world society and the brotherhood and sisterhood of humankind. Since the culture of Java is different from that of Ghana, 'there is no basis for preferring Javanese concepts of human rights to Ghanaian ones' (Vincent, 1986, p.48). Therefore, rights can only be enjoyed within, or claimed against, one's own society. No single culture can claim that its version of human rights or system of government is superior.

Somewhere between the two extremes is the idea of discovering human rights by careful study of all cultures to establish core values, common to all. Such an enquiry would hope to generate a list of rights to which all societies subscribe. Although this approach would be open to the criticism that the core rights it identified represented the lowest common denominator, it would have the virtue of commanding wide acceptance. However, several difficulties are encountered in this approach. In the first place, it is unlikely that agreement could be reached on many particular rights. For example, how could we deal with the claim of many societies that men and women have different rights and duties, which assign men to the public world and women to the private (Mayer, 1995)? Merely drawing up a list that attempts to attract wide agreement does not solve the problem of moral abhorrence to some cultural practices. Second, even if we could agree on a list of rights that attracted wide agreement, our list would also include rights that a minority did not recognize. Different cultures would point to those rights that offered a fit with existing societal values and practices and reject those that offered a challenge. Again, we must ask if such a 'pick and choose' approach offers a satisfactory solution to agreeing a list of universal human rights.

The third solution to the problem of cultural relativism tends towards the universalist end of the argument. This solution looks to processes of globalization for justifying the universality of human rights. As globalization reaches out to touch all the peoples of the world, from the smallest village high in the Andes to the largest corporate office in New York, it brings with it a single cosmopolitan culture that pulls people away from their traditional life and values. While cultural differences remain important, the demand for universal human rights is a response to changing economic, social and political practices that characterize globalization. Human rights are said to be universal because, for the first time, the people of the world are living a single history. These processes are 'transforming the international polity, away from a society of states, towards a broader social framework for ordering the relations among the world's peoples, a framework that some have called a "world society"' (Ruggie, 1983, p.105). Universal human rights are therefore a justified claim because of the single dominant culture associated with processes of globalization.

While this may seem an attractive foundation on which to press for universal human rights, it does not avert the charge of cultural imperialism. As long as the distinction between globalization and Westernization is unclear, conflict will remain a feature of the human rights debate. The West is often accused of attempting to gain global legitimacy for a set of values that support a particular way of life and their own sense of superiority; a charge the West seeks to avoid by calling it 'a world social process', or 'modernization', or 'an emerging global social structure' (Vincent, 1986, p.51). Therefore, basing human rights claims upon processes of globalization runs the risk of substituting cultural conflict over rights for the ideological conflict of the Cold War. While democratizing global society might be one way of mediating such conflict, the outcome remains uncertain. For the first time in the modern history of rights, countries other than those from a Judeo-Christian tradition

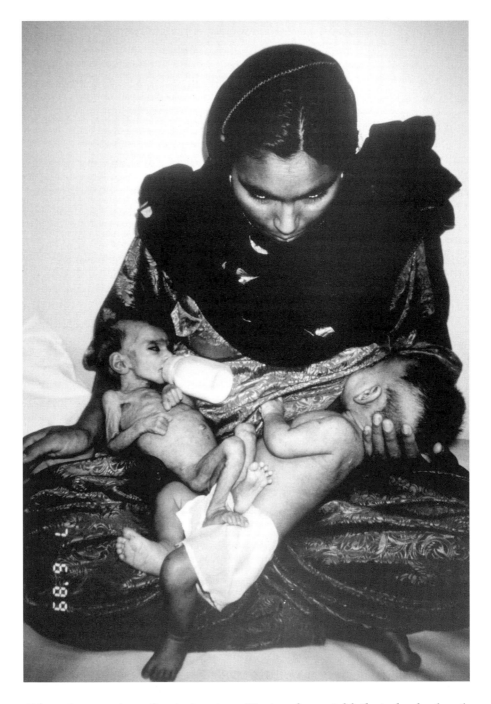

Education against discrimination: Having been told that she had only enough milk for one child, and in keeping with cultural biases in favour of the male, this mother in Pakistan opted to breastfeed her son and bottlefeed her daughter. Receiving a fraction of the essential nutrients as her twin brother, the daughter died the next day.

are gaining in geo-political prominence, particularly the newly emerged economies of Asia. Democratization may indeed lead to a fruitful dialogue that develops a cross-cultural notion of rights, eventually 'finding a balance between a pretentious and unrealistic universalism and a paralysing cultural relativism' (Kausikan, 1993, p.32). On the other hand, such a dialogue may provide a platform for the politics of difference and assertions of moral superiority.

Pointing to all the difficulties that cultural relativism and power present can leave us with the distinct feeling that human rights are anything but universal and we should give up any thought of promoting them as such. However, our failure to assert that at least some rights are universal leaves us in the uncomfortable position of accepting the values of other societies, no matter how repressive they might be. Is the practice of female infanticide acceptable simply because another culture asserts its traditional rights?

Furthermore, in many countries, particularly those engaged in programmes of rapid growth, the state itself remains the greatest violator of human rights. Can we in the West continue to enjoy the benefits of globalization, knowing that the rights of those living in less developed states are violated to maintain our own standard of material life? While tolerance may be a virtue of liberal democracy, in the field of human rights it can be fatal, literally.

Lists of rights

Following the difficulties presented by power and cultural relativism is the problem of agreeing lists of rights. The disagreement over understanding human rights as a point of 'departure' or 'arrival' has been mentioned above. Although the UN Declaration expresses both political and economic rights, there is general agreement that this is a political compromise intended to facilitate a rapid response to the moral outrage of Nazism (Humphrey, 1984). Following the Declaration, Western states used their political influence to ensure that the distinction between political and economic rights was reinforced by insisting on a separate covenant for each. While in formal terms the two covenants are given equal weight, in practice greater attention is given to civil and political rights.

According to some scholars, although economic claims might be utopian ideals, they are not rights. This argument is supported in several ways. First, civil and political rights can be protected by the simple expedient of passing laws that forbid the violation of rights. The enactment of legislation on rights requires no material means and bears no costs. Second, while civil and political rights can be implemented through legal means, the attainment of economic rights is dependent upon the level of development a country has achieved. To claim economic rights is therefore unrealistic for many people. Third, economic claims, like the right to a certain standard of living, are culturally bound and no universal standards can ever be achieved. The most often quoted example of this is Article 24 of the UN Declaration, which gives the right to holidays with pay. For many of the world's peoples, particularly those who live in agrarian or hunting societies, the concept of holidays, or even pay, is alien. Fourth, to establish a right a correlative duty holder must be found. In the case of negative rights we all accept a duty not to take actions that infringe the rights of other citizens. No such duty holder can be identified for economic rights. Lastly, since the right to life is the basic right from which all other claims follow, and the right to life is one of forbearance, this must be prioritized over other claims (Cranston, 1973).

While at first sight these seem powerful arguments, Henry Shue has attempted to refute them. Shue argues that there are basic rights without which no other rights can be enjoyed. These are the rights to life, security and subsistence. According to Shue, the economic right of subsistence is a basic right, because 'no one who is deprived of subsistence is able to enjoy any other rights until the deprivation is corrected. To claim to be fulfilling civil and political rights while postponing fulfilment of subsistence rights for the same people can only be deception or self-deception' (Shue, 1980, p.159).

Shue refutes the claims of writers like Cranston in the following way. First, Shue attacks the assumption that civil and political rights are cost-free. He argues that Western democratic societies are so accustomed to paying taxes that support the legislature, the legal system, police and prisons, that the cost of taking action in support of rights is often forgotten. Second, Shue argues that, although it is clear we all have a duty to protect and aid the deprived, the duty to avoid future deprivation is often forgotten. Thus, if the structures of the global economy produce outcomes that make some groups wealthy while denying subsistence to others, the wealthy have a clear duty to respond to a claim for food and shelter. Accordingly, the distinction between positive and negative rights is not clear. This leads Shue to question why Cranston thinks rights can only be delivered through legal means rather than the transformation of economic, social and political structures. Finally, Shue argues that while culture may determine the type and level of subsistence a people understand as adequate, subsistence is an essential part of being human and achieving a dignified life. In short, if you are so weakened by hunger that you cannot get to the poll, what does it mean to have right to vote?

These opposing sets of arguments have provided an enduring theme throughout the recent history of human rights. During the Cold War, poor countries could rely on the support of the USSR in their claim for prioritizing economic rights. While this did nothing to weaken the West's resolve that economic rights were not human rights, it did at least keep the issue alive. With the continued expansion of the global economy, and the emphasis on liberal values, economic claims are perhaps less likely to be accepted as human rights. Without global democratization, the voice of the poor, who represent the majority, will go unheard.

International law and human rights

If it was possible to solve the problem of lists of rights, and to overcome the difficulties over cultural relativism, we would then have to confront the problem of implementation. The most visible aspect of the human rights regime is the extensive body of international law developed by the United Nations and in the three regional regimes (section 6.2 above). However, as Barkun has reminded us '[a] narrow concern for the assertions of documents or for the power of legally constituted organs of government mistakes appearances for reality, confuses visibility with significance and substitutes (however inadvertently) sophisticated description for explanation' (Barkun, 1968). Those who think and write about human rights through an examination of the law have been called notoriously 'wishful thinkers' because they are prone to confuse formal agreements that describe a normative order with the existence of that order (Vincent, 1986, p.45). This is not to argue that the law is an ass, or that the law has no part to play in the protection of human rights. International agreement on human rights norms does reflect the global demand for human rights and offers non-state actors a focus for pursuing that demand. However, it is important to consider why reports of torture, genocide and starvation remain so common in the face of widespread agreement on human rights.

The first issue to consider is the distinction between 'law' prefaced by 'domestic' and 'law' prefaced by 'international'. In liberal democratic states, the rule of law is taken for granted so that the distinction between domestic and international law usually goes unnoticed. But the character and functions of domestic law are quite distinct from international law. For example, if a citizen of a liberal democratic society breaks the law, they can expect to be detected, brought before the courts and punished, all under a code of law applied equally to all citizens. In this sense, domestic law is coercive. It relies upon enforcement procedures that ensure compliance whatever the immediate social and political environment in which it is applied. International law, on the other hand, relies upon reciprocity and some version of 'do to others as you would have them do to you' under similar circumstances. The sovereignty principle means that enforcement is at best weak and at worst non-existent. Note the self-reporting system for human rights law mentioned earlier (Section 6.2). In the field of human rights the need for reciprocity is particularly difficult to establish, since how another state treats its citizens is of little consequence to others. Large transnational movements of refugees are the only area of human rights that attracts regular attention, exactly because they do threaten the political and social stability of other states.

Furthermore, the subjects of international law are sovereign states, not citizens, and sovereign states decide for themselves which pieces of international law they accept. Unlike citizens who are subject to the law of the land, even if they disagree with it, states are subject only to that international law they choose to formally ratify. While it might be argued that customary international law is regarded as binding on all states, regardless of whether they have ratified it or not, the modern development of international law suggests that states must give their explicit consent (Sighart, 1985, pp.48–9). Even if a state does decide to ratify an international law, it can take out derogations, reservations and declarations against certain articles that are not to its liking. In effect, this means that a state can pick and choose which parts of a treaty to accept or reject, thus gaining the political status that ratifying a treaty might bring, without accepting the complete range of responsibilities that it defines. Recently the United States has been criticized for this when ratifying the Covenant on Civil and Political Rights (Henkin, 1995). It is not difficult to imagine the effects that picking and choosing would have on a liberal democratic society. Furthermore, as far as enforcement goes, it is clear that the UN has little authority and few resources to act against law breakers.

A further distinguishing feature is that in domestic society the law is generated by a central, legislative body. In Britain, parliament fulfils this role. This is not so in international law, where no central authority exists for either creating or enforcing the law. Although the United Nations has taken this role upon itself, and acts as a clearing house for all international treaties, this is clearly not the same function as that of a democratically elected parliament.

Finally, it is important to remember that the mere existence of international law may not lead to changing behaviour and a reduction in human rights violations. Even if states ratify a human rights treaty in good faith, the argument that globalization supports social, political and economic structures that are themselves a cause of violations must be kept in mind. Since structures cannot be subjects of law, the legal approach to reducing violations may therefore offer an illusion of doing something without doing anything. What is required is the reformation, perhaps transformation, of those structures so that the cause of violations is removed. This requires political rather than legal action, strengthening the case for global democracy in the name of human rights.

———————————— *Summary of Section 6.3* ————————————

- Human rights are socially constructed and therefore power is an important element in assessing the role and nature of rights in a globalized world.

- Cultural relativists claim that each community has the right to live by its own customs, traditions and values, no matter how repugnant others might find them. Therefore, universal rights are illusory. Radical universalists disagree.

- The dominant view of universal human rights is that of the Western liberal democratic tradition, which prioritizes civil and political rights over economic, social and cultural rights. Civil and political rights offer moral legitimacy to capitalist social relations and economic globalization.

- International law attempts to regulate relationships between states. Although a large body of international law on human rights now exists, implementation remains in the hands of national governments. Those sanctions that do exist for ensuring implementation remain weak.

6.4   Rights and the democratization of world order

A question of central importance to this chapter is to ask whether there is a normative case to be made for the democratization of world order. If we accept the arguments of the cultural relativists, that all moral and political values emerge from the educational experience of living together in society, then any attempt to establish a universal system of morality or government must be rejected (Brown, 1987). At the international level, the only common experience is that which comes from states having to exist within the society of states. This has generated a system of rules that govern inter-state relationships, most obviously seen in international law. Since international law governs relations *between* states, as opposed to a system of law that is common *to* all states, the claim to be governed democratically comes up against the same problems of all universal claims. Keeping to the norms expressed in international law is all a government needs to do to claim international legitimacy.

Hoffman has pointed out that this position is no longer tenable under conditions of globalization. While accepting that legitimacy may still include the need for external recognition by other members of international society, two further sources of legitimacy are important. First, there is growing recognition that a legitimate state is one that receives the endorsement of its own citizens, and what better way to demonstrate this than through liberal democracy? Internal and external recognition offer a concept of legitimacy which 'relates the individual to the state in some sort of morally cogent fashion, and which relates the state to other states in the international community' (Hoffman, 1988, p.68). Second, the existence of a global civil society changes the political context of state behaviour. Even if states would prefer to continue to behave in the traditional way, and ignore the human rights behaviour of other states, NGOs and public opinion can threaten to delegitimate a government. Under conditions of globalization the claim that states are morally autonomous is difficult to sustain (Beitz, 1979). To reiterate an example given earlier, while the USA and Britain remained uncommitted to imposing sanctions on South Africa, public opinion forced financial, industrial and business interests to withdraw from the South African economy.

Taken together, these three sources of legitimation point to a rights-based society, including freedom of expression and electoral rights, supported by a liberal democratic system of government. Thomas Frank has argued that a right to democracy is already accepted under international law, and is increasingly observable in the actual practice of states (Frank, 1988). Frank argues that this right is built upon the right to self-determination, which replaced the previously accepted norm of colonialism at the end of the Second World War (Article 1, UN Charter). Since then, the right to self-determination has received widespread acceptance. For example, the first article in both major global covenants on human rights asserts the right to self-determination through democratic means. Article 25 of the CCPR further asserts that everyone has a right to 'take part in public affairs, directly or through freely chosen representatives'. Further evidence is seen in Article 21 of the Universal Declaration. This gives everyone 'the right to take part in the government of his [sic] country ... expressed in periodic and genuine elections which shall be by universal suffrage and shall be held by secret vote or by equivalent free voting processes'. Similarly, the regional regimes of Europe (Article 3 of Protocol 1) and Africa (Article 5 of the African Charter) acknowledge the right to democratic representation.

Frank's argument, however, remains embedded in the idea of national democracy, with democratically elected national governments achieving legitimacy through their acceptance of acknowledged international standards for liberal democracy. To reiterate, under conditions of globalization this may not be enough. If, as accounts of globalization suggest, the life chances, economic well-being and social welfare of people are affected by the decisions and actions of transnational actors free of democratic control, national democracy by itself is of limited value (Held, 1995). What globalization demands is a right to democracy that includes participation in both national and international decision-making. Only then will the principle of self-determination be achievable.

Importantly, the claim to be a liberal democracy must rest upon something more than the introduction of formal institutions, which often do nothing to provide for social, economic and legal reforms or the rights of the people. In countries where this type of 'low intensity democracy' is found, little attention is given to developing an open, rights-based culture (Gills, Rocamora and Wilson, 1993). For example, trade unions are weak, wages are kept at a level beneath that necessary for a dignified life, non-governmental organizations are marginalized or illegal, press censorship operates and access to public office is restricted. While the claim to be a liberal democracy may help to legitimate external relations, particularly where established democracies remain squeamish over trading with non-democratic countries, universal standards for human rights are not a necessary part of that claim.

Although it might be argued that 'low intensity democracies' are at least making the first tentative steps towards creating a culture of democracy, the processes of globalization may not favour such a view. For the activities of transnational corporations, multinational banks and global and regional trading organizations play a significant role in shaping the social, political and economic context in which human rights must be protected. Even in the more established liberal democracies, the activities of these institutions and organizations are often incompatible with the push to create greater equality, justice and rights. In 'low intensity democracies', which are primarily less-developed economies with few opportunities to exert control over global economic forces, those democratic institutions that do exist are weakened further by globalization.

This raises some important questions about the potential for the democratization of world order, including human rights. On the one hand some authors, like Hoffman for example, suggest that liberal democracy and a good human rights record are increasingly necessary if a state is to achieve and maintain global legitimacy. The future for liberal democracy and human rights therefore seems bright, because globalization means that no state can escape detailed public scrutiny. The work of NGOs and their use of communications technology is significant in this respect. On the other hand, if the state has less political and economic significance under conditions of globalization, legitimacy may not be of great importance. To achieve democracy and rights might require us to abandon traditional thinking on international relations and replace it with a more inclusive view that allows us to create democratic institutions on a global scale. Frank's optimistic view – that a right to democracy is already accepted under international law – may therefore offer unintended support to those whose interests are best served by maintaining the centrality of the state system when thinking about the democratization of world order.

────────────────── *Summary of Section 6.4* ──────────────────

- Globalization brings the technical capacity for us to scrutinize the democratic and human rights records of all states. A failure to live up to international standards of human rights threatens state legitimacy.

- The right to democracy may already be embedded in international law. However, this seems to express a right to national democracy and has nothing to say about democratizing world order.

- We must be careful to distinguish between liberal democracy as formal institutions and liberal democracy as outcome when thinking about human rights.

6.5   The future for democracy and human rights

This chapter began by noting the difficulties of expressing a universal value, like human rights, within a global order characterized as a system of states. The present world order of states is based upon the principle of sovereignty, including domestic jurisdiction and non-intervention. This means that all states reserve the right to decide their own political, economic, social and cultural future, without fear of outside interference. Therefore, any attempt to introduce a set of universal values offers a challenge to the central principle on which the current order stands. If a state decides that the rights of women, guest workers, indigenous people, ethnic and religious minorities are not equal to those of other groups, any attempt at intervention threatens not only the sovereignty of the state concerned but the state system itself. Justifying intervention on grounds of human rights is made even more complex when the problems associated with cultural relativism are taken into account. While the existence and importance of the 'idea' of universal rights is now widely acknowledged, sovereignty and the preservation of the system of states still seem to be valued more highly.

This is the traditional view of international relations, and one that is challenged increasingly by the idea of globalization. The post-war project to place universal human rights at the centre of international politics suggests a more inclusive view of international relations that goes beyond a narrow view of world order as simply a society of sovereign states. With the recognition of globalization, this project has gained in importance, so that now people throughout the world are aware of their rights as human rights. With the growth of social movements, particularly those associated with women and the environment, traditional thinking that puts states first and human beings second is being reversed. The work of global NGOs is seen by many as evidence of new forms of social and political association, creating an extension of civil society that goes beyond traditional national political communities. An important catalyst for this development is the realization that important decisions are being taken by multinational corporations, international organizations and international financial institutions beyond the control of the state. This is one of the central paradoxes of globalization. While globalization provides the conditions for thinking beyond our own immediate community, allowing us to engage in ideas with universal consequences, it simultaneously weakens the effectiveness of the traditional institutions of liberal democracy. Just at the moment when liberal democracy and human rights are achieving global legitimacy, the ability to create the necessary institutions may elude us.

Although establishing the idea of human rights must be an important step towards constructing a world order that delivers the conditions for human rights and human dignity, the problems outlined in this chapter are grave, and are likely to remain so for the foreseeable future. At the formal level, states continue to focus on international law and large international conferences as a way of demonstrating their commitment to human rights. However, sovereignty, cultural relativism and conflicting ideological views of rights continue to present problems that impede agreement on ensuring a reduction in rights violations. While developing a body of international law that achieves wide formal acceptance is important, unless local and global institutions make a commitment to rights, and reflect that commitment in their activities, the future will remain uncertain. If we are to continue to think of human rights and democracy as two sides of the same coin, the conditions of globalization must be acknowledged and reflected in the political, economic and social institutions we create.

References

Barkun, M. (1968) *Law Without Sanction*, London, Yale University Press.

Beitz, C. (1979) *Political Thought and International Relations*, Princeton, NJ, Princeton University Press.

Bergeson, H.O. (1982) 'The power to embarrass: The UN human rights regime between realism and utopia', Paper presented to the World Congress of the International Political Studies Association, Rio de Janeiro.

Boyle, K. (1995) 'Stock taking on human rights: the world conference on human rights, Vienna 1993', *Political Studies,* vol.43, pp.79–95.

Brown, C. (1988) 'Not my department? Normative theory and international relations', *Paradigms: Kent Journal of International Relations,* vol.1, no.2, pp.213–22.

Bull, H. (1977) *The Anarchical Society*, Basingstoke, Macmillan.

Carothers, T. (1993) 'Democracy and human rights: policy allies or rivals?', *The Washington Quarterly,* vol.17, no.3, pp.109–20.

Cranston, M. (1973) *What are Human Rights?*, London, Bodley Head.

Donnelly, J. (1986) 'International human rights: a regime analysis', *International Organization,* vol.40, no.3, pp.599–642.

Donnelly, J. (1989) *Universal Human Rights in Theory and Practice,* New York, Cornell University Press.

Donnelly, J. (1993) *International Human Rights*, Boulder, CO, Westview Press.

Dworkin, R. (1987) *Taking Rights Seriously*, London, Duckworth.

Evans, T. and Wilson, P. (1992) 'International regimes and the English school of international relations: a comparison', *Millennium,* vol.21, no.3, pp.329–52.

Evans, T. (1995) 'Hegemony, domestic politics and the project of universal human rights', *Diplomacy and Statecraft*, vol.6, no.3, pp.616–44.

Evans, T. (1996) *US Hegemony and the Project of Universal Human Rights*, Basingstoke, St.Martins Press.

Farer, T. (1987) 'The United Nations and human rights: more than a whimper, less than a roar', *Human Rights Quarterly*, vol.9, pp.550–86.

Fischer, D. (1982) 'Reporting under the covenant on civil and political rights: the first five years of the human rights committee', *American Journal of International Law*, vol.70, pp.142–53.

Frank, T.M. (1988) 'The emerging right to democratic government', *American Journal of International Law*, vol.86, pp.46–91.

Galtung, J. (1994) *Human Rights in Another Key*, Cambridge, Polity Press.

Gills, B., Rocamora, J. and Wilson, R. (eds), (1993) *Low Intensity Democracy: Political Power in the New World Order*, London, Pluto Press.

Held, D. (1995) *Democracy and the Global Order*, Cambridge, Polity Press.

Henkin, L. (1995) 'US ratification of human rights conventions: the ghost of Senator Bricker', *American Journal of International Law*, vol.89, no.2.

Hoffman, M. (1988) 'States cosmopolitanism and normative international relations', *Paradigms: Kent Journal of International Relations*, vol.2, no.1, pp.60–75.

Humphrey, J. (1984) *Human Rights and the United Nations: The Great Adventure*, Dobbs Ferry, Transnational Publishers.

Kausikan, B. (1993), 'Asia's different view', *Foreign Affairs*, vol.92, pp.24–41.

Kudryartov, V.N. (1986) 'Human rights and the Soviet constitution' in *Philosophical Foundations of Human Rights*, New York, UNESCO.

Mayer, A.E. (1995) *Islam and Human Rights*, Boulder, CO, Westview Press.

Onuf, N.G. and Peterson, V.S. (1984) 'Human rights from an international regime perspective', *Journal of International Affairs*, vol.32, no.2, pp.329–43.

Quinn, J. (1992) 'The general assembly in the 1990s' in Alston, P. (ed.), *The United Nations and Human Rights: A Critical Appraisal*, Oxford, Clarendon Press, pp.55–106.

Raphael, D.D. (1987) 'Human rights old and new' in Raphael, D.D. (ed.), *Political Theory and the Rights of Man*, London, Macmillan, pp.54–67.

Ruggie, J.G. (1983), 'Human rights and the future of international community', *Daedalus*, vol.112, no.4, pp.93–110.

Sakamoto, Y. (1991), 'The global context of democratization', *Alternatives*, vol.16, pp.119–27.

Salim, J. (1993) *Violence and the Democratic State*, London, Zed Books.

Shue, H. (1980) *Basic Rights: Subsistence, Affluence and US Foreign Policy*, Princeton, NJ, Princeton University Press.

Sighart, P. (1985) *The Lawful Rights of Mankind*, Oxford, Oxford University Press.

Stammers, N. (1993) 'Human rights and power', *Political Studies*, vol.XLI, pp.70–82.

Stammers, N. (1995) 'A critique of social approaches to human rights', *Human Rights Quarterly*, vol.17, no.3, pp.499–508.

Tetrault, M.A. (1988) 'Regimes and liberal world order', *Alternatives*, vol.13, pp.5–26.

Vincent, R.J. (1986) *Human Rights and International Relations*, Cambridge, Cambridge University Press.

Watson, J.S. (1979) 'Legal theory, efficacy and validity in the development of human rights norms in international law', *University of Illinois Law Forum*, vol.3, pp.609–41.

Further reading

Donnelly, J. (1993) *International Human Rights*, Boulder, CO, Westview Press.

Galtung, J. (1994) *Human Rights in Another Key*, Cambridge, Polity Press.

Mayer, A.E. (1995) *Islam and Human Rights,* Boulder, CO, Westview Press.

Vincent, R.J. (1986) *Human Rights and International Relations,* Cambridge, Cambridge University Press.

CHAPTER 7

Multinational corporations and democratic governance

Grahame Thompson

Introduction

In the mid-1990s there were an estimated 40,000 parent-firm multinational corporations (MNCs) with over 250,000 foreign affiliate companies. Two-thirds of these parent firms were from just fourteen of the major capitalist states, with some 90 per cent from the developed world as a whole. These MNCs were estimated to employ 73 million persons at home and abroad. In addition to this direct workforce, through backward linkages via subcontractors and suppliers, direct and indirect MNC employment totalled approximately 150 million.

As well as being important employers, MNCs are also prodigious generators of sales and trade. Foreign affiliates generated nearly US$5 *trillion* of sales in 1993, which was slightly more than the total of world exports. MNCs are thought to be responsible for nearly two-thirds of world exports, and some 30 per cent of world trade is estimated to be intra-MNC trade, i.e. the trading of goods and services across frontiers but within the same firm.

Of course, it is as the medium through which foreign direct investment is conducted that MNCs are best known. Direct investment is investment which involves some managerial and organizational control on the part of the investing firm. Foreign direct investment (FDI) implies the 'internationalization of production', and it is this internationalization that poses the question of the relationship between MNCs and territorial democracy. How far can there be any democratic control over corporations whose activity spreads across international frontiers and whose objectives are the unbridled pursuit of competitive advantage and the maximization of profits? There might seem to be an inherent conflict between, on the one hand, the demands of democratic accountability and, on the other, the private pursuit of economic advantage, particularly as MNC activity increasingly spreads beyond defined national boundaries – the traditional arena for democratic organization.

The modern day MNC arose with the development of international manufacturing as the industrial revolution took hold. Technical and organizational developments after the 1870s allowed a wider variety of similar products to be produced domestically and abroad within the same firm, while the exploration and development of minerals and other raw material products also attracted large amounts of FDI (Dunning, 1993, Ch. 5). It was during this period that the issue of the relationship between such companies and democracy first began to be explicitly posed.

Two different aspects to this relationship can be delineated. The first involves the 'internal' democratic control of MNCs; the second, their 'external' impact upon development and democracy in those countries in which they operate. Thus the issue is how they can be made accountable and democratic on two fronts:

a) in terms of their activities as important economic players in their 'home' economy, and

b) in terms of their activities where these impinge upon the conduct of economic activity in foreign countries.

Because MNCs are so large and powerful they present problems in the home domestic arena as well as being important international economic players. Indeed, to some extent they continue to present more important problems domestically than they do internationally. This is because, despite being the repositories of vast overseas investments and assets, collectively MNCs still conduct some 70 per cent of their business activity in their home territories. In aggregate, only about 30 per cent of their operations, measured along various dimensions, are conducted abroad (Hirst and Thompson, 1996, Ch. 4). As we shall see this can be important for the whole debate about accountability, democratization and regulation of MNCs.

We can tackle these matters either at the level of the firm, the nation-state or in terms of international regulation. Indeed, the analysis of MNCs has oscillated between these three different arenas as the primary focus for democratic regulation. First, in the immediate post-war years the level of the *firm* occupied the central ground: what was the MNC doing as a business unit, what was its impact, how did it operate internally, how could it be made more accountable to shareholders? Secondly, there is the *national* arena: how can MNC activity be made compatible with national mechanisms of democratic accountability? Most recently the emphasis has switched to the *international* arena: what policies can governments collectively develop to manage the impact and consequences of MNCs or to develop mechanisms for their democratic governance? This has served to raise further issues concerning the role of intergovernmental organizations and regimes in the regulation of MNC activities.

We begin this chapter with a discussion of why MNCs have been, and continue to be, considered a 'problem' for national democratic regulation and management in an internationalizing economic environment. Sections 7.3–7.5 concentrate upon the 'internal' government of the firm as a business unit, which in turn raises issues of economic democracy more generally. The difference between 'shareholder' democracy and 'stakeholder' democracy is stressed here. This also serves to shift the focus of the analysis away from the individual firm and on to the role of 'external' governance mechanisms, that is to national governments and intergovernmental organizations in respect of their scrutiny of MNC activity. Finally, in Section 7.6, we look at some of the policy responses to the problems posed by the activities of MNCs for national systems of democratic accountability, and also at policy prescriptions for the democratization of MNCs, and their more effective democratic regulation.

7.1   Attitudes towards the democratic control of MNCs

In this section we review the changing general perceptions of MNCs in the post-war period. Why, and in what way, have MNCs been considered to be a problem to which a democratic, or regulatory, response is needed?

The traditional approach

The term MNC was only introduced in the 1950s, so it was effectively in the 1960s that the relationship between MNCs and democracy was first problematized. Most of the early post-war MNCs were American in origin and they grew on the back of the post-war expansion of US economic power across the globe. Thus MNCs and American global power, and later the global power of the advanced industrial world as a whole, were closely tied to one another. Prevailing attitudes toward the rise of American economic power also coloured attitudes towards those MNCs that were thought to embody that power. Broadly speaking, host countries looked on MNCs with some suspicion, and at times outright hostility. FDI was often seen as the spearhead of an aggressive American imperialism, particularly by many of the less developed countries (LDCs). Foreign investment was for the profit and competitive advantage of the US and European economies; thus it involved an exploitative relationship between the investing and host nations. Not only did this generate economic inequality, but also political power. US multinationals acted in the interests of the US government, particularly the big oil firms and those involved with mineral extraction and the production of agricultural goods. A number of notorious examples of the blatant use of MNCs as instruments of US foreign policy in Latin America and the Middle East helped consolidate the prevailing attitude. FDI became controversial and confrontational. Set in the context of Cold War tensions, MNC economic activity became increasingly viewed as an important and even key element in the international struggle between capitalism and socialism. The 'Socialist Bloc' was isolated from most FDI activity which it viewed as an aggressive challenge to its own economic integrity and to its ambitions for revolutionary social change in less developed countries and other peripheral areas.

Thus the 1960s and 1970s saw the debate about the economic benefits or otherwise to be derived from FDI and MNC activity conducted very much in the context of the Cold War conflict. However, this did not exhaust the nature of the reservations expressed about the behaviour of MNCs.

Current attitudes towards MNCs

The worry about MNCs as the advance guard of an exploitative American style capitalism waned somewhat in the late 1970s and 1980s. This had to do with a number of developments, both international and domestic.

To start with, the world gradually got used to MNCs. They were novel and potentially threatening organizational forms in the 1960s. By the 1990s they were commonplace and acceptable. The world had become used to consumption goods being produced by MNCs, many of which became household names.

Secondly, the 1980s saw an underlying change in the sentiments associated with economic organization. Anything involving 'market exchange' became fashionable and virtuous, while anything associated with regulation, intervention and control was viewed with deep suspicion. This affected MNCs and FDI just like it affected everything else. Deregulation, liberalization and privatization were the banners under which this transformation in ideology and practice was inflected into economic matters. Fixed exchange rates were abandoned, capital controls lifted, financial and domestic production systems liberalized (see Chapter 3). All this added up to an environment that was conducive to the extension of the activities of MNCs and FDI across the globe. Although the issue of 'deregulation' was central to this change in policy stance, it was ambiguously embraced by the international economic community in respect to the activity of MNCs, as we shall see later. In the case of MNCs, a programme of what is perhaps better described as 're-regulation' rather than outright and sustained deregulation was initiated.

Thirdly, as the prospects for any large-scale socialist advance receded in the Third World, there was a considerable dilution of the previously highly politically charged atmosphere in which MNCs operated. With the demise of the Cold War at the end of the 1980s a more propitious political climate for MNCs' operations was consolidated.

In addition, as economic growth in certain Latin American and East Asian countries took off rapidly, MNCs from these regions entered the world scene as important players and helped to quell the idea that it was only the USA and Europe that were the home countries of large MNCs. Japanese multinationals in particular became key players in the international economy, and have been followed by MNCs from other fast expanding East Asian economies.

But perhaps the main reason for the decline in the overtly 'political' controversy surrounding MNCs in the post–1970s period has been a realization that the key arena for their operation is not within the LDCs but within the home regions of the advanced industrial states themselves. Between 1985 and 1991, 75 per cent of the total accumulated FDI stock and 60 per cent of FDI flows were located in just three regions in the international economy: North America, Europe and Japan. *Foreign direct investment and MNC location are fundamentally intra-advanced country phenomena*. But, it must be added, the quickly growing Asian–Pacific economies were also showing the fastest regional growth of FDI; in 1994, for instance, the People's Republic of China became the largest single LDC recipient of FDI in the world.

Of course, this *relative* concentration of FDI in the advanced industrial countries was already recognized by some in the late 1960s. The French, in particular, worried about the 'American Challenge' to their own indigenous manufacturing base and the difficulty this would create for their ability to create 'National Champions' (later converted to 'European Champions'). In addition, although FDI and MNC activity in the LDCs is relatively small by world standards, it may be large in absolute terms in the particular economies concerned. However, this should not divert our attention from the significance of the intra-advanced country nature of MNC activity. To a large extent, popular concern surrounding MNCs in the LDCs is misplaced. The LDCs remain *marginal* to the 'global economy', measured in terms of FDI, trade and income levels (Hirst and Thompson, 1996, Ch. 3; Ruigrok and van Tulder, 1995, Ch. 7; Lipsey, Blomstrom and Ramstetter, 1995).

─────────────── *Summary of Section 7.1* ───────────────

- When the term MNC was coined in the 1950s the attitude towards MNCs was generally hostile. They were considered to be exploitative institutions often spearheading an expansionary capitalist ideology, bent on undermining the democratic control of domestic and foreign economies alike.

- This popular attitude changed in the 1980s to a more benign and resigned approach, leading to the expectation that MNCs could be regulated and controlled much like other aspects of international economic activity.

7.2   Issues and concerns in the conduct of MNC activity

Why, then, should we be concerned about MNC activity in relation to issues of national democracy and accountability? Despite something of a 'sea-change' in the discernible prevailing attitudes towards MNCs, as registered in the above discussion, it should not be concluded that MNCs' activities are now all driven by an unambiguous enlightened benevolence. There remain good reasons for both advanced and less developed economies to be suspicious and vigilant in respect to MNC activity.

The first reason for this involves an issue mentioned before, the sheer size and importance of these organizations. A lot of MNCs are bigger, measured in terms of economic output, than even quite large and developed economies. The turnover of the US company General Motors, for instance, was US$132.4 billion in 1992, bigger than the entire GNP of Finland. Despite the fact that, overall, MNCs remain much more important in their home territory, the really big ones exercise enormous international economic power as well. For instance, the top 100 non-banking multi-nationals (measured in terms of overseas assets) – all based in the advanced countries – were estimated to account for about US$3.4 *trillion* in global assets in 1992, of which US$1.3 trillion were held outside their respective home countries (UN, 1994). Such a concentration of assets and stocks of investment raises their profile in terms of global patterns of trade, technological flows and employment.

One consequence of this overseas orientation to their activity is that MNCs are now important organizations in the conduct of diplomacy, both economic and political. They negotiate with governments over the terms and conditions of their FDI and other aspects of their business activities, though this is mostly done 'invisibly', behind the scenes and out of the public eye. Some authors have gone so far as to argue that MNCs now act akin to nation-states; they are the 'new sovereigns' in a rapidly globalizing economy where traditional nation-states are losing their relevance. Even if one does not agree that they have yet usurped national sovereignty, there is a question concerning the democratic accountability and transparency of these institutions as centres of diplomatic activity .

Indeed, this connects to another reason for concern about the activity of MNCs. How far does FDI now represent 'footloose capital', continually searching the globe for low-cost locations and competitive advantage, with no real commitment or embeddedness in any particular national economy? In contrast to the tone of the discussion above, this conception of the international economy sees it as one increasingly dominated by MNCs that have no clear home-base. They are genuinely 'disembedded' and represent a new ruling financial oligarchy, one that cannot be regulated, even by national governments, let alone made subject to any deeper or wider democratic processes.

One does not have to go quite this far, however, to share concerns over some of the business practices that pervade even the most enlightened and 'nationally-embedded' MNCs. There is a lot of potential for abuse. Whilst some MNCs no doubt still engage in deliberate profiteering and market-eering, which can amount to outright exploitation at times, there now exists such an array of developed national and international regulatory bodies that it would be very difficult to sustain this kind of activity over a long period. (These bodies are discussed further in Section 7.6.) If nothing else, the insatiably inquisitive attitude of the world's media means this type of behaviour is likely to be quickly brought into the open (e.g. the case of the US Union Carbide chemical company, whose activities in the Indian city of Bhopal caused such suffering to the local population, was subject to an intensive exposure by the international media in the 1980s).

However, there remain some less dramatic but legitimate reasons to be concerned with the activity of MNCs. As mentioned above, a third of the international trade conducted by multinationals takes place within the companies themselves. These kinds of transfers are thus not 'openly' registered. The terms of their exchange remain hidden within the physical flows and accounting conventions of the firms themselves. Here is a potential for abuse associated with what is termed 'transfer pricing'. At what 'price' should the transfer of components, half-finished goods or commodities be registered within firms? Supposing there is a different tax rate between two countries in which a company has integrated production plants. It would pay the firm to declare all its output in that country with the lower rate of company tax. However, most of the value added to that output may have been produced in the higher tax country and should legitimately be declared there and taxes paid accordingly. In addition, if the company transfers its output between countries at an artificially high internal 'price', then profits will be lower in the low tax country (because the company is paying 'more' for its inputs into production there than is warranted) and its overall tax bill will be lower as a consequence. By these and other means, companies can move their losses and profits around the international system in the hope of avoiding taxes altogether.

This is a very simplified example of a transfer pricing practice – the basis of a larger number of similar commercial practices going under the same name – which have worried those analysing MNC activities. In particular, regulatory bodies have taken this issue very seriously, as a result of which rules and monitoring arrangements have been put in place to prevent abuses along these lines. Building on this concern with transfer pricing, these bodies have developed a wide range of rules and regulations that touch on many aspects of international business practice, including accounting conventions, general taxation issues, terms and conditions for financial transfers and investments, company operating practices, local content agreements, and the like. All of these rules and procedures can, of course, be flouted, as they probably regularly are by devious but usually perfectly legal means, but they exist nonetheless as a restraint on abuse. (Further discussion of these regulatory institutions can be found in Section 7.6.)

Finally, there remain some important ethical and environmental considerations associated with MNCs' activities, particularly in the LDCs. It is often thought that MNCs have used their LDC business activity as laboratories for 'experimental' programmes which would not be tolerated in their home or other advanced country locations. This is because of the differential power relations between the MNC and the LDC governments. The latter are often desperate to attract FDI in the name of their modernization programmes or economic development strategies. Their own monitoring capacities are also often weak or corrupt, so that MNCs have a freer hand. Even if there is no deliberate policy on the part of the MNC to use these country locations in this way, they may drift into it almost unnoticed through a lack of local opposition or by force of inertia. Environmental degradation is an easy by-product of industrial development. Exploitation of a cheap workforce is tempting if there are few or no checks or alternative employment opportunities. The production and selling of sub-standard or dangerous products can be lucrative when there is no competition. Of course, these or similar practices go on in the advanced world as well. But the weaker governments and civil societies in the LDCs are thought to render them particularly vulnerable to these kinds of practices.

─────────────── *Summary of Section 7.2* ───────────────

- MNCs are not all benevolent organizations simply wishing to help and foster the economies of the countries in which they invest.

- There are a series of economic, political and ethical issues, associated with the operation of MNCs which are a cause for serious concern to those responsible for the management of national economies and the international economy overall. (The connection between these concerns and the characteristics of a liberal democratic order is explored in the following sections.)

7.3   A democratic governance of the firm?

What is the nature of the modern corporation and how is it governed? MNCs are in principle no different from wholly nationally located and incorporated firms, other than that they operate 'abroad' as well as 'at home'. So how are ordinary companies incorporated and governed, and in what sense is such governance democratic?

Governance of the modern company is traditionally conceived through the twin concepts of ownership and control. An incorporated company is 'owned' by its shareholders who have the rights, powers and duties to determine how that company is run; it should be run exclusively in their interests. The second concept is that of control. Who controls the company? Is it the shareholders or the managers? The introduction of managers renders the relationship between ownership and control problematic. The traditional view is that managers are appointed by the shareholders to run the company, and they have a duty to run it in the interests of those shareholders. In this sense, the shareholders are the controllers *and* the owners. Insofar as there is any democracy in the firm, the democratic mandate rests with the constituency of shareholders, who 'elect' a set of managers to run the company on their behalf. This is a (very restricted) form of representative democracy: shareholder democracy.

But the history of the modern corporation is typified by the rise in power of managers relative to that of shareholders. In the 1950s and 1960s this was recognized in the 'divorce of ownership and control' (Berle and Means, 1968). As the role of managers expanded, they were increasingly able to wrest control of the company away from the owner–shareholders and run it in their own interests, hence the notion of a 'divorce'. While *de jure* the shareholders still formally appoint the managers, who are accountable to the shareholders through the yearly company meeting, *de facto* it is very difficult to remove control from management (though individual managers may come and go). Managerial theories of the firm thus stress the ability of the managers to forge their own conception of the objectives and role of the firm.

As a result of these developments it is now generally agreed that shareholders do not in any way 'democratically' control the firm. It is only in times of 'crisis' for a company, when there is a takeover-bid perhaps, or when the performance of a company is so dire that it is threatened with liquidation, that the shareholders can exercise any 'power' to decide the fate of a company.

Insofar as any 'control' of companies can be exercised by the shareholders in this way, it is generally accepted that this requires a lot less than a 51 per cent majority of the shareholder votes. Control can be exercised with as little as 10–15 per cent of the total shareholding when this portion is held as a consolidated block. This is because shareholding is usually quite diverse and spread amongst different institutions and individuals (mainly institutions – shareholding amongst individuals still represents a small, and declining, proportion of all holdings). Any agent that consolidates a shareholding of 10–15 per cent is thus able to exercise effective 'control' over managers despite this being a relatively small proportion of the overall shares. Thus this seems to be a case of financial oligarchy rather than of democracy.

One reaction to this in the UK context has been to try to promote an extension of 'shareholder democracy', by encouraging shareholding amongst the population at large with tax incentives on the one hand, and the selling-off of public assets at attractively low prices on the other. Implicit in this programme is the notion that shareholders really can exercise the power over managers that conventional theory suggests. To achieve this more effectively requires widening the spread of shareholding. However, by and large, this attempt to extend the range and effectiveness of shareholding has not much altered the conventional problems thrown up by the original divorce of ownership and control (see, for example, Kay and Silberston, 1995).

What has arisen in its wake is an explicit attempt to challenge the orthodox view as an increasingly discredited exclusive shareholder oligarchy. An alternative idea has been promoted for the recognition of a range of 'stakeholders' in the firm, which are not just confined to owners, shareholders or managers. The stakeholder conception broadens the ambit of firm democracy, seeking to promote the interests of those traditionally excluded from any say in the organization of the firm, by incorporating their interests into the firm's decision-making structure. Such excluded groups could include the employees of the firm, its creditors other than shareholders, its customers, its suppliers, the local community, the 'national interest', even environmental interests. All these, it is suggested, have a legitimate stake in the firm and its future, alongside the managers and owners, and there should be some explicit recognition of this in company law. A new form of representative 'stakeholder democracy' would thus be forged by this conception.

However, this conception presents a particular problem in the context of the MNC form of organization. Independently of the theoretical and philosophical considerations associated with stakeholder democracy (more of which later), there are a set of operational problems with the idea. How are the various stakeholder constituencies to be formulated in practice? With the internationalization of production, the shareholders of the MNCs are themselves liable to be widely dispersed internationally, let alone the workers, the customers, the suppliers, environmental interests, various local interests, and so on. How, in an MNC, could these be brought into an effective 'democratic' working partnership, even if there was support from within the firm for such a governing structure?

Clearly, any practical arrangement is unlikely to involve the standard democratic procedures of direct voting by constituency. These constituencies would be spread internationally and would in most cases be extremely difficult to constitute properly. Instead it has been suggested that the idea of 'champions' or 'stewardship' should be introduced in its place: there would need to be some mechanism by which appointments to MNC governing institutions were instituted – not 'democratically' – but in relation to persons who would champion a particular cause, say 'the consumer interest' or 'environmental interests', and act as steward(s) for that interest within the company's governing structure. Worker and shareholder interests could be handled more easily in terms of traditional notions of democracy, since they already have an institutional base within most international companies – the shareholder meeting and the works council. But any wider conception of stakeholding would rely upon goodwill on the part of any MNC involved, and the active participation of reputable and concerned stewards or champions in the 'civic duties' of the firm. Whilst difficult then – indeed doubly difficult for MNCs compared to wholly nationally operated companies – the problems associated with extending a more democratic notion of stakeholding to international companies are not completely insurmountable.

Summary of Section 7.3

- This section has examined how the 'internal' economic activities of a company are governed, and their relationship to conceptions of representative democracy.

- The traditional notion is that shareholders govern the firm. This has been challenged by the notion that the managers are the ones who really control it.

- But dissatisfaction with both these approaches has given rise to the idea of an extended 'stakeholder' conception of the firm, which is argued to provide a potentially more democratic and representative form of governance than either of the two traditional approaches.

7.4 Property rights, companies and the law

The previous section introduced the notions of shareholder and stakeholder democracy in terms of the firm. To a large extent these two conceptions represent competing 'visions' of the way MNCs should be run. In this section we analyse the distinction between them a little more deeply. This also serves to raise a second level of conceptual issues framing the discussion of MNCs, namely the way these firms might be 'externally' democratically regulated in an international context. This engages the general 'economic democracy' debate and its application to the case of the MNC.

Economic freedom and liberty

Any discussion of economic democracy must confront the classic triptych: democracy, liberty, equality (Dahl, 1985). Why is there such political sensitivity surrounding issues of economic democracy? The classic arguments here involve whether economic democracy threatens individual liberty, or whether it is absolutely essential for its effective exercise.

Those that feel liberty would be threatened by economic democracy see this threat coming by way of greater equality. One of the key conditions securing liberty, it is argued, is the private ownership of property. If this results in political and economic inequality, so be it; it is a price worth paying for the benefits afforded by liberty and freedom. Liberty and freedom are fundamentally 'negatively' inscribed in this view. They represent freedom *from* constraint – at its strongest, as an absence of coercion (Hayek, 1994). The private ownership of capital and wealth is the foundation stone of the capitalist system, and that capitalist system in turn guarantees those freedoms and liberties it so readily invokes in its own name. An excessive concern with equality challenges the proper outcomes that emerge from the operation of the market system. Any compromise in respect to individual liberty, occasioned by an over-zealous consideration for equality, would act to undermine that system. In as much as democracy fosters an excessive consideration for equality, by placing it above the consideration of liberty, it becomes suspect and should be circumscribed. It is this conception of the centrality of ownership that underpins the idea of shareholder democracy.

On the other hand, we have an approach that sees economic democracy and equality as absolutely central to the securing of liberty, rather than as a potential threat to it. Indeed, in this case economic inequality and a lack of economic democracy pose serious threats to the effectiveness of capitalism. This is because the political legitimacy of capitalism is at risk when inequalities are large and democratic decision-making absent. Here liberty and freedom are more 'positively' associated; they relate to the capacity for action rather than to a lack or otherwise of constraint (Wootton, 1945). Liberty becomes the effective ability to initiate action and implement programmes in a range of arenas. Thus there is no necessary 'sacrifice' of liberty under conditions of economic equality or democratic decision-making. Indeed, from this position it is the *plurality* of arenas and forms of economic organization that is celebrated. A pluralism of freedoms and liberties, of spheres of justice and of fairness, of ethical considerations and deployments, is what counts (e.g. Walzer, 1983). In this case the existence of a range of 'stakeholders' would be welcomed rather than considered as a potentially sinister intrusion or threat.

These philosophical considerations inform the debates about economic democracy. But they suffer from a certain formalism and abstractness where the modern corporation is concerned. As we shall see, the modern corporation represents a very specific instrument of economic and legal organization in advanced capitalism.

The company in law

To push the discussion forward, we first need to clarify the nature of the company as a 'subject' in law. But doing so presents a problem for the argument conducted so far, in so much as it relies upon a rather traditional – but widespread – confusion over the relationship between ownership and control. Briefly, the argument compressed ownership (a legal relation) and control (an economic relation).

Companies are incorporated in law as subjects independently of those who 'own' them. This means, for instance, that firms can sue, or be sued, in their own name, independently of those who either work in them or own them. Strictly speaking, then, the shareholder does not 'own' the assets of a company. These are invested in the company itself. The shareholder 'owns' a right to share in the distribution of any surplus generated by the company (itself decided by management). In this respect the shareholder is in a similar legal position to any other creditor *vis-à-vis* the company as legal subject – they are both creditors and have no proprietary entitlements in the company's assets as such. The company owns itself. Similarly, although the managers may be (formally at least) elected by the shareholders, they are legally constrained to work in the best interests of the company in the first instance, not the shareholder (Hadden, 1977). Their role is to supervise the continuing financial and legal reproduction of the firm – to maintain it as 'a going concern', to 'keep its capital intact', and so on. Obviously a different set of legal conditions hold if the company is in liquidation, creditors having prior interest over shareholders in this instance. But even under these circumstances creditors or shareholders cannot seize the company's assets at will, so they do not 'own' it in this sense. Here both shareholders and creditors are similarly constituted as 'claimants' with only a contingent title in respect to the company's assets.

In addition, with regard to these assets and the firm, claimants must act in accordance with due legal process. What this means is that legal rights in respect to company law are always highly specific, and what they impart to different agents are differential capacities and capabilities to undertake actions and engage in litigation. Legal rights do not exclusively or unconditionally guarantee access to 'ownership' or anything else but only impart possibilities for taking action or undertaking litigation.

This point is important in the debate about economic 'property rights', for here such rights are largely thought to impart an exclusive, unconstrained and unconditional possession to a definite subject or agent. Any attenuation of these rights is thus thought to be a circumscription or restraint on the exercise of those rights, usually imposed by the state or the political process. However, if we consider 'property rights' as attributing no more than a capacity or capability to initiate something (like a claim on the assets of a firm), then that guarantees nothing in terms of outcomes but only contingently and conditionally arranges a series of possibilities for legal disputation and action.

With this conception there is no general public or private possession of, or exclusion from, 'ownership'. In principle the law could thus establish a set of 'rights' that impart capacities and capabilities to any number of stakeholders without that undermining a deeper or more fundamental 'ownership' relation (because rights in law are never rendered with respect to an exclusive *possession* but only in respect to a claim). Here we see the way a discussion of the nature of the company in law can establish the principles for the wider notion of stakeholder democracy.

─────────────── *Summary of Section 7. 4* ───────────────

- This section has considered two types of argument. The first involved the difference between 'negative' conceptions of liberty as a freedom from coercive constraint upon actions compared to the pluralistic nature of 'positive' liberties. The argument was that the latter allowed a wider interpretation of the prospects for democratic accountability than the first.

- Secondly, it was suggested that the company in law represents a legal subject, in which associated property rights are more accurately considered as contingent claims rather than as possessions.

- These two arguments allow us to think more creatively about the democratization of the firm, particularly in respect to the idea of 'stakeholder democracy'.

7.5   Financial systems, corporate control and MNCs

A further issue raised by this discussion is the extent of its relevance in the international domain. For the way companies are incorporated varies between countries, which have their own particular philosophical and legal traditions. Is the analysis conducted so far too 'Anglo-American' in its orientation to apply to MNCs?

Whilst the analysis is mainly based upon the Anglo-American practice, it is universal enough to adequately describe the contemporary position of MNCs. Most are incorporated broadly in the manner described, though national traditions do vary and there are important differences in how they are controlled or governed. In part this has to do with the national characteristics of different financial systems. Broadly speaking, these can be divided into so-called 'outsider' and 'insider' systems. The 'Anglo-American' (UK and USA) tradition is an example of an 'outsider' system. Here the stock exchange and a decentralized market-based approach to corporate control predominate. By comparison, in the 'Continental' model, typified in the popular imagination by Germany and Japan, and to a lesser extent in Europe by France and Spain, the banks hold greater power and a more centralized, administrative approach prevails – an 'insider' system (Thompson, 1996).

These different systems pose an important question: what are the consequences of the outsider and insider systems in terms of economic performance and democratic corporate governance? This is the subject of fierce controversy. In principle, the competitive market-based outsider system would seem to offer the most efficient and attractive method of corporate governance – self-regulation on the basis of the pursuit of clear interests. But it has increasingly come under attack. In the first place, the mode of gaining control tends to be highly antagonistic and conflictual. Contested takeovers are the order of the day in outsider systems whereas they are rare in insider ones. This is costly and distracting, leading to all manner of pre-defensive strategies by managements to prevent takeovers. Secondly, the form of corporate control represents only shareholder interests. The interests of other stakeholders tend to be ignored. Thirdly, it is accused of leading to 'short-termism', that is the inability of management to develop a long-term investment strategy, devote enough resources to R & D (research and development) and training, think in terms of organic internal growth rather than external growth through merger or acquisition, and the like. It leads to a great emphasis on competition for corporate control and a consequent neglect of competition in product markets. The insider system, by contrast, stresses long-term co-operation between producers and the providers of finance.

A recent study found that shareholders and other 'owners' were more able to exercise control within the company in German, Japanese and French multinationals than they were in UK and US multinationals. In addition, there were a wider variety of stakeholders who had an input into decision-making in the former group than in the latter (Fukao, 1995). On both counts, then, the insider system seems to have had the edge over the outsider system in terms of corporate democracy.

─────────── *Summary of Section 7.5* ───────────

- A key feature of the way firms are regulated and governed involves the form of the financial system into which they are inserted. The Anglo-American 'outsider' system can be contrasted to the Continental 'insider' system in terms of its democratic potential.

- Broadly speaking, the outsider system confirms a narrower shareholder/manager control compared to the wider stakeholder democracy of the insider system of corporate control.

7.6   Approaches to democratization

Here we move beyond the level of the firm to consider national and international approaches to the democratization, or democratic regulation, of MNCs.

National approaches

Historically, there have been a number of attempts to democratize the corporate world, some of which still retain a contemporary relevance. The clearest of these is represented by the socialist tradition. This has always been hostile to corporations and highly suspicious of their motives. They are the embodiment of a corporate capitalism which works to exploit the working classes. A number of alternative 'democratic' programmes have been suggested from within this tradition. These range from:

1   the overthrow of the capitalist order altogether and the establishment of a worker's state under the 'dictatorship of the proletariat', through

2   the idea of syndicalism where corporations are put under direct worker control but together co-ordinate themselves as autonomous co-operatives, and

3   the nationalization of particular industries (the 'commanding heights'), to

4   various forms of 'partnership' schemes (between labour and capital) and workers' councils.

These programmes tend to be prescriptive in character – they are emphatic in saying what must be done to overcome the 'contradictions in capitalism', democratize society in the name of the exploited classes and save the world from ruination and environmental degradation.

The most enduring of these traditions is probably represented by various forms of the 'mutual sector' (co-operatives, partnerships, workers' councils, municipal socialism, etc.). The outright 'socialization of the means of production' and full-scale nationalization are heavily discredited in the wake of the demise of communism and the socialist systems of the East. Workers' control looks ominously restrictive in a democratic sense. Where would one set the limit as to how much control should be given exclusively to the workers in any organization? Would we be happy, for instance, for only police officers to control the police force, or for prisons to be run exclusively by prison wardens?

On the other hand, there are very well-developed and viable examples of effective co-operative organization in the industrial and financial spheres. Several hundred plywood manufacturing companies in the Pacific Northwest of the USA continue to be run as democratic co-operatives. The Mondragon co-operative movement in Northern Spain comprised more than 150 primary and hybrid co-ops, involving 25,300 workers, had US$6.3bn assets in 1992, and was responsible for $3bn sales and $380m exports (Turnbull, 1994, p.336). The UK hosts the world's largest single workers' co-operative – the John Lewis Partnership. Extensive and complex control and decision-making procedures typify these well-established and efficient examples of co-operative organization.

The reason for mentioning these successful examples of the 'mutual sector' (and they could be multiplied) is to indicate a possible way of dealing with the potential adverse consequences of MNCs. Given the liberal nature of the international trading system, governed by the World Trade Organization (WTO), it is difficult for a single country to unilaterally 'impose' more democratic governance on either its own or foreign multinationals. This is because international treaties involved with organiza tions like the WTO and the Organization for Economic Co-operation and Development (OECD) forbid 'discriminatory' measures in trade and invest-ment matters.

But measures designed to stimulate the domestic mutual sector, organized along democratic lines, need not contravene any international trading or investment treaties. Fiscal and monetary incentives could be employed to stimulate mutually organized local industrial initiatives, regional economic networks and the like. This represents a real possibility for 'bypassing' the undemocratic nature of existing national and multi-national corporate governance structures, and any potential harmful effects of MNC operations. Although the mutual sector is on the defensive in the present period – it is viewed with suspicion by all those promoting market-led solutions to anything economic – there remains a rich history of traditions involving various forms of guild socialism and associative democracy on which to draw for suggestions as to how to democratize contemporary corporate life (e.g. Hirst, 1994, Chs 4 and 5).

A second way to go about increasing the accountability of MNCs, in particular, would be to introduce a system of national monitoring of the activity of home-based MNCs (Bailey, Hart and Sugden, 1994). Countries like the UK have no such monitoring structure, though they are common in other comparable advanced countries. Bailey *et al.* suggest the introduction, development or strengthening of these forms of scrutiny across the advanced world, so they at least provide good quality information and analysis on what the exact impact of both inward and outward investment is on an economy. They propose setting this in an elaborate social accounting framework, measuring the wider social impact of any MNC investment on the economy, not just the private advantage for the company or its shareholders. Their argument is that this could be extended to incorporate the general business issues mentioned above in connection with intra-MNC trade. This would then form the basis for developing consensus policy measures, both domestically and between the major nation-states, to bring to account adverse MNC activity. Given the fact that the bulk of MNC business activity is still conducted on the home-country territory, the option of making MNCs more accountable in this way remains a distinct possibility.

In fact, this would provide the basis for what Kapstein (1994) has termed 'international co-operation based upon home-country control'. This is the major contemporary form of international governance in economic matters, and in the next section we explore this in respect to MNC regulation.

Internationally-based approaches

Economic relations between the major advanced economies are managed multilaterally through a variety of international institutions and regimes (see Chapter 3). In the case of MNCs these international institutions and regimes include the UN, the GATT and WTO, the OECD, the EU, the G7 (the western club comprising Canada, France, Germany, Italy, Japan, UK and USA), the ILO (International Labour Organization) and the Basel Committee. All these have an impact on the multilateral regulation and governance of MNC activity. These bodies serve to bridge the principal mismatch in the governance of MNCs which characterizes the present period – that is, an institutional gap between the increasingly international nature of the financial systems and company activities but the still predominantly 'national' remits of central banks and domestic regulatory mechanisms for companies, financial markets and institutions.

How has this institutional gap been closed? To begin with there is the G7 summit meeting system which provides the widest possible arena in which broad issues about FDI have been addressed. But this still lacks a proper institutional base: there is no permanent secretariat attached to these summits; their business is conducted in an informal atmosphere without

Finance Ministers from the Group of Seven (G7) after talks at the French Finance Ministry, Paris, 20 January 1996

tight procedural rules or functionally specified agendas; and there is no proper external accountability for decisions taken, with few, if any, sanctions applied to national actors if implementation is not forthcoming.

International banking and financial activity

By contrast, a relatively developed and institutionalized area of regulation characterizes the supervision of those multinationals conducting banking and financial market business. Here the landmark policy initiative was the G20 (later G30) 1975 Basel Concordat that established the leading role of the Bank of International Settlements (BIS) in the supervision of international financial activity. Following from this, the Basel Committee's 1988 Capital Accord was probably the most significant international agreement to date in the field of multinational bank supervision. This established both a framework for further developments and a set of rules fixing minimum standards of business conduct for banks involved with international activities. The Basel agreement has been mirrored by developments within Europe, where the EU approved a comprehensive Capital Adequacy Directive for banks in 1989.

Although the Basel Committee maintains its original informal atmosphere, its evolution has been toward much more involvement in hardheaded rule-making and monitoring of rule implementation. Led by the demands of banks, security houses and governments for a more codified and ordered international financial environment, the Committee has responded to the effects of liberalization of international financial markets, rather than initiating discretionary action on its own part.

The Basel Committee's activity with respect to the banking community is paralleled by the International Organization of Securities Commission (IOSCO), a younger and less robust body dealing with other aspects of international financial transactions, notably security market supervision. This was established in 1986 and, although in a dialogue with the Basel Committee framework, has yet to mature to the same extent. In addition, it is argued that this Commission has yet to establish a political legitimacy and accountability in the face of the relentless imperative of marketization (Underhill, 1995).

The emergence of these bodies (and other similar ones discussed in a moment) raises the question of why and how they came about in an era of increased ideological emphasis on market-led solutions to international economic relationships. Why create new regimes to regulate and manage markets and transactions when such regulation and management is supposed to be increasingly frowned upon by policy makers? Part of the answer is that the Basel Committee responded to the demands made both by governments, through their central banks, and by commercial companies involved in financial activity itself. National liberalization and deregulation of financial markets in the 1980s and technological development of information and communication systems led to a sense of organizational 'loss of national control' experienced by both central bankers and the managers of the private financial institutions.

These developments undermined well established and understood practices of commercial management within those firms and countries.

The players no longer quite understood what their 'capital base' was nor how it functioned in terms of credit and market risk. The rapidity of the introduction of new financial instruments, the very pace of trading activity itself, and the necessity of 'on the spot' decisions having to be made by floor dealers, meant that even managers of commercial banks became unsure of their risk exposure and the real worth of their firms. Bank officials, along with their traditional national supervisors, the central banks, thus had an interest in re-establishing greater transparency and accountability in the light of the new circumstances they faced.

Central bankers, governments and mainstream commercial banks were also concerned with the number of international banking crises/failures in the 1970s and 1980s. These banking crises were successfully 'managed' by the judicious intervention and co-operation of national governments. So the trend was set for *national governments* to co-operate with each other more fully over a wider range of supervisory and monitoring tasks. According to Kapstein (1994) it is national governments that remain central to the nature of these new supervisory regimes. For instance, it was the USA that took the lead in securing the 1988 Basel Capital Accord. Within this framework, home-country supervision of financial institutions came to take precedence over host-country supervision, following the principle of *international co-operation based upon home-country control* (Kapstein, 1994).

This remains, nevertheless, the limited *supervision* of a market-led international economy. Regulation does not attempt to alter price-fixing by markets or the direction of financial flows. In as much as it operates democratically, it is another form of a broadly representative (and realist) form of democracy. The different national entities, or their central banks, form the 'constituency' and these each then 'dispatch' a representative to the international body to make decisions on their behalf. Accountability, weak though it may be, is ensured by the normal channels of domestic politics as these representatives report back to their respective governments and legislatures.

Manufacturing and other productive services

We now look at the way manufacturing and other service multinationals are internationally regulated and managed. To do this we need to describe the forerunners of the present arrangements for 'international co-operation based upon home-country control'. This involves the GATT mechanism and the period of hostility towards MNCs mentioned above, broadly encompassing the 1960s and 1970s.

Generally speaking, the tactics of the inter-governmental organizations committed to the preservation of a multilateral and liberal trading environment, principally the OECD, have been to attach FDI governance issues to the GATT/WTO negotiating framework. They have attempted to ride on the back of the past successes of GATT by grafting FDI negotiations directly on to it. This was aided by the traditional close linkage between trade and investment matters.

The post-war GATT system has involved a series of multilateral conferences in which governments negotiate the reduction of global trade barriers. The latest round of these negotiations – known as the Uruguay

Round – ended in 1995. Previous rounds of GATT negotiations were successful largely because they concentrated on one main aspect of trade – the reduction of various forms of trade barriers on the international exchange of raw materials and manufactured goods. But the Uruguay Round was different. It took on some rather difficult issues that were not obviously intrinsically linked.

A key issue was trade in services, i.e. banking, insurance, intellectual property. Here FDI is progressively substituting for trade because it is not possible to trade internationally in many services; they are locationally specific, so MNCs must invest abroad to provide these services in-country. In the Uruguay Round an attempt was made to negotiate a comprehensive accord on trade and investment in services so as to liberalize them. The results of this Round were only partially successful in liberalizing trade in services, and GATT's successor, the WTO, has become burdened with many FDI-related issues, which it is ill-equipped to deal with.

However, GATT/WTO is not the only international organization involved in initiatives in this area. Both the World Bank and the OECD have been in the forefront of attempts to generate new instruments to codify and regulate aspects of FDI and MNC activity. Perhaps the most comprehensive attempt to come to terms with these issues is represented by the UN Economic and Social Council's efforts to negotiate a *Draft Code of Conduct for TNCs* (Dunning, 1993, Appendix to Chapter 21). The work on this code began in the early 1970s but, by the early 1990s, it had come to nothing and represented a stalled initiative without momentum. The main reason for this is that it was begun in a different era as far as attitudes towards MNCs and FDI are concerned. It represents the final phase in that long post-war hostility towards MNC activity, referred to earlier.

Rethinking these issues in a new political context less concerned with autonomous development has led to the revival of another old idea from the 1970s but presented as a new start: a comprehensive multilateral agreement on international investment or international corporations – a General Agreement on International Corporations (GAIC) (Bergsten and Graham, 1993; Kline, 1993; Scaperlanda, 1993). The objectives of such an agreement would be to codify and bring together the legitimate goals of both business and government in the conduct of FDI.

What might such an agreement involve?

1   It would define, codify and guarantee the property rights of MNCs.

2   The rights of labour and conditions of work would be protected.

3   It would recognize the rights of governments to defend certain of their legitimate national functions in respect to the economy – support for R & D, defence considerations, balance of payments issues, etc.

4   It would establish binding protocols on company taxation.

5   It would establish a disputes mechanism that would be written into international law.

6   There would be some strengthened protocols on environmental protection as well.

However, in the current international climate this kind of a comprehensive agreement would be very difficult, if not impossible, to achieve. It would require a degree of political commitment and negotiating convergence not so far seen amongst the G7 countries.

Labour market issues

The labour market is a further area of governance of MNCs that potentially, at least, straddles the international and the national as the appropriate level of regulation. Although often neglected as a governance issue, labour is likely to become increasingly important as the significance of MNCs in employment matters grows. One possibility is to build on the work of the International Labour Organization (ILO) to lay down common international rules for employment conditions and contracts, industrial relations procedures, ethical working standards, etc. The existing structures in this area are extremely weak, however, so the attempt to build a new international labour regime would prove very difficult. These are particularly sensitive areas of economic policy-making. Up until now international co-operation has been aimed rather at restricting than expanding the scope of international bodies in dealing with national labour market matters.

An alternative approach would be to think along rather more regional or sub-regional lines. This would build on current trends, and emerging arrangements, which increasingly mirror the regionalization of trade and investment. But even here handing over further policy formation and control to intergovernmental bodies would prove politically difficult. Within the EU, the most advanced of the regional configurations, developments have progressed unevenly. Thus for the foreseeable future we might expect that national governments will continue to preserve their prerogatives in these sensitive matters.

_____ *Summary of Section 7.6* _____

- There are a large number of international institutions involved in the monitoring and regulation of MNC activities, organized at a number of different levels (national, regional and transnational).

- These bodies provide different degrees of democratic accountability to the national territories they represent, mainly through the principle of 'international co-operation based upon home-country control'.

- However, there remain real possibilities for extending these organizational procedures to strengthen levels of democratic accountability, though whether there exists the political will to do this remains to be seen.

Conclusion

As we have seen, whilst there are substantial difficulties in setting MNCs into a democratic framework, this is by no means impossible. There are different levels at which it can be tackled. Traditionally it is the shareholders that are thought to exercise legitimate democratic control over MNCs. However, increasingly a wider set of interests have been drawn into the debate as the idea of stakeholder democracy has developed. In the case of MNCs, stakeholder democracy would be rendered doubly difficult, however, since the stakeholders are more geographically dispersed than even the shareholders are likely to be. The internationalization of business activity has dispersed not only shareholding but also supplier and customer involvement.

This is the main reason why governance issues have shifted to the international level in recent years, and into the jurisdiction of multilateral institutions. At this level, there is a reasonably developed system of limited accountability operating through the normal political processes of diplomatic representation to international bodies. This is not particularly democratic in a direct sense, however, but it looks the best achievable under contemporary international conditions. Thus, for the foreseeable future, extensions of the principle of international co-operation based upon home-country control look the most promising and likely. The possible strategies and tactics for achieving this in a number of areas have been discussed in this chapter. This is indicative of the continuing lively and widespread concern, registered amongst the governments and international bodies involved, about the limited democratic accountability of MNCs.

References

Bailey, D., Harte, G. and Sugden, R. (1994) *Making Transnationals Accountable*, London, Routledge.

Bergsten, C.F. and Graham, E.M. (1992) 'Needed: new international rules for Foreign Direct Investment', *The International Trade Journal*, vol.VII, no.1, Fall, pp.15-44.

Berle, A. and Means, G. (1968) *The Modern Corporation and Private Property*, New York, Brace and World.

Dahl, R.A. (1985) *A Preface to Economic Democracy*, Cambridge, Polity Press.

Dunning, J.H. (1993) *Multinational Enterprises and the Global Economy*, Wokingham, Addison-Wesley.

Fukao, M. (1995) *Financial Integration, Corporate Governance and the Performance of Multinational Companies*, Washington, DC, The Brookings Institution.

Hadden, T. (1977) *Company Law and Capitalism*, London, Weidenfeld and Nicolson.

Hayek, F.A. (1994) *The Road to Serfdom*, London, Routledge and Kegan Paul.

Hirst, P.Q. (1994) *Associative Democracy: New Forms of Economic and Social Governance*, Cambridge, Polity Press.

Hirst, P.Q. and Thompson, G.F. (1996) *Globalization in Question: The Myths of the International Economy and the Possibilities of Governance*, Cambridge, Polity Press.

Kapstein, E.B. (1994) *Governing the Global Economy: International Finance and the State*, Cambridge, MA, Harvard University Press.

Kay, J. and Silberston, A. (1995) 'Corporate governance', *National Institute Economic Review*, August, pp.84–97.

Kline, J.M. (1993) 'International regulation of transnational business: providing the missing leg of global investment standards', *Transnational Corporations*, vol.2, no.1, February, pp.153–64.

Lipsey, R.E., Blomstrom, M. and Ramstetter, E. (1995) 'Internationalized production in world output', *NBER Working Paper 5385*, Cambridge, MA, NBER.

Ruigrok, W. and van Tulder, R. (1995) *The Logic of International Restructuring*, London, Routledge.

Scaperlanda, A. (1993) 'Multinational enterprises and the global market', *Journal of Economic Issues,* vol.XXVII, no.2, June, pp.605–16.

Thompson, G.F. (1996) 'The market system' in Mackintosh, M. *et al.* (eds) *Economics and Changing Economies*, London, International Thompson Business Press/The Open University.

Turnbull, S. (1994) 'Stakeholder democracy: redesigning the governance of firms and bureaucracies', *The Journal of Socio-Economics*, vol.23, no.3, pp.321–60.

Underhill, G.R.D. (1995) 'Keeping governments out of politics: transnational securities markets, regulatory co-operation, and political legitimacy', *Review of International Studies*, vol.21, no.3, July, pp.251–78.

United Nations (1994) *World Investment Report 1994: Transnational Corporations, Employment and the Workplace*, New York and Geneva, UN.

Walzer, M. (1983) *Spheres of Justice: A Defence of Pluralism and Equality*, Oxford, Blackwell.

Wootton, B. (1945) *Freedom under Planning*, London, Allen and Unwin.

Further reading

Casson, M. (ed.) (1992) *International Business and Global Integration*, Basingstoke, Macmillan.

Dunning, J. (1993) *Multinational Enterprises and the Global Economy*, Wokingham, Addison-Wesley.

Gereffi, G. and Korzeniewicz, M. (eds) (1993) *Commodity Chains and Global Capitalism*, Westport, CT, Praeger.

Julius, D. (1990) *Global Companies and Public Policy: The Growing Challenge of Foreign Direct Investment*, London, RIIA/Pinter.

CHAPTER 8

The European Union: reconstituting democracy beyond the nation-state

James Goodman

Introduction

It is widely recognized that the European Union (EU) institutions that emerged out of the Maastricht Treaty suffer from a profound 'democratic deficit'. This phrase, first coined by the European Parliament, has gained wide currency and usefully sums up the 'power without accountability' wielded by EU institutions. It also illustrates the limits of conventional liberal democratic forms of government in the EU. Somewhat simplistically, it applies financial concepts of deficit and surplus to democratic life, leading many to assume that such a 'deficit' can simply be corrected by applying a new liberal democratic 'blueprint' – with some favouring a regrounding of liberal democracy in the nation-state, others preferring to reconstruct it in a new pan-EU federal state and still others arguing that it must begin at the substate regional level.

All these prescriptions, while interesting, fail to acknowledge the growing transnational character of political relations in the EU. As it becomes harder to contain political life in territorial units, democratic participation has become increasingly delinked from liberal democracy – at whatever institutional 'level'. The pressures reconstituting EU democracy are not reducible to one or other 'level' – on the contrary, they range across them and derive their strength from such transnational interaction. EU democracy will be deepened only by harnessing, not containing, these pressures. This requires a multitude of representative structures that transcend often outmoded distinctions between 'domestic' and 'foreign' affairs. These need to be geared to many different constituencies – above, across, below and between existing states – and they would need to discharge different responsibilities and be founded on new structures of accountability designed to express active participation beyond the limits of territorial liberal democracy.

The main reason for this rethinking is the impact of globalization on legislative capabilities and institutional structures. Globalization imposes a new range of policy-making dictates that undermine the ability of national states – or any other territorial unit short of a global government – to act as a vehicle for popular democracy. A range of alternative structures and movements have emerged in the EU that are proactively redefining democracy and, in some respects, contesting the disempowering impacts of globalization. EU institutions are included in this as they respond to globalization and open up new transnational political agendas – primarily to maximize their political legitimacy. Even national democracies and 'official' nationalisms are being recast as internationalized vehicles for democracy. At the same time, substate regional and nationalist movements are finding new transnational ways of arguing for and extending substate democracy. Meanwhile, social movements are also becoming powerful vehicles for strengthening and extending democracy into new transnational realms of political participation.

All are in some sense contesting the logic of globalization and can be seen as potential carriers for EU democracy. This chapter examines these various aspects to the process of reconstituting EU democracy.

It begins in Section 8.1 by tracing the linkages between globalization and EU integration. Globalizing pressures are linked to recent policy developments – in particular the Single European Market (SEM) and the proposed Economic and Monetary Union (EMU). These are not legitimated through new pan-EU democratic structures but through a range of initiatives designed to maximize social, regional and civic cohesiveness which, it is argued, open up new transnational political agendas.

Section 8.2 outlines three contending models of European democracy – a 'Europe of nation-states', a 'federal Europe' and a 'Europe of the regions'. It is argued that these are ideal types rather than workable models and that, in practice, neither the national, federal or regional 'level' of democratic representation is likely to become the 'foundational' element in the European democratic system. Democratizing pressures do not conform to these models and perhaps require a broader rethink of liberal democracy.

This is attempted in Section 8.3, drawing on the concept of 'cosmopolitan democracy' (Held, 1995). The EU response to globalization – in the form of accelerated regional integration – is seen as opening up new transnational democratic spaces. These are being claimed by the pan-EU Parliament and by national assemblies and also by substate authorities and transnational social movements. These four aspects to the emerging EU system of democracy are examined, highlighting the degree to which they breach the state 'container' and constitute a 'post-Westphalian' or 'cosmopolitan' polity. The chapter concludes by discussing the broader political implications of these developments.

8.1 Globalization and regionalization: EU integration

The European Community (EC) was established in 1957, drawing on the Benelux and European Coal and Steel Community (ECSC) experience. Having lived through two major wars, several Western European political leaders hoped that economic integration through the Community would make war-mongering amongst them an impossibility and that, in time, economic unity would lead to political unity. This idealism combined with pressures to unify Western Europe against the Soviet-dominated Eastern bloc. The Cold War lent an urgency to negotiations between the six founding states, and culminated in the Treaty of Rome which set up the EC and its associated institutions.

In the late 1960s these regional issues were overtaken by a broader concern to defend the EC economies against a growing 'Americanization' of global and West European markets. This stimulated a wave of renewed integration in the early 1970s – nothing less than an 'alliance for economic defence' to achieve parity with the USA (Galtung, 1973, p.58). In 1971 heads of state agreed to relaunch the EC as an 'Economic Union' with 'the principal decisions of economic policy ... taken at the Community level' and agreed to transfer the required powers to EC institutions (CEC, 1970). This new Economic Union was to become an integrated 'global region' through 'economic and monetary union', with political and social union to follow. But the proposed relaunch proved over-optimistic. The global regulatory framework that had underwritten EC convergence began to collapse after 1971 with the breakdown of the Bretton Woods System (see Chapter 3), followed by the OPEC crisis which sent prices and wages spiralling in most EC countries. The resulting economic divergence stalled proposals for renewed integration and six years later the Commission was forced to admit there was 'no agreement on how to achieve a common economic and monetary policy' (CEC, 1976, p.21).

European integration was revived in the early 1980s, again in the context of intensifying global pressures. In 1983, the European Parliament (EP) debated how the EC could avoid being economically subordinated to the twin 'global regions' – East Asia centred on Japan, and North America centred on the USA. There was a growing sense that the EC urgently needed to overcome 'Euro-sclerosis' and the only way to do this was to relaunch a programme of integration. In the first instance this was aimed at increasing the efficiency of EC economies – and, given the political complexion of EC governments at this time, the preferred way of doing this was to 'restructure' production, concentrate industries on a European scale, improve industrial co-operation and co-ordinate investment in new technology. In effect, deregulation in a Single European Market was paired with greater technological assistance to pan-EU firms able to compete in global markets.

EU regulations were used to open up markets for public procurement and to restrict the role of the public sector in the economy. Deregulation for the state sector was paralleled by minimal intervention in private industry, while in trade policy there was some selective protection of industry. There was a marked increase in financial interdependence and EU trade also became highly integrated. At the same time, there was increased integration of productive capital with a wave of mergers and takeovers. Market share of the EU's top 100 firms rose by five per cent to a fifth of total sales and a relatively unified 'European corporate system' began to emerge (Amin and Tomaney, 1995).

With increased regional integration, national and EU priorities had to be more closely co-ordinated to avoid clashes of interests and resulting instability. The Maastricht Treaty aimed to resolve this problem through economic and monetary union. The Treaty maps out a convergence process between national economies with targets for minimizing government debt and inflation rates and co-ordinating interest rates and exchange rates. These 'convergence criteria' and the proposed creation of an independent 'European Central Bank' seek to institutionalize global financial constraints and, in effect, to internationalize national economic policies.

To legitimize this intensification of regional integration, a range of compensatory policies were introduced. The integration process was expected to create losers as well as winners – and the former had to be persuaded of the merits of integration through a range of policies designed to prevent the growth of social, spatial and political divergence. In the area of social protection, a so-called 'social dimension' was introduced under the 1989 Social Charter and the Social Protocol of the Maastricht Treaty (1991). While this has amounted to little more than a series of 'symbolic gestures, general policy commitments, and a few hotly debated, specific EC proposals', it has opened up new pan-EU political agendas (Lange, 1992, p.229). Legislation has been hesitant, especially since the UK opt-out from the Maastricht Protocol – only one Directive was implemented in the first three years of the Protocol, albeit the highly significant Works Council Directive. Yet the joint committees and advisory groups set up under the 'social dimension' have increasingly defined social issues – such as working conditions and mass unemployment – as pan-EU issues. In doing so they have shed light on 'larger questions about what kind of values and vision will shape the welfare states within Europe' (Benington and Taylor, 1993, p.131; Cochrane, 1993a).

With the recession of early 1990s, EU integration quickly became associated with 'job killing' and Commission officials were acutely aware of the need for job-creation policies at the EU level. But Commission proposals for new expenditure were heavily pruned by EU Finance Ministers and in 1994 it was the 'supply-side', cost-reducing aspects of the Delors Report on 'Growth, Competitiveness and Employment' that received most member-state support. Nonetheless, more extensive measures to resolve the Union's unemployment crisis did gain wider currency – with the European Parliament, for instance, demanding that states should commit themselves to establishing a 'social union' at the same time as an economic and monetary union, enforceable through new social 'convergence criteria'.

EU policies have also been developed to compensate regions 'lagging behind' in the SEM. Inter-regional divergence sharpened in the 1980s as regional economies became increasingly exposed to EU and global pressures. Limited financial redistribution under the European Regional Development Fund (ERDF) was doubled in 1988 and was focused on those most 'in need'. But at a mere 0.24 per cent of EU GDP, it compared unfavourably with the expected efficiency gains of the SEM, largely accruing to core regions (Perrons, 1992). In contrast, in the USA, 9 per cent of GDP was redistributed through Federal Government fiscal policy where maximum per capita disparities of GDP stood at 140 per cent, compared with 240 per cent in the EU (Suarez-Villa and Roura, 1993). Yet, while inadequate, EU regional policy has politicized cross-border regional inequality. This was not on the political agenda before the ERDF – and even within many EU states, regional policy was either non-existent or undeveloped. Indeed, like the 'social dimension', regional policy has created new transnational political agendas that affect national states as much as they affect regions and EU institutions.

EU citizenship policies have also been introduced, primarily to promote political cohesiveness. As outlined under the Maastricht Treaty, EU citizenship is built on a melding of national and supranational rights and serves both to encourage popular consent for the integration process and to increase political convergence across the Union. The Treaty widened the EP's franchise to include the nationals of all EU states, regardless of their place of residence within the Union, and strengthened pan-EU civil rights by guaranteeing the right of EU citizens to free movement (except for those dependent on state welfare), and the right to diplomatic protection from member-state embassies (CEC, 1993a). This is defined against non-nationals of EU states – 'outsiders' who are in their millions spatially 'inside' the EU yet are denied EU citizenship rights. While EU citizenship may acquire a logic of its own, it remains rooted in statist conceptions of nationality. This undermines attempts at forging an inclusive European civic identity as many member states confer nationality on the basis of 'blood' or place of birth rather than place of residence (MacLaughlin, 1993).

But as a result of these policy developments, EU political elites have been forced to address the contradictions between 'internal' inclusivity and 'external' exclusion, often for the first time. The European Parliament, for instance, has called for a charter of rights for 'non-citizens', spelling out the degree to which they are to be excluded from political and social systems. Whether or not such a charter emerges, the exclusion of a large proportion of the Union's population from access to citizenship rights poses a profound challenge to liberal democracy as it de-legitimizes political structures within member states and, by extension, de-legitimizes the EU itself. In this way the commitment to cultural inclusivity embodied in the Maastricht Treaty legitimizes increasing pressures for more explicit diffusion of cultural rights and resources – suggested more positively in the proposed European Cultural Charter which has been promoted as a counterpart to the 1989 European Social Charter (Garcia, 1993, p.27).

Overall, EU policy-making has created a range of policy contradictions and legitimacy deficits. These politicize issues at the EU level, such as social and regional cohesion and common citizenship, and stimulate related demands for a greater role in EU decision-making. Boundaries between domestic and external affairs are transgressed and integration directly undermines the institutional solidity of politics both within and between member states. As this transnational and potentially open-ended policy dynamic emerges, it directly raises the question of how to democratize the emerging policy-making system.

--------------------- ***Summary of Section 8.1*** ---------------------

- Economic globalization stimulated EU integration and shapes EU economic policies.

- Regional integration is legitimized by EU social, regional and citizenship policies.

- This transnational policy framework generates pressures for increased democratic involvement in EU institutions.

8.2   A democratic Europe? Models of EU democracy

This section analyses the three main 'models' that dominate academic and public debate about EU democracy – an EU of national parliaments, a federal EU and an EU of the regions. First though, the existing institutional structure is briefly outlined.

The Treaty of Rome created five central institutions. The heads of state provided for their respective ministers to agree common policies in the 'Council of Ministers' – later supplemented by meetings of the 'European Council' of state leaders. Policy proposals would be drawn up and implemented by the EC 'Commission' with a new European Court of Justice and European Court of Auditors ensuring compliance. In addition, a 'European Assembly' of representatives drawn from national parliaments would play an advisory role – as would an 'Economic and Social Committee' (ECOSOC) of non-parliamentary representatives appointed by national governments.

The European Parliament in session

In 1979 the Assembly became a directly elected 'European Parliament' and later acquired a stronger advisory role, including in some instances the right to 'co-decision' with the Council of Ministers. From the 1980s a plethora of advisory groups emerged, often sponsored by the Commission as its range of responsibilities widened. One of these, the 'Consultative Council of Local and Regional Authorities', set up in 1988, became the 'Committee of the Regions' (CoR) under the Maastricht Treaty. This committee is constituted by elected regional representatives with powers similar to ECOSOC. The Maastricht Treaty also created two new 'pillars' of policymaking: 'Foreign and Security Policy' and 'Justice and Home Affairs'. Both are separated from the 'Community' pillar, are subject to the national veto and are effectively dominated by the Council of Ministers, with the Commission and the Parliament accorded relatively minor roles.

Ministers, representing national governments, remain central to EU decision-making while appointed Commission officials retain the power to propose policy and ensure policy implementation. Directly elected MEPs remain largely subordinate as do representatives in the ECOSOC, the CoR and other advisory bodies. In effect, EU decision-making is dominated by state executives and Commission officials. This is illustrated in Table 8.1 which highlights the limited role accorded to directly elected as opposed to indirectly elected (government-appointed national or locally elected politicians) or appointed representatives under the 'Community' pillar. Decision-making under the additional Maastricht pillars, meanwhile, is entirely restricted to indirectly elected state representatives, with the Commission and Parliament retaining only strictly limited powers.

Table 8.1 The Community 'pillar': roles and composition

	Appointed	Indirectly elected	Directly elected
Proposing	European Commission	European Council	—
		Council of Ministers	
Advising	Committee of Permanent Representatives	Committee of the Regions	European Parliament
Deciding	—	European Council	(European Parliament)
		Council of Ministers	
Implementing	European Commission	—	—
	National civil service		
Enforcing	European Court of Justice	—	—
	European Court of Auditors		
	National courts		

This raises the question of how to democratize the increasingly powerful EU institutions – a question that was implicitly recognized in the Maastricht Treaty commitment to holding an 'Institutional Review' in 1996. This has been an issue of concern to EC policymakers since the creation of the Community in 1957 – and before, during the deliberations of the Spaak 'Committee of Enquiry into European Union' in the early 1950s. But never has it been so sharply posed.

The hard-fought and narrowly successful Danish, French and Irish referenda on the Maastricht Treaty, together with the escalating costs of German reunification and worldwide recession, combined to precipitate an intense crisis of confidence in EU institutions in the early 1990s. This threatened to undermine the carefully encouraged 'permissive consensus' that had begun to emerge in the 1980s (Reif, 1993). As recorded by the Commission's public opinion survey, *Eurobarometer,* public acceptance of an EU dimension to political life had grown so that, by 1992, 50 per cent of respondents would have 'regretted' if the EU had been dissolved. By 1993, expressions of regret had plummeted, reversing earlier gains, and post-1993 confidence only grew at a faltering pace as EU economies were beset by unemployment, fiscal and monetary crises, all in some sense attributable to the SEM and the proposed EMU.

No wonder, then, that the Institutional Review was widely seen as an opportunity to legitimize EU policy-making and re-ground European democracy. In 1995 the Commission defined two priority tasks for the Review – to improve the Union's legitimacy and its effectiveness, both of which had to be addressed if the EU was to develop successfully (CEC, 1995). The resulting discussions about how to improve accountability reflected broader debates between advocates of one or other of the models for revived liberal-democracy in the EU.

A Europe of 'nation-states'

The first approach argues that European democracy is best constructed on the existing nation-state model. This draws on the 'realist' tradition of international relations which emphasizes the role of states in maintaining domestic and international order. National traditions and institutional forms weld the citizenry to its national state, creating stable and resilient political communities able to meet the requirements of a globalizing age. Consequently, it is argued that national institutional identity should provide the basis for European democracy – and the legitimacy for EU policies. Insofar as member states decide to participate in joint EU institutions this should be strictly on the basis of mutual self-interest – if those interests are threatened states should reserve the right to 'opt out'.

Advocates of the Europe of 'nation-states' argue that the EU should be reformed, but only to strengthen the role of national states. The power of the European Parliament to intervene in decision-making should be reduced; the Commission's autonomy should be reined-in; and the Court's role in enforcing EU Directives should be subordinated to national jurisdiction. EU policy-making should always defer to national policy-making and the Maastricht principle of 'subsidiarity' (decisions taken at an approriate level to the task in hand) should grant primacy to national governments. Most important perhaps, decision-making in the Council of Ministers should be by unanimity, with member states reserving the right to opt out at a later date.

This Europe of 'nation-states' has been characterized as a 'Gaullist Europe', after General de Gaulle who advocated the pursuit of French national interests through EC institutions. It has been adopted as a model by various governments – most notably by the British Conservative government from 1979 – while it has informed various position-papers drawn up by pan-EU groups of anti-federalists, including the European Research Group and the European Policy Forum (ERG, 1993; EPF, 1995).

This position though, even on its own terms, is vulnerable to accusations of naivety. Decision-making in the Council of Ministers is on the basis of proposals drawn up by Commission officials acting in tandem with the Committee of Permanent Representatives (COREPER) – officials appointed by, and directly responsible to, national governments – and is already largely in 'national' hands. The same is true of decision-making in the European Council of Heads of State. Meanwhile, the Parliament, the Committee of the Regions and the Economic and Social Committee have, at most, minimal powers of intervention in the decision-making process (see Table 8.1). More important than the loss of powers to EU institutions is the vesting of power in unaccountable state officials (COREPER) who set the agenda with Commission officials, advise state representatives and monitor implementation of the various decisions. A Europe of nation states may serve well as a rallying cry but it fails to address these central democratic issues.

Attempts have been made to reformulate this state-centred perspective, primarily through strengthening the role of national assemblies, as proposed by the European Policy Forum (EPF, 1995). There is a broad consensus – including the European Parliament and the Commission – that elected assemblies at the national level should have increased powers of review, but there is disagreement on how this can be achieved. One option is simply to ensure that all EU policy is ratified by national assemblies before it reaches the Council of Ministers – thereby adding a new, highly complex process of referring back to 15 separate assemblies. An alternative, proposed by the EPF, is to create an indirectly elected 'assembly of national assemblies' at the EU level. This could either be a standing assembly, an 'upper house' of the directly elected European Parliament, or an ad hoc assembly meeting to consider key policy initiatives. An approximation of the latter option already exists in the form of the European 'Assizes', composed of 173 delegates from national parliaments and 53 from the EP, which met in 1990 to consider the Maastricht proposals.

But such a body, in whatever form, does not generally find favour amongst those preferring a Europe of nation-states – primarily because it would create a potentially powerful assembly at the EU level, not unlike the European Assembly that existed before direct elections to the European Parliament. This presents a dilemma for those favouring the national route to EU democracy. How can an increased national role in EU decision-making be squared with the separate territorial sovereignties of member states? The obvious response, suggested by the European Research Group, is to 'repatriate' policy-making and restrict the EU to realms of public policy that ostensibly do not impinge on national sovereignty. This nationalist reaction, though, leaves governments with no effective response to globalization or regionalization.

A federal Europe

European federalists in the European Movement and the Union of European Federalists have long argued that the solution to any democratic deficit in EU institutions is to create new representative structures at the EU level. Under the federal model, the EU-elected legislature and its government would become the primary unit for democracy, rather than the member states. The EU would devolve powers to state parliaments, rather than the other way round, and states would not have the right to secede from the resulting EU Federation or to conduct 'independent' foreign and defence policies. This contrasts with an EU 'confederation', in which states would retain sovereignty, devolve powers to EU bodies and retain the right to 'opt out'. At present, EU institutions hover between this state-centred confederalism and the more EU-centred federalism. They retain the claim to formal sovereignty but have granted the Commission a federal-like legal jurisdiction, through the European Court of Justice and the Court of Auditors, and the European Parliament has been granted limited, but significant, powers of 'co-decision'.

Euro-federalists argue that this 'in-between' condition seriously undermines EU authority, creating legitimacy deficits in national states as well as in EU institutions. The way to resolve this is to write a pan-EU constitution for a European federal state in which there would be clear lines of responsibility and accountability to an elected pan-EU assembly and also to still separate and autonomous national assemblies (Wistrich, 1991).

This is embodied in the European Parliament's proposals for the 1996–97 Institutional Review, in which MEPs argued that they should have 'equal status' with the Council of Ministers in all aspects of Union responsibility. The EP argued that it represents the peoples of the Union while the Ministers represent individual states and that neither should be given priority over the other in EU policy-making. This was reflected in the demand for 'co-decision' with the Council in all fields of EU policy-making and for qualified majority voting in all Council sessions, except on treaties and constitutional issues (EP, 1994, 1995). This would create a loose EU federal state, with the Commission as the executive and a legislature composed of the EP and the Council. The Commission was less ambitious in its suggestions, but still promoted the federalist option of strengthening the EP, arguing that MEPs should have a greater role in all aspects of Union policy (CEC, 1995).

This model for EU democracy has a striking simplicity to it. If the national state is increasingly undermined by globalization and it becomes necessary to create powerful pan-EU institutions, then, logically, new democratic structures have to be constructed at the EU level. To fail to do so, as national states are disempowered and EU bodies are de-legitimized, would be to drift into the worst of both worlds. But perhaps ongoing 'drift' is more likely than re-imposed stability. To entrench federal democracy, member states would have to sign a pan-EU constitution. No longer would the Union be founded on ad hoc inter-state treaties, but on the firm constitutional guarantee of a '*democratic acquis communautaire*' (acquired democratic community) (Kuper, 1995, p.6). Such a prospect is highly unlikely – state elites are not about to fall on the sword of federal democracy. Instead, the institutional and symbolic tug of war between state sovereignty and popular sovereignty is likely to persist.

More fundamentally, some have criticized this approach as a 'Gulliver' fantasy which assumes away all the failings of the liberal democratic state when faced with globalization (Walker, 1993, p.126). Global economic forces are by definition transnational and create transnational communities of interest in policy areas well beyond the existing limited territorial conception of the public realm. Any pan-EU federal state would be under the same pressures as the national state to reduce social overheads and promote EU 'champions' and in all likelihood would be taking the same neo-liberal policy pathway as existing institutions, albeit with greater legitimacy.

More generally, a federal EU implies greater centralization. There is no guarantee that stronger state-like institutions in the EU would serve popular as opposed to elite interests. Formal democratic structures may broaden popular participation in tandem with national assemblies but by constructing formal legitimacy, such structures may simply amplify existing elite domination of EU decision-making, giving it a centralized authority with greater autonomous power than existing institutions.

A Europe of the regions

One possible corrective to this fear of centralization, and to the failings of the existing national state, is to argue for a Europe of central institutions *and* substate regions. In this 'Europe of the regions' it would be possible to celebrate 'diversity in unity' and leave 'the Europe of competing nationalisms behind us' (Kearney, 1988, p.15). Such a Europe would not be a centralized superstate but would be like a 'great sponge', able to soak up and express the needs of its many and varied regional units (Ascherson, 1991, p.7). The capital city of this regional EU would not be the centre of a highly centralized multinational state like London – but would be more like Berne, the capital of the Swiss Federation (Martin, 1991). Under the regionalist model, local forms of participative democracy are prioritized over less accessible national institutions and are paired with pan-EU democratic forms to create a 'unity in diversity'. This, it is argued, would both respond to globalization and be sufficiently rooted in existing democratic practices. In effect, state sovereignty would be removed from the equation as European democracy is rebuilt 'from below' (Harvie, 1994).

There are a variety of proposals as to how strong the pan-EU bodies should be *vis-à-vis* regional bodies. Some European federalists argue that the Council of Ministers should be reconstituted as a council of substate regions and nations, to become a second chamber of the existing Parliament (Martin, 1991). This two-chamber, federal pan-EU parliament would have extensive Union-wide powers. Others argue for a more 'confederal' structure, with the Parliament exercising powers subject to the consent of regional and national assemblies (Harvie, 1994). But the general consensus amongst advocates of a 'regional Europe' is that democratic institutions have greater legitimacy the closer they are to the people they represent – demonstrated in *Eurobarometer* polls which consistently show that EU citizens feel closest to their local and regional assemblies. On this basis it is argued that democracy must be rooted in the 'local' if popular participation is to increase and the pitfalls of over-centralized liberal democracy are to be avoided.

This is reflected, for instance, in the Committee of the Regions (CoR) submission to the 1996 Institutional Review which demanded that subsidiarity be rewritten to explicitly define local and regional bodies as the 'primary' units of European democratic culture (CoR, 1995). Initially this would apply to states where such bodies had gained significant powers and would be enforceable through the European Court, with the Committee taking on a 'watchdog' role. The Committee would gain equal institutional status with the Parliament and the Council, enabling it effectively to act as the Parliament's second chamber. These proposals found enthusiastic backing from the EP Regional Policy Committee, although they were later watered down by the main EP assembly to an open commitment simply to strengthen the role of the CoR (EP, 1995).

But, like European federalists, EU regionalists exaggerate the degree to which national states are being undermined in the EU. They consequently underestimate the barriers to the creation of a regionalist institutional structure. Despite this, the regionalist version of reconstructing EU democracy highlights developments that have previously remained off the political agenda, and to a considerable extent overturns the ideological counter-positioning of state-centred nationalism and centralist federalism that has hitherto characterized political debates on the EU.

The three models for reconstituting EU liberal democracy are each deficient in their own ways but also in their common assumption that a new territorial or spatial 'fix' is both possible and desirable. Democratization thus becomes simply a matter of *scale* rather than of *process* – although under the 'Europe of the regions' version there is some acknowledgement of the potential cross-cutting impacts of both EU and regional structures. In many respects globalization is likely to undermine such 'fixes', just as it undermines existing democratic institutions. Instead, enquiry should focus on how to harness transnational forces – be they economic, social or political – in the name of democracy. Rather than devise a new blueprint for democracy, the aim should be to identify the potential vehicles for a democratized EU.

―――――――――――――― *Summary of Section 8.2* ――――――――――――――

- EU institutions undermine state-centred liberal democracy.

- Some argue that EU democracy should be reconstructed using national parliaments; others argue that there should be a pan-EU federal parliament; still others argue that local and regional assemblies should become the primary units of EU democracy.

- Given the impact of globalization, these attempts at re-grounding democracy are unlikely to be successful.

8.3   Democratizing the EU

This section argues that EU democracy should be reconceptualized in terms of 'cosmopolitan democracy', as discussed in Chapter 1. It commences with an exploration of the idea of 'cosmopolitan democracy' as applied to the EU polity. This is followed by analysis of four key potential vehicles for democratizing the EU: pan-EU institutions, national assemblies, substate authorities and transnational social movements.

The EU as a 'cosmopolitan democracy'

Many of those recognizing that EU integration undermines state power argue that this presages a more 'rational' reassessment and reconstruction of public power in the EU (Preston, 1994). Whether leading to a more explicitly confederal framework (Wallace, 1994), or to a looser configuration of 'confederal public power' (Thompson, 1993), there are strong assumptions – or hopes – that the current situation is one of transition. But there is little to indicate that such expectations will bear fruit. Attempts at guaranteeing democratic participation, either in EU institutions or in substate regional and national units, have been at best uneven, suggesting that perhaps a radical reassessment of concepts of public accountability and liberal democracy is required.

In the various conflicts between regional, state and EU institutions, none is likely to win out. State, regional and federal forms intermingle to constitute a new form of 'cosmopolitan polity' which remains more or less permanently in-between national states and a federal state. While to a great extent politics remains defined by territoriality, and in many policy areas 'singular sovereignty' remains dominant, whether exercised by the member states or by the EU, there is a significant move towards an 'unbundling' of state sovereignty such that in some realms of social life it is no longer possible to determine which public policies are derived from which 'level' of political responsibility (Anderson and Goodman, 1995a). Whole realms of public policy are no longer defined solely or even largely by state institutions, but instead are the outcome of a variety of political conflicts between state and non-state sources of political authority. Partly as a result, it is nigh impossible to separate out a specifically European Union public sphere, existing independently of national public arenas – they intermingle and become mutually constitutive.

In this 'post-Westphalian' scenario there is no fixed 'quantity' of democratic involvement and accountability to be shared between states, EU institutions and substate regions (Linklater, 1996). Only if political power is conceived as vested in a single, primary territorial unit, is democracy understood in zero-sum terms: that is, if power is confined to the 'nation-state' unit, an increased role for EU institutions necessarily means less power for the national assembly. Once it is conceded that societies require a range of democratic channels to exercise democratic rights effectively, supra-national, transnational and substate aspects of political authority can be understood to extend rather than delimit popular empowerment. Strengthened institutions at one 'level' do not imply weakened institutions at other levels; on the contrary, the overall 'quantity' of democracy rises as democratic accountability increases across the various levels. In a transnational context, non-state democratic institutions complement state democracy rather than undermine it, and have a positive-sum rather than a zero-sum effect.

Just as the autonomy of the state has become more 'relative' with globalization, so also must its democratic structures (Gross, 1995). There can be no foundational or 'absolute' claim to democratic sover-eignty when the world of territorial absolutes is increasingly emptied of meaning. This requires a move away from reliance on a single source of democratic legitimation – rather than seeking the 'primary' unit of EU democracy, there has to be democratization at all levels of democratic life. From this perspective, pan-EU democracy for instance could complement and strengthen national democracy, rather than undermine it. This move to a form of 'cosmopolitan democracy' perhaps permits the construction of new political forms that can more effectively meet popular needs in the context of advancing globalization and regionalization (Held, 1995). The following discussion focuses on the institutional structures, political processes and social movements that could potentially bring this about.

EU institutions and liberal democracy

The Treaty of Rome created an institutional 'tug of war between the intergovernmental and the Community approach' (Wessels, 1991, p.151). This is expressed, for instance, in constant tensions between Commission officials formally committed to promoting 'an ever closer Union' and national politicians sitting in the Council of Ministers.

This combining of roles is perhaps most clearly exposed by the attempts to establish an EU institutional jurisdiction. In 1963 the European Court of Justice ruled that the Treaty of Rome created a 'constitutional regime' rather than simply an agreement between sovereign states. It went on to establish the doctrine that EU legislation had 'direct effect' on states and had 'supremacy' over national law (Shapiro, 1992). With the Maastricht Treaty, constitutional lawyers were forced to strike a 'compromise between the inadequate and the impossible' in their attempts to bridge the ideological gap between national sovereignty and regionalization (Hoffmann, 1994, p.18). This was expressed in the German Constitutional Court ruling that the EU constituted a *Staatenverbund* – not a federal European state, nor a confederation, nor simply a concert of states, but an 'association' of states that has no competence to determine its own sphere of competence (Wieland, 1994, p.263).

As greater powers have been ceded to the Commission, national governments have strengthened their political control. From 1974 they began setting the pace for integration through the European Council, using the COREPER to shape Commission proposals. Further, as already noted, the Maastricht Treaty constructed an arbitrary distinction between so-called 'high' politics in the two new 'pillars' (Foreign and Security Policy; Justice and Home Affairs) where the national veto is sacrosanct, and 'low' politics in the Community 'pillar' where more co-operative decision-making is possible.

Nonetheless, pan-EU institutions retain a central role. In 'Community' affairs, the Maastricht Treaty has, more than ever, forced states into a process of shared policy-making. In the Council of Ministers, distinctions have been drawn between issues of policy, implementation and procedure in which only issues of policy extending Treaty agreements, or directly affecting particular national interests, require unanimity. Issues of implementation, where a policy has been established, require a qualified majority and procedural proposals require only a simple majority. This dilution of states' veto powers, envisaged in the Treaty of Rome, introduced under the 1985 Single European Act (SEA) and strengthened with the Maastricht Treaty, transforms the way in which member states exercise sovereignty. Whole swathes of economic and social policy dominated by previously agreed 'framework' policies – in external trade, currency control, agricultural, regional and competition policy – are determined through qualified majorities, through 'co-decision' with the European Parliament and through consultation with the Economic and Social Committee and, from March 1994, the Committee of the Regions. Indeed, even in policy areas related to the other two intergovernmental 'pillars', the Commission and Parliament have been granted limited powers – with the Commission gaining powers of policy initiation, and Parliament gaining powers of policy review, in areas previously beyond the remit of the EC.

Paradoxically, EU institutions are autonomous international actors subordinated to member-state executives. There are few pan-EU rights of participation in the decision-making process except indirectly, through the political executives of elected governments. This is, in some degree, addressed by the Maastricht Treaty which, as noted, gives the European Parliament greater powers of 'co-decision' with the Council of Ministers. Ironically though, even the European Parliament, the cradle of EU democracy, is built on national divisions. From 1979 MEPs have been directly elected on an EU basis every four years. But they are not elected on the same polling day nor even under the same electoral system, since member states could not agree on the appropriate timing or system for the elections. In anticipation of the first direct elections European political parties were formed – the European Socialist Party in 1974, the European Peoples' Party and the European Liberal Democrats in 1977. Twenty years later there are still constant confusions and contradictions between European and national party manifestos and European parties tend to act primarily as parliamentary groupings, offering support to national groupings during EP elections rather than campaigning on a pan-EU basis.

In general terms, EU institutions stand, to a varying degree, somewhere in between national governments and supranationalism (above states). This undermines liberal democracy at all levels, and has stimulated a profound democratic riposte. This is only partly expressed through the European Parliament – it is also embodied in democratizing pressures from national parliaments, substate authorities and transnational social movements.

National democracy in the EU

National assemblies are the firmest basis for liberal democracy in the EU. They retain wide-ranging powers, especially in the realms of social reproduction and social control and remain centre-stage in the political arena. Indeed, while powers are devolved to EU or substate authorities, the symbolic power of national sovereignty has, at least in formal terms, been preserved intact. Greater devolution of power to substate authorities reduces the central state's responsibilities without reducing its sovereign powers. Meanwhile, national governments have maintained a grip on EU decision-making which in many respects strengthens rather than under-mines their power. By acting together, state executives have gained greater leverage over economic forces and greater influence in global arenas – in effect, 'the increasing density of global society gives states new geopolitical roles' (Mann, 1993, p.158).

Yet states are also internationalized (see Chapter 3) as they are integrated. The state has ceased to hold sway over the increasingly open and internationalized 'national' economy and policy options have narrowed as the EU has become increasingly receptive to global economic pressures. This strengthens the state's managerial and bureaucratic roles, downgrading its role as a vehicle for popular aspirations – which are increasingly directed elsewhere, especially into substate authorities and transnational movements. The contact points between 'national' (in fact 'internationalized') state bodies and EU institutions have acquired a vastly enhanced significance, yet are far removed from the reach of national democratic assemblies. Decisions can be made behind closed doors by state executives and their officials in relative isolation from the 'national' parliaments to which they are formally accountable.

In many respects this undermines liberal democracy. National frameworks for political legitimation are under constant pressure as permanent conflict between the different sources of public authority disrupts democratic structures forcing changes in national political ideologies. Paradoxically, state nationalism has become increasingly inter-nationalized. Across the EU, mainstream national parties have attempted to marry their 'official' nationalisms with EU integration with the result that amongst EU politicians, 'the nationalist European is the most common breed of all' (Gibb and Wise, 1993, p.36).

State elites assiduously present themselves as pursuing national interests in the EU, using the EU platform to enhance their national political profile (Preston, 1994). The deep contradiction between preserving national sovereignty while pursuing 'national interests' at the EU level leads mainstream political parties into a series of recurring policy quagmires. They are forced into 'defending' the symbolic, while in practice conceding to EU policymaking. In 1991 for instance, the British government insisted that the word 'federalism' be removed from the Maastricht Treaty – a concession that ironically enabled the Conservative government to agree the Treaty's decision-making structures unamended.

As nationalisms are Europeanized, so are national assemblies. Post-Maastricht there has been no assault on the power of EU institutions – rather, national parliaments have sought to strengthen their influence over EU policy. Some have gained a stronger role in ratifying major policy developments. The German Constitutional Court, for instance, ruled that any further institutional changes at the EU level, beyond the Maastricht Treaty, would have to be ratified by a two-thirds majority in both the Bundesrat and the Bundestag. Meanwhile, the Danish and the British Parliaments gained a direct role in determining if and when their countries would enter Monetary Union.

Across all EU national parliaments, involvement in EU policy-making has substantially increased, especially in the two 'intergovernmental' pillars of Foreign and Security Policy and Justice and Home Affairs (Westlake,

1995). Knowledge of, and active engagement with, EU-related issues has mushroomed. Involvement has been institutionalized in policy committees and reporting procedures that, in many cases, are entrenched in national law – in the French case via a new Article of the national Constitution. Greater involvement has also led to the creation of an autonomous pan-EU conference of national parliamentary committees specializing in EC affairs, which has met twice a year under each EU presidency since 1989 to consider how to deepen EU democracy.

This combining of national democracy and EU integration could be seen either as a nationalization of EU policy-making or as a democratization and deepening of the EU integration process. Whichever interpretation is adopted, national state-centred politics is strengthened in parallel with a strengthening of pan-EU institutions, in what has been characterized as the 'organic evolution of a Parliamentary Europe' (Westlake, 1995, p.72). As the distinction between 'foreign' and domestic political relations begins to blur, new policy contradictions open up and, paradoxically, nationalist ideology is internationalized, perhaps into a form of 'cosmopolitan nationalism'.

Substate democracy in the EU

Resistance to undemocratic structures at the EU level is also expressed in burgeoning regionalist and nationalist movements from 'below' national states. During the 1970s and 1980s regional devolution was often introduced to democratize state structures – for instance, in France, Spain, Italy, Portugal and Greece – and by the mid 1980s elected substate authorities (such as Catalonia in Spain) had become a permanent feature of democratic life in four of the five largest EU states and in several of the smaller ones (Keating, 1988). Subsequently these sub-national vehicles for EU democracy have assumed a central role in the implementation of EU policies – they have developed direct 'foreign' relations with EU institutions and have emerged as a political force at the transnational level. This has Europeanized substate regional and national groupings who now demand greater political autonomy from member governments as part of the EU. This in turn has bolstered their support-base and stimulated an 'explosion of political activity' at the substate level (Anderson, 1990, p.428).

As the Single European Market has widened disparities between substate regions, local elites have maximized their autonomy from central government and have acquired a key role in stimulating economic development (European Dialogue, 1993; Leonardi et al., 1992). The increased EU-orientation is expressed in a burgeoning of the EU regional lobby, with numerous authorities opening offices in Brussels – competing and sometimes collaborating with existing Brussels-based state re-presentations in the COREPER. Bavaria was the first region to fund a representative in Brussels in 1986, following a breakdown in relations between the regional and German Federal governments on EU-related issues. By 1992 all 16 German Länder had joined Bavaria, along with many other EU regional and local authorities – including 26 authorities from the UK.

A plenary session of the Parliament of Catalonia

The Commission has been a loyal ally of substate authorities – reflected in its proposal at the Maastricht negotiations that a Committee of the Regions (CoR) should be set up as an 'upper house' of the European Parliament. In the event the Committee has purely consultative powers, yet substate politicians and Commission officials anticipate that in time it will become a potential rival to states in the EU (Grey, 1994). Indeed, in the second year of its existence, there was some limited evidence that the Committee was developing its own distinctive perspective on the integration process (CEC, 1995).

As well as participating in the CoR, substate authorities have worked with the Commission to establish new cross-regional associations. In 1989 cross-border association agreements gained legal recognition under Community Law as 'European Economic Interest Groupings'. By 1992 there were 322 of these groupings, many acting as 'holding' organizations of broader inter-regional associations, often formally recognized as 'Euro-regions' by the Commission, such as the relationship between Nord Pas de Calais and Kent across the Channel (CEC, 1993b; Cochrane, 1993b). Unsurprisingly the more prosperous regions took the lead in forging these new inter-regional links. Catalonia, Lombardy, Baden-Würtemberg and Rhône-Alpes, for instance, set up an association in September 1988 – the so-called 'Four Motors' – that was explicitly designed to help these stronger regions take a 'pathbreaking role' in the new Europe as a new 'intra-European, high-technology cartel' (Harvie, 1994, p.65). A similar 'High Technology Route of Southern Europe' has been established, linking Catalonia with the two adjoining French regions of Languedoc-Roussillon and Midi-Pyrenees (Gibernau, 1995). This links French and Spanish Catalan speakers and brings together two major growth centres in the emerging European political economy – Barcelona and Toulouse. Others are organized along sectoral lines, for instance in the 'Regions of Traditional Industry' or the 'Motor Industry Cities and Regions'.

Associations are only rarely aimed at linking the interests of core and peripheral regions; the latter often resort to bargaining for individual membership of 'core' associations – in the case of Wales, as part of the 'Four Motors'. This has encouraged the less prosperous to define their common interests more clearly at the EU level – jointly campaigning for changes in EU policies and linking with neighbouring peripheries, for instance in the case of the north and south of Ireland (Goodman, 1995a).

As substate authorities have become more bound into EU institutions and transregional associations, substate regionalists and nationalists have redefined their aspirations, in effect Europeanizing their demands for increased substate autonomy or independence (Goodman, 1996). Such redefinitions have been particularly marked in the UK where Scottish, Welsh and Irish nationalists have all become enthusiastically pro-European. The Scottish Nationalist Party (SNP), the Welsh Plaid Cymru, the Irish Social Democratic and Labour Party (SDLP) and, most recently, Sinn Fein, all welcome increased EU integration. With the exception of the SDLP, they had opposed EC membership in 1975, seeing it as a threat to potential national sovereignty. Subsequently their nationalist agendas have been combined with Euro-regionalism and they now define themselves as part of the EU political 'mainstream', accusing the Euro-sceptic British government of 'separatism' on EU issues. This has helped to give all four an electoral boost – particularly in European Parliament elections where the SNP share of the vote rose from 26 to 33 per cent between 1989 and 1994; the Plaid Cymru vote rose from 13 to 17 per cent; and in Northern Ireland, the combined Sinn Fein and SDLP vote rose from 34.7 to 38.9 per cent.

At the same time, UK regionalism has intensified. In England, the Campaign for a Northern Assembly, the North-West Regional Association and the West Midlands Regional Forum have argued that regional autonomy is urgently required in the SEM. They submitted bids for the 1995–99 tranche of regional funds independently of Whitehall (Birch and Holliday, 1993; Rose, 1992). In London, the need to lobby jointly for European regional development funds brought together the Conservative-controlled London Boroughs Association and the Labour-controlled Association of London Authorities, while in Northern Ireland a cross-community coalition including business organizations, local authorities and politicians set up the Northern Ireland Centre in Europe in 1992 to lobby for Northern Ireland interests at the EU level (Anderson and Goodman, 1995b).

There were similar developments in other parts of the EU. In Spain, for instance, Basque and Catalan nationalists became enthusiastic Euro-regionalists when Spain joined the EC in 1986 (Keating and Jones, 1995). In the Basque country, where the total nationalist vote rose to 66 per cent of the electorate in 1990, the Nationalist Party leader Xabier Arzalluz argued that the key to Basque independence lay in an EU constitution which would override the Spanish one, offering the region a 'future within an EU which, with the disappearance of nation-states, would dissolve its tensions with Madrid' (*Independent,* 17 May 1993). In Belgium, the Flemish regional government linked its campaign for increased independence to the process of EU integration, with the slogan 'Flanders–Europe 2000', and in 1993 Luc van den Brande, President of the Flanders Government, argued that the Committee of the Regions would speed up the region's transition to independence (*Financial Times*, 6 March 1993). In Northern Italy, Umberto Bossi, leader of the Lega Lombardy, a regionalist party which emerged in the late 1980s and early 1990s, argued that the party was 'in the avant garde of a new politics in Europe which you could say was made up of regions under the umbrella of the EU rather than the nation-states' (*Guardian,* 30 January 1993).

Across the EU, substate regionalists and nationalists have used integration to imbue their message with an 'internationalist vision' (Lindsay, 1991, p.95). This ideological redefinition has bolstered support for substate political movements. As a result, relatively marginalized separatist anti-federalism has given way to a significantly more popular politics of inclusive autonomy in a federalized EU (Müller-Rommel, 1994).

In sum, EU integration has released new substate democratizing pressures. It has increased the power of substate authorities – most of which are directly elected. It has also increased popular involvement in substate politics through new or invigorated social and political movements.

Social movements in the EU

Substate pressures are paralleled and complemented by increased citizen involvement in transnational social movements, which have also exerted a powerful democratizing influence on EU politics. As state legitimacy falters and is not reconstructed at the EU level, new political spaces are opened up in which such groupings can claim a strengthened role in defining public policy (Hirsch, 1995). Some social movements *react* to the increased melding together of national politics in the EU, reasserting the myth of national homogeneity or reconstructing it in the guise of Euro-racism. Others have developed more *proactive* responses, often establishing linkages between global concerns and specific but highly symbolic political actions. These movements embody the demand for wider participation in EU decision-making and constitute 'communities of conscience' beyond the territorial state. Indeed, by defining and mobilizing transnational constituencies they are capable of posing a democratic alternative to increased transnational economic integration.

However, many social movements, far from being vehicles for popular participatory democracy, are simply subscription organizations and can be dominated by elites rather than by the peoples whose interests they aim to serve. They are often strongly associated with state agencies and lack political autonomy. Alternatively, if fully autonomous, they may be unstable and lacking in political influence. Yet many such organizations retain a 'radical reformist' agenda that, crucially, involves autonomous self-organization around issues that are constructed and articulated beyond the state (Hirsch, 1995).

In this respect, many social movements offer a means of linking with democratizing pressures beyond the immediate EU region – embodied in a range of proactive global movements that challenge the social, environmental and developmental costs of economic globalization (Sakamoto,

1996). In doing so, they offer a means of extending democratization both to the EU's internal 'minorities' and to other 'majorities' beyond its borders. Democratic structures confined to the EU will remain vulnerable to global pressures and the emphasis should be on extending democratic rights and participation beyond its borders as well as within them. This requirement is perhaps best satisfied by transnational social movements.

Since the early 1980s there has been an exponential increase in social movement lobbying at the EU level (Andersen and Eliassen, 1991). EU policy-making catalyses local action which then rebounds back onto national governments and EU institutions in a dialectical process of transnational politicization (Goodman, 1995b). As a result, a wide range of social movements that previously were largely or exclusively focused on their separate national jurisdictions have been strengthened through increased transnational collaborative efforts.

This has particularly affected the environmental movement as EU Environmental Action Programmes, begun in 1973, have legitimized locally-defined demands. This in turn has strengthened such programmes, from piecemeal directives affecting specific environmental issues, to process-orientated directives, for instance requiring Environmental Impact Assessments of all major infrastructure projects from 1985. These have been followed by more ambitious institutional initiatives – such as the creation of the European Environmental Protection Agency in 1993. With the Maastricht Treaty, there were broader ideological advances – for instance, introducing the 'polluter pays' principle and questioning traditional growth concepts – which were described by one observer as 'potential dynamite' (Weizsacker, 1994).

Similarly, EU declarations of intent on issues of social protection, embodied in the 1989 Social Charter, have provided a useful source of legitimation for trade union and broader labour movement demands. This was encouraged by Commission President Jacques Delors who sought the support of the European trade union movement in 1988 for a 'social dimension' to complement the economic aspects of integration implemented under the Single European Act. In May 1988 he addressed the European Trade Union Confederation (ETUC), arguing that the Community should adopt a base of social rights, including rights to continuing training and limited workplace democracy through works councils. He followed this with a speech to the 1988 British TUC, which emphasized the need for a 'social Europe' to complement economic integration. This mobilized support for the Commission's Social Charter proposals, approved in watered-down form by the Council of Ministers in December 1989.

Subsequently the ETUC has gained some access to EU decision-making structures. Member unions have been able to use EU directives to defend members' interests. The ETUC has gained new roles and pan-EU industry committees – for instance, the European Public Services Committee – have been strengthened. National trade unions have linked up with social democratic and ex-communist groups in the Parliament; some have established their own offices in Brussels; and there have been moves towards pan-EU 'super-unions' able to organize industrial action in the more unified EU corporate system (Greenwood *et al.*, 1992). From 1992 this has been encouraged by Commission funding for trans-frontier co-operation between employee organizations and by 1994, for instance, British trade unions were involved with their counterparts in over 90 pan-EU company specific negotiations, despite the British government's opt-out from the Maastricht Treaty Protocols on social policy (Wendon, 1994).

EU policy-making has also influenced the women's movement – in some respects leading to 'spontaneous, flexible and sometimes enduring transnational contacts among women' (Hoskyns, 1994, p.233). Again, the EU legislative programme has stimulated transnationally orientated local action. In the UK, for instance, the process of challenging the government's failure to fully implement EU Directives on equal pay (1970), equal treatment in the workplace (1975) and equal treatment under the benefits system (1985), has had a crucial consciousness-raising impact (Hoskyns, 1986). In all three cases, women's organizations took cases to the European Court and forced amendments to the British 'enabling' legislation.

ETUC Conference on Jobs and Social Rights, 2–3 December 1996

Partly as a result, in the UK at least, pan-EU organization on gender issues is most advanced amongst women trade unionists, where there has been a 'huge shift' in orientation (Sperling and Bretherton, 1995). EU Action Programmes on equal opportunities, begun in 1982 after a European Parliament Resolution, have played a similar role, leading to the strength-ening of pan-EU womens' organizations, such as the European Network of Women, the European Forum of Socialist Feminists and the European Women's Lobby. At the same time, transnational linkages associated with particular issue areas, for instance relating to women refuges and migrant women, have also been strengthened.

Other social movements have similarly demanded access to EU policy-making and used EU Directives to gain leverage over national states. The lesbian and gay movement, for instance, has become organized on a more transnational, pan-EU basis and has had some limited, although ground-breaking, success. From 1984 the European Parliament repeatedly called for Commission action on the issue of discrimination against lesbians and gay men, arguing that it constituted a barrier to free movement within the SEM and required Commission action under the 1985 Single European Act. In 1991 this culminated in the first explicit recognition by the Commission that discrimination in the workplace on grounds of sexual orientation was unacceptable and in 1992 the issue was directly addressed in the European Parliament's Charter on Sexual Harassment in the Workplace (Tatchell, 1992, p.22).

Anti-racist movements have also become more organized on an EU basis, often in response to the increasingly restrictive and explicitly racist immigration policies emanating from the process of pan-EU police co-operation. The European Migrants Forum has become increasingly prominent, although it has remained primarily a forum rather than a movement, and in 1995 it was joined by a new pan-EU organization of anti-racist movements and refugee support organizations. Also, human rights organizations, such as the Helsinki Citizens' Assembly (HCA), lobby EU institutions, and pan-European security organizations, such as NATO, the Western European Union and the Organization for Security and Co-operation in Europe, as does the anti-nuclear movement (Overby, 1990).

Many of these movements challenge national divisions both in the EU and beyond it. The HCA, for instance, is heavily critical of new East West divisions in Europe, and reaches out beyond them to promote inclusive and democratic political principles. It was, for instance, instrumental in promoting the creation of a multi-ethnic EU protectorate in Mostar and in supporting multi-ethnic municipalities elsewhere in Bosnia – such as in Tuzla, where the Assembly met in 1996.

Such movements are generally both participatory and democratic, yet are mostly forced to the margins of EU decision-making. The ETUC, for instance, represents 86 per cent of unionized labour in Western Europe, and as such has a larger constituency than most member states, yet its influence is limited to clearly demarcated areas of EU policy-making, centred on the Social Affairs Directorate (Greenwood et al., 1992). This contrasts with the business and employers' lobby which is able to influence, if not set, the EU agenda on a range of issues, from Economic and Monetary Union to External Policy. Through organizations such as the Union of Industrial and Employers Confederations, employers are able to exert an 'astounding' degree of influence, especially when compared to the subordinate roles accorded to more representative and democratic regional and social groupings (Rhodes, 1991).

The environmental movement is also forced to the margins, with business organizations, for instance, stalling implementation of the Maastricht 'polluter pays' principle (Seager, 1993). Indeed, national disre-gard for environmental degradation is sharply reproduced at the EU level, where policy is more clearly driven by the competitive pressures of economic globalization, while alternative avenues for a more 'co-operative globalization' pursued by more universal organizations such as the United Nations Environment Programme, tend to be ignored (Hooghe, 1993).

The women's movement is similarly relegated to the fringes. Like trade union bodies, women's organizations have difficulty in gaining access beyond the social affairs directorate. This 'ghettoization' ensures, for instance, that whole swathes of EU policy which centrally involve women's issues – such as training policy, the social charter and the poverty programme – are developed with little or no acknowledgement of their impact on women (Hoskyns, 1994, p.236). This gender blindness reflects the tendency for the national states' untouchable 'private' realms – for instance, of personal and social relationships – that depoliticize issues of 'domestic' labour and sexual violence and deny reproductive rights, to be simply transposed to the EU level.

In general terms, the overall tendencies are surprisingly similar. Social movements are orientated to transnational ideals that have an inherent mobilizing potential at the EU level. This is true of the labour movement – a so-called 'old' social movement – as much as, for instance, new social movements such as the women's and environmental movements. In contrast with more narrowly defined business groupings with direct access to EU decision-making, pan-EU associations of marginalized social movements can claim a popular legitimacy that in many ways reaches out and builds new alliances beyond as well as within EU borders – a process of transnational political empowerment that is underway, but is as yet very weak relative to other channels of political power (Tarrow, 1994a).

Nonetheless, social movements and the policy-making structures associated with them are challenging elite governance in the EU. A dialectical relationship has emerged between bureaucratic and business elites, and social movement 'challengers'. Such challengers are powerful vehicles for democracy in an increasingly transnationalized EU. As popular movements can no longer be forced into their respective national 'containers', they retain their transnational radicalism. In a sense then, EU integration lets the social movement 'genie' out of the nation-state 'bottle' – a precondition of moving towards a non-statist, cosmopolitan and participative democracy capable of challenging globalizing pressures (Tarrow, 1994b; Wainwright, 1994).

─────────────── *Summary of Section 8.3* ───────────────

- In place of a single territorial foundation for democracy, a form of 'cosmopolitan democracy', with several sources of democratic participation, is likely to emerge in the EU.

- The pan-EU Parliament, national assemblies, substate authorities and social movements are all potential vehicles for EU cosmopolitan democracy.

- They are increasingly orientated to pan-EU agendas and, in some respects, offer an alternative to the de-democratizing effects of economic globalization and regionalization.

Conclusion

This chapter began by emphasizing that the recent history of EU integration is rooted in advancing globalization. It was argued that the EU's economic policies and related initiatives on social, regional and political cohesion open up new transnational political agendas. Democratic involvement in this policy-making process is restricted to national and Commission executives, with a limited role accorded to the European Parliament and other advisory bodies. This undermines liberal democracy – expressed in arguments that it should be 're-grounded' in national parliaments, in a pan-EU federal parliament or in regional assemblies. These were discussed and it was argued that liberal democracy is unlikely to be reconstructed on a single territorial 'foundation'. Instead, a form of 'cosmopolitan democracy' is likely to emerge. This was illustrated, focusing on new transnational democratic spaces in the EU. It was argued that these are being claimed by the pan-EU Parliament and by national assemblies and also by substate authorities and by transnational social movements. Concrete illustrations were offered and the extent to which these democratizing vehicles breach the state 'container' and constitute a 'post-Westphalian' or 'cosmopolitan' polity were discussed.

Overall, EU integration has created sharp disjunctures between the claims of liberal democracy and increasing disempowerment of state structures. In 1970, one observer predicted that growing economic 'interpenetration' in the EC would lead to the creation of political institutions beyond the reach of formal democracy (Mandell, 1970). To a great extent this prediction has been borne out. The vertical organization of political life in which the nation-state is the primary locus of public power, is being replaced by a more horizontal organization in which a variety of spheres of authority – of which the nation-state is only one – impinge on the individual.

As transnational networks, regulatory regimes and other non-state forms of governance become more important, the nation-state can no longer be seen as the exclusive 'container' of democratic political life. This proliferation of power sources short-circuits liberal democracy and is profoundly disempowering for those not served by transnational corporations or by suprastate organizations. Indeed, subject to the limited sanctions of state executives, EU institutions are able to act in the interests of EU business to a degree that national states, subject to the dictates of liberal democracy, never could (Mann, 1993).

To survive, liberal democracy must 'resist the spatial and temporal constraints which the state imposes upon the political process' (Hoffmann, 1995, p.196). This requires an extensive re-democratization of the 'hybrid' EU political system, in which states coexist with as yet unaccountable transnational power structures. Yet there is no prospect of economic and political elites simply granting such democracy 'on request'. Re-democratization beyond the nation-state, to a new 'cosmopolitan democracy', will only emerge out of transnational mobilization. Here, the transnational working of national assemblies, substate authorities and an array of 'old' and 'new' social movements point the way to a reconstituted democracy that flows through and beyond the state – to match the transnational constituencies emerging from increased globalization.

References

Amin, A. and Tomaney, J. (1995) 'The regional dilemma in a neo-liberal Europe', *European Urban and Regional Studies*, vol.2, no.2, pp.170–87.

Anderson, J. and Goodman, J. (1995a) 'Regions, states and the European Union: Modernist reaction or postmodernist adaptation?', *Review of International Political Economy*, vol.2, no.4, pp.600–32.

Anderson, J. and Goodman, J. (1995b) 'Euro-regionalism and national conflict: the EU, the UK, Ireland north and south' in Shirlow, P. (ed.) *Development Ireland*, London, Polity, pp.39–54.

Anderson, J. (1990) 'Sceptical reflections on a Europe of regions: Britain, Germany and the ERDF', *Journal of Public Policy*, vol.10, pp.417–47.

Andersen, S. and Eliassen, K. (1991) 'European Community lobbying', *European Journal of Political Research*, vol.20, pp.173–86.

Ascherson, N. (1991) 'Europe as a sponge?' in *The Future of Europe*, Guardian Studies, no.6, pp.7–9.

Benington, J. and Taylor, M. (1993) 'Changes and challenges facing the UK welfare state in the Europe of the 1990s', *Policy and Politics*, vol.21, no.2, pp.121–34.

Birch, M. and Holliday, I. (1993) 'Institutional emergence: The case of the North-West of England', *Regional Politics and Policy*, vol.3, no.2, pp.29–51.

Cochrane, A. (1993a) 'Looking for a European welfare state' in Cochrane, A. and Clarke, J. (eds) *Comparing Welfare States*, London, Sage, pp.239–68.

Cochrane, A. (1993b) 'Creating a planning region' in Bullmann, U. (ed.) *Die Regionen in EG-integrationsprozess*, Giessen, Giessen University Press.

Commission of the European Communities (1970) *Report to the Council and the Commission on the Realisation by Stages of Economic and Monetary Union in the Community*, 'Werner Report', Luxembourg, Office for the Official Publications of the EC.

Commission of the European Communities (1976) *Comprehensive Report on European Union*, 'Tindemans Report', Luxembourg, Office for the Official Publications of the EC.

Commission of the European Communities (1993a) *The Citizenship of the Union*, 21 December 1993, Com (93) 702, Luxembourg, Office for the Official Publications of the EC.

Commission of the European Communities (1993b) *EEIG, the Emergence of a New Form of European Co-operation*, Luxembourg, Office for the Official Publications of the EC.

Commission of the European Communities (1995) *Inter-governmental Conference 1996: Commission Report for the Reflection Group*, Luxembourg, Office for the Official Publications of the EC.

Committee of the Regions (1995) *Institutional Reform*, 'Pujol Report', Brussels, Committee of the Regions.

European Dialogue (1993) *Power to the People? Economic Self-determination and the Regions,* Conference Report, Roberts A. (ed.) London, European Dialogue/Freidrich Ebert Foundation.

European Parliament (1983) *The Recovery of the European Economy,* Albert-Ball Report.

European Parliament (1994) *Draft Constitution of the European Union,* vol.9, no.2, 'Herman Report'.

European Parliament (1995) *Resolution on the Finalizing of the Treaty on European Union,* 17 May 1995.

European Policy Forum (1993) *Proposals for a European Constitution,* Brussels, EPF.

European Research Group (1995) *A Europe of Nations,* London, ERG.

Galtung, J. (1973) *The EC: a Superpower in the Making,* London, Allen and Unwin.

Garcia, S. (ed.) (1993), *European Identity and the Search for Legitimacy,* London, Pinter.

Gibb, R. and Wise, M. (1993) *Single Market to Social Europe,* Harlow, Longman.

Gibernau, M. (1995) 'Spain: a Federation in the making?' in Smith, G. (ed.) *Federalism: the Multi-ethnic Challenge,* Harlow, Longman, pp.239–55,.

Goodman, J. (1995a) 'The Northern Ireland question and European politics' in Catterall, P. (ed.) *Northern Ireland in British Politics,* London, Institute of Contemporary British History and Macmillan, pp.212–29.

Goodman, J. (1995b) 'The EU: towards a transnational politics of movement?', *Via Europa,* Rhone, Diagonales Est-Ouest, vol.1, pp.23–33.

Goodman, J. (1996) *Nationalism and Transnationalism: The National Conflict in Ireland and European Union Integration,* Aldershot, Avebury.

Greenwood, J. *et al.* (1992) *Organized Interests in the European Community,* London, Sage.

Grey, C. (1994) 'The Committee of the Regions' in Brouwer, F. (ed.) *Economic Policy Making and the EU,* London, Federal Trust, pp.103–9.

Gross, A. (1995) 'Why Europe needs a European constitution for a transnational democracy', Paper to the British Political Science Association, April 1995.

Harvie, C. (1994) *The Rise of Regional Europe,* London, Routledge.

Held, D. (1995) *Democracy and the Global Order: From the Modern State to Cosmopolitan Governance,* Cambridge, Polity Press.

Hirsch, J. (1995) 'Nation-state, international regulation and the question of democracy', *Review of International Political Economy,* vol.2, no.2, pp.267–84.

Hoffmann, J. (1995) *Beyond the State,* Cambridge, Polity Press.

Hoffmann, S. (1994) 'Europe's identity revisited', *Daedalus,* vol.122, no.2, Spring, pp.1–25.

Hooghe, M. (1993) 'Success through lack of competition: the political opportunity structure for EC environmental policy in Belgium' in Holder, J. *et al.* (eds) *Perspectives on the Environment,* Aldershot, Avebury, pp.141–51.

Hoskyns, C. (1986) 'Women, European law and transnational politics', *International Journal of the Sociology of Law,* vol.14, pp.199–315.

Hoskyns, C. (1994) 'Gender issues in international relations: the case of the European Communities', *Review of International Studies*, vol.20, pp.225–39.

Kearney, R. (1988) *Across the Frontiers: Ireland in the 1990s*, Dublin, Wolfhound.

Keating, M. (1988) *State and Regional Nationalism: Territorial Politics and the European State*, London, Harvester Wheatsheaf.

Keating, M. and Jones, B. (1995) *The European Union and the Regions*, Oxford, Clarendon.

Kuper, R. (1995) 'The many democratic deficits of the EU', Paper to the ECPR conference, Oslo, September 1995.

Lange, P. (1992) 'The politics of the social dimension' in Sbragia, A. (ed.) *Europolitics*, Washington, the Brookings Institution, pp.225–57.

Leonardi, R. *et al.* (1992) 'The regions and the European Community: the regional response to the Single Market in the underdeveloped areas', *Regional Politics and Policy – An International Journal*, Special Issue, vol.2, no.1.

Lindsay, I. (1991) 'The SNP and the lure of Europe' in Gallagher, T. (ed.) *Nationalism in the Nineties*, Edinburgh, Polygon, pp.84–102.

Linklater, A. (1996) 'Citizenship and sovereignty in the post-Westphalian state', *European Journal of International Relations*, vol.2, no.1, pp.77–103.

MacLaughlin, J. (1993) 'Defending the frontiers: the political geography of race and racism in the EC' in Williams, C. (ed.) *The Political Geography of the New World Order*, London, Belhaven, pp.20–46.

Mandell, E. (1970) *Europe Versus America? Contradictions of Imperialism*, London, New Left Books.

Mann, M. (1993) 'Nation-states in Europe and other continents: diversifiying, developing, not dying', *Daedalus*, vol.122, no.3, Summer.

Martin, D. (1991) *Europe: An Ever Closer Union*, Nottingham, European Labour Forum and Spokesman.

Müller-Rommel, F. (1994) 'Ethno-regionalist parties in Western Europe: empirical evidence and theoretical considerations' in de Winter, L. (ed.) *Non-statewide Political Parties in Europe*, Barcelona, ICPS, pp.181–97.

Overby, L. (1990) 'West European peace movements: an application of Kischelt's political opportunity structures thesis', *West European Politics*, vol.13, no.1, pp.1–12.

Perrons, D. (1992) 'The regions and the Single Market' in Dunford M. *et al.* (eds) *Cities and Regions in the New Europe*, London, Belhaven, pp.170–95.

Preston, P. (1994) *Europe, Democracy and the Dissolution of Britain*, Aldershot, Dartmouth.

Reif, K. (1993) 'Cultural convergence and cultural diversity as factors in European identity' in Garcia, S. (ed.) *European Identity and the Search for Legitimacy*, London, Pinter, pp.131–54,.

Rhodes, M. (1991) 'The social dimension of the SEM: national versus transnational regulation', *European Journal of Political Research*, vol.19, pp.245–80.

Rose, E. (1992) 'A Europe of regions – the West Midlands of England: planning for metropolitan change in Birmingham', *Landscape and Urban Planning*, vol.22, pp.229–42.

Sakamoto, Y. (1996) 'Democratization, social movements and world order', in R. Cox *et al.* (eds) *International Political Economy: Understanding Global Disorder*, London, Zed, pp.129–44,.

Seager, J. (1993) *Earth Follies*, London, Earthscan.

Shapiro, M. (1992) 'The European Court of Justice' in Sbragia, A. (ed.) *Europolitics*, Washington, Brookings Institution, pp.191–225.

Sperling, L. and Bretherton, C. (1995) 'Women and public policy: women's networks and the EU' in Lovenduski, J. and Stanger, J. (eds) *Contemporary Political Studies*, York, Proceedings of the UKPSA, no.3, pp.1309–16.

Suarez-Villa, L. and Roura, J. (1993) 'Regional economic integration and the evolution of disparities', *Papers in Regional Science*, vol.72, no.4, pp.369–87.

Tarrow, S. (1994a) 'Social movements in Europe: movement society or Europeanisation of conflict?', European University Institute Working Paper, RSC 94/8.

Tarrow, S. (1994b) *Power in Movement: Social Movements, Collective Action and Politics*, Cambridge, Cambridge University Press.

Tatchell, P. (1992) *Europe in the Pink*, London, GMP.

Thompson, G. (1993) *The Economic Emergence of a New Europe?*, Aldershot, Edward Elgar.

Wainwright, H. (1994) *Arguments for a New Left*, Oxford, Blackwell.

Walker, R.B.J. (1993) *Inside/Outside: International Relations as Political Theory*, Cambridge, Cambridge University Press.

Wallace, W. (1994) 'Rescue or retreat? The nation-state in Western Europe 1945–93', *Political Studies*, vol.XLII, pp.52–76.

Weizsacker, E. (1994) *Earth Politics*, London, Zed.

Wendon, B. (1994) 'British trade union responses to European integration', *Journal of European Public Policy*, vol.1, no.2, pp.243–61.

Wessels, W. (1991) 'The EC Council: the Community's decision-making centre' in Keohane, R. and Hoffmann, S. (eds) *The New European Community: Decision-making and Institutional Change*, Oxford, Oxford University Press.

Westlake, M. (1995) 'The European parliament, the national parliaments and the 1996 intergovernmental conference', *Political Quarterly*, vol.3, pp.59–73.

Wieland, J. (1994) 'Germany in the EU: the Maastricht decision of the Bundesverfassungsgericht', *European Journal of International Law*, vol.5, no.2, pp.259–66.

Wistrich, E. (1991) *After 1992: the United States of Europe*, London, Federal Trust and Routledge.

Further reading

Newman, M. (1996) *Democracy, Sovereignty and the European Union*, London, Hurst.

Preston, P. (1994) *Europe, Democracy and the Dissolution of Britain*, Aldershot, Dartmouth.

Taylor, P. (1996) *The European Union in the 1990s,* Oxford, Oxford University Press.

Wallace, W. (1994) *Regional Integration: the West European Experience*, Washington DC, Brookings.

CHAPTER 9

Geo-governance without democracy? Reforming the UN system

Mark Imber

Introduction

Global governance exists in many forms; it occupies the space between the extreme positions of 'international anarchy', that is the complete absence of government and law in international relations, and its logical opposite, a 'world government' which would replicate at the global level all the forms of government (legislature, executive and judiciary) found in the domestic polity of every independent state. Global (geo-)governance should not be confused with 'world government'; the latter is associated largely with the idea of world federalism (Falk, 1975). This chapter will attempt to explore the connections between globalization, the democratization of world order, and the forms and quality of geo-governance. It addresses, in particular, three questions.

First, is democracy relevant to international relations? That is, to relations between a large number of independent states that may them selves be liberal-democratic, partially democratic or authoritarian? More specifically, can the international regimes and international organizations created by states be judged against standards or models of democratic institutions and practices originally intended for application to domestic politics?

Second, how far do existing mechanisms of geo-governance reflect democratic principles and values? In this context the discussion concentrates upon the prospects for, and also the limits to, democratic reform of the UN system. The growth of the UN system since 1945 has witnessed a gradual extension of international co-operation and a degree of international authority over a wide range of social, scientific and economic activities. However, the UN is now over 50 years old, and is open to criticism in respect of both its competence to undertake its many designated tasks and its limited 'democratic' credentials; for example, the veto which exists in the Security Council gives very real powers to just five states. Furthermore, some of the subsidiary organs of the UN, such as the World Bank, which when taken together comprise the 'UN System' of over twenty organs and agencies, are also subject to similar criticisms and speculation concerning democratic reform.

Third, although citizens can participate *indirectly* in processes of geo-governance, through the election of governments which conduct this multilateral diplomacy, can citizens participate *directly*? The enormous expansion of Non-Governmental Organizations (NGOs), such as Amnesty International or Friends of the Earth, and their international affiliates and confederations (INGOs), does now allow this to occur. However, the emergence of an international, or even global, 'civil society' has certain limits. Most obviously, the variety of political regimes – liberal-democratic, partially democratic and authoritarian – each tolerate different levels of NGO activity, which reflect traditional attitudes towards domestic civil society.

Whilst globalization has been primarily associated with the expansion of mechanisms of geo-governance, the growth of co-operation and integration between some regional groupings of states, such as the European Union (EU) and the new North American Free Trade Area (NAFTA), may also be interpreted as a defensive *reaction* to globalization. These groupings are seeking to insulate and strengthen regional economies against global competition. In the case of the EU, as the previous chapter indicates, democratization and globalization may be in tension. The creation of geo-governance therefore involves *competitive* as well as *co-operative* institutions. Elements of power politics as well as democratic politics are present in these arrangements. These tensions will be explored shortly, in the debate between schools of thought which characterize international organizations variously as instruments of state policy, as arenas for negotiation between them, or exceptionally as actors in their own right.

This chapter commences with an examination of the growth of geo-governance in the post-war era. In Section 9.2, it explores the nature of the UN system as the core institution of existing forms of geo-governance. Finally, in Sections 9.3 and 9.4, the democratic credentials of the UN system are critically analysed alongside the contemporary debate about its reform. The Conclusion returns to the issue of the prospects for the democratization of geo-governance and world order.

9.1   The growth of geo-governance

Geo-governance, as Chapter 1 discusses, is a form of 'governance without government' (Rosenau and Cziempel, 1992). There are many formal and informal arrangements for co-operation between states, known as *international regimes*, which together provide the world's 191 legally independent states with a partial and imperfect system of governance, and also formal, legally constituted *international (or inter-governmental) organizations* (Archer, 1992; Keohane and Nye, 1977). Regimes and inter-

> ### *Box 9.1 International regimes and organizations*
>
> *International regimes:* 'By creating and accepting procedures, rules or institutions for certain kinds of activity, governments regulate and control transnational and international relations. We refer to these governing arrangements as international regimes.' (Keohane and Nye, 1977, p.5)
>
> *International organization:* 'A formal continuous structure established by agreement between members (governmental or non-governmental), from two or more sovereign states with the aim of pursuing the common interest of the membership.' (Archer, 1992, p.37)

national organizations allow independent, or *sovereign,* states to create norms, laws and programmes of co-operation between them. This allows a degree of order in their relations; in this way, the so-called international anarchy is tempered by elements of international society (Bull, 1977).

Explaining the growth of geo-governance

Underlying the twentieth-century rise of inter-governmental organizations (IGOs) is a struggle between power politics and democratic politics. Conventionally, the International Commission for the Navigation of the River Rhine, or Rhine Commission, is credited as the first IGO. It was founded in 1815. Growth was steady (see Table 9.1) until the First World War and most rapid in the period 1945–60.

Table 9.1 The growth of IGOs

Date	No. of IGOs
1815	1
1909	37
1960	154
1981	337
1994	263

Source: *Yearbook of International Organization* (31st edn, p.1625)

The very recent decline reflects the dismantling of a range of IGOs associated with the demise of communist governments in Eastern Europe. The 1994 figures also *exclude* religious orders (816), international conferences (610) and international treaties (1,838), which may be included in other counts.

Why do states create regimes and international organizations? Different motives and ideologies have variously risen and decayed, and with this the commitment of states to international institution-building has varied. The twentieth century has seen institutions created to fill one or more of three broad purposes: security, welfare (functional co-operation), and regional governance.

Some IGOs were created to provide *security.* The League of Nations (1919) and the United Nations (1945) were both founded in an attempt to control the use of force by independent states, to transcend the instabilities associated with the balance of power, and replace these with a system of *collective security* in which the world organization would be the only legitimate body to authorize the use of force to suppress acts of aggression. The failure of the League of Nations members to act on this principle in the cases of Japanese aggression against Manchuria, Italian action against Ethiopia, and German actions in Austria and Czechoslovakia, which all occurred in the 1930s, did much to discredit the proposition that security could be maintained in this way. Resurrected in the form of the United Nations in 1945, the full provisions for collective security have only been invoked since in two highly controversial cases,

The League of Nations at its opening session, Geneva,
15 November 1920

namely the war against North Korea in 1950 and that against Iraq in 1991. The more limited and ubiquitous form of UN *peacekeeping*, as in Cyprus since 1964, and more controversially in Bosnia-Herzegovina during 1992–95, is a sort of scaled-down version of collective security. It is based on the principle of armed force being deployed by the legitimating authority of the UN, but strictly limited by mandate and resources, to provide third-party policing of agreed cease-fires and to protect the provision of humanitarian relief to all parties. In some cases quasi-governmental roles have been fulfilled, such as organizing militia surrenders, supervising post-war elections and repairing infrastructure.

Recent elaborate peacekeeping missions in Namibia (UNTAG 1989–90) and in Cambodia (UNAMIC and UNTAC 1992–93) illustrate this enlarged competence. In these cases, internationally legitimated governance has been brought to terminate two civil wars in accordance with the original intention of limiting the effects and duration of wars between states. Since the end of the Cold War, the veto-free Security Council (see Section 9.2) has massively expanded the provision of peacekeeping, as Table 9.2 demonstrates.

A more modest rationale for international co-operation promotes joint actions in technical, economic and humanitarian affairs. This *functionalist* (or welfare) scheme takes its name from the 'functions' of government which may be more efficiently provided by international co-operation (Mitrany, 1975; Imber, 1989). Just as governments provide physical *public goods* such as roads, street lights, and sewers, and more conceptual 'goods' such as economic stability, issuing currency and setting interest rates, and also provide, or used to provide, basic welfare services, these 'functions' have their equivalent *international* public goods. International air-traffic control, telecommunications and posts, the control of contagious diseases, the humanitarian welfare of refugees and victims of natural disasters, the

Table 9.2 UN peacekeeping operations in place, 31 July 1995

	Location	First mandate
UNTSO	Jerusalem	1948
UNMOGIP	Kashmir	1949
UNFICYP	Cyprus	1964
UNDOF	Golan	1974
UNIFIL	S. Lebanon	1978
UNRSO	W. Sahara	1991
UNIKOM	Kuwait	1991
UNPROFOR	Bosnia	1992
UNOMIG	Georgia	1993
UNOMIL	Liberia	1993
UNMIH	Haiti	1993
UNAMIR	Rwanda	1993
UNCRO	Croatia	1994
UNPREDEP	Macedonia	1995
UNAVEM III	Angola	1995

protection of the ozone layer and the prevention of climate change (see Chapter 4) are examples of 'goods' which require co operation between states to work effectively. They are goods beyond the capacity of any one state to produce, and they are 'goods' vulnerable to damage caused by states if allowed to go unregulated, such as air or river pollution which crosses international boundaries.

Whilst the distinction between private and public sectors can change over time, similarly the scope of what is a national or an international public good can change. In the UK the boundary between private and public sector has undergone a radical shift in the last 15 years. Industries which were regarded as firmly in the category of public goods, such as water, telecommunications and electricity supply, have been transformed into commercial firms. Other sectors such as health and roads have also been subject to charges and tolls, although still publicly owned. This shift has been detected almost globally, in the USA, the ex-communist countries of Eastern Europe and increasingly in Third World countries as well. It raises a fundamental challenge to the functional approach to international regimes and organizations.

If the welfare state and public goods are subject to privatization 'at home', can the 'welfare world' and 'international public goods' remain immune to this, or to similar pressures? It is no coincidence that the radical right in the UK and USA which has been in the vanguard of 'rolling back the frontiers of the state' at home, has also been an exponent of limiting the growth, credibility and competence of the UN and its agencies' pretensions to 'international government'. However, privatization and the expansion of international trade do require a legal minimum of regulatory standards to facilitate orderly market transactions. Therefore, whilst standardizing, say, the use of English language in international civil aviation does not offend the radical right, the attempt by UNESCO to set international standards to reportage and broadcasting was denounced as censorship in the 1980s by the UK and the USA. Closer to home, the tension between the UK and the EU over the opt-out from the social chapter of the Maastricht Treaty exactly demonstrates the British preference for deregulation compared to the EU's attempt to maintain social welfare programmes in the face of global competition (see previous chapter).

Collective security and functionalism are necessarily globally organized. But the UN system (see Box 9.2) of global economic and social agencies predates the intensification of 'globalization' during the 1980s. As will be

Box 9.2 United Nations organs and specialized agencies

The UN system consists of the following:

1   UN organs

These were created by the General Assembly after 1945. They are funded from the UN's own budget raised by membership contributions and by additional voluntary contributions. Taken together they embrace the 'welfare' functions of the UN.

Acronym	Name	HQ
UNCTAD	UN Conference on Trade and Development	Geneva
UNICEF	UN Children's Fund	New York
UNHCR	UN High Commission for Refugees	Geneva
UNDP	UN Development Programme	New York
UNEP	UN Environment Programme	Nairobi
WFP	World Food Programme	Rome
UNFPA	UN Fund for Population Activities	New York

2 UN 'specialized agencies'

These are legally separate organizations. Many pre-date the UN, with their own membership (i.e. non-members of the UN like Switzerland, can join), their own budgets and programmes. Nominally, the specialized agencies are subject to co-ordination with the UN via its Economic and Social Council, and an annual heads of agencies meeting, called the Administrative Committee on Co-ordination. Listed below by their founding date, they illustrate the emergence of 'new' functional problems requiring international governance, as 'new' technologies such as civil aviation and nuclear energy were developed over the course of the century. The expansion of Third World membership is also reflected in the emergence of developmental themes and programmes.

UN 'specialized agencies'			
Acronym	**Title**	**Founded**	**HQ**
ITU	International Telecommunications Union	1865	Geneva
WMO	World Meteorological Organization	1873	Geneva
UPU	Universal Postal Union	1874	Bern
ILO	International Labour Organization	1919	Geneva
ICAO	International Civil Aviation Organization	1944	Montreal
IMF	International Monetary Fund	1944	Washington DC
IBRD	International Bank for Reconstruction and Development (World Bank)	1944	Washington DC
FAO	Food and Agriculture Organization	1945	Rome
UNESCO	United Nations Educational Scientific and Cultural Organization	1945	Paris
WHO	World Health Organization	1946	Geneva
IMCO	International Maritime Consultancy Organization	1948	London
GATT (WTO)	General Agreement on Tariffs and Trade (now World Trade Organization)	1948	Geneva
IFC	International Finance Corporation (IBRD subsidiary)	1956	Washington DC
IAEA	International Atomic Energy Agency	1957	Vienna
IDA	International Development Association (IBRD subsidiary)	1960	Washington DC
UNIDO	UN Industrial Development Organization	1967	Vienna

explained shortly, the UN system is curiously inhibited, by its one-member–one-vote structure and by its weak financial base, from fulfilling the global role it is now theoretically better poised to fulfil than at any time since 1945.

The system has evolved piecemeal over 50 years to meet functional needs, but has lagged in its level of provision and authority due to Cold War inhibitions, limited efficiency and the frequent preference of major 'hegemonic' actors to establish and promote regimes only very loosely associated with the UN, such as the US-led international monetary system of 1944–71. So, although formally and historically the organs of geo-governance have preceded the contemporary process of globalization, it is the acceleration of globalization today which is outstripping the capacities of the UN system.

Furthermore, it would be overly simplistic to assume that the growth of international organization and the intensification of globalization are always mutually reinforcing. Whilst the work of many functional UN agencies is consistent with globalization, other organs of the UN system are mandated

Headquarters of the United Nations, New York

to protect their clients against the more divisive consequences of economic globalization (see Chapter 2). For example, the role of the World Bank in receiving a net surplus of funds from Third World debt repayments in the late 1980s conflicts with the mandate of WHO, FAO and the UNICEF to protect some of the world's poorest citizens from reductions in social, medical and educational expenditure by those governments carrying heavy debt burdens, especially in Africa and Latin America. As argued below, some tension may therefore exist between global and regional interests.

Regionalism provides the third dominant explanation of why states create international regimes and organizations. Many groupings of states such as the European Union, Arab League and Organization of African Unity are committed to greater or lesser degrees of regional co-operation and integration. These reflect a mix of security and functional concerns, which may be more readily restricted to the regional level rather than the universal level of organization, and in the context of trade blocs may actually seek to protect a regional group from the full onslaught of deregulated global economic competition. Unusually in the case of the EU, its commitment to democratization is explicit, as the previous chapter noted.

Regional and ideological associations create something akin to a party-system in international relations. In global negotiations such as trade talks in GATT and its successor WTO, in measures to protect the ozone layer (Montreal Protocol, 1990) at the Rio 'Earth Summit' (UN Conference on Environment and Development, UNCED) of 1992, and in the long negotiations to create the Convention on the Law of Sea (UNCLOS) 1970–82, 'bloc politics' predominates. As Section 9.2 argues, the process of bargaining and compromise between blocs, through the mechanisms of international conference diplomacy, has become the central political process of global governance in the past 25 years.

Mechanisms of informal geo-governance

The UN is the most familiar of the many organs of geo-governance established since 1945. Some others, such as the International Monetary Fund (IMF) and the International Bank for Reconstruction and Development (IBRD), better known as the World Bank, are formally linked to the UN but in fact control multi-billion dollar assets many times larger than the monies available to the UN. Other institutions, such as the meeting of the seven largest industrial powers, the Group of Seven (G7), operate quite independently of the UN. Although it comprises democratic member-governments (USA, Japan, Germany, UK, France, Canada and Italy), the G7 conducts confidential policy debates and generates only limited public interest, mostly centred on the so-called world economic summits.

As well as inter-governmental organizations (IGOs), the contemporary system of geo-governance includes *non*-governmental organizations (NGOs and INGOs), such as the World Wide Fund for Nature (WWF), Greenpeace, Amnesty International and the Red Cross. The rate of growth for INGOs has been more rapid than that for IGOs (see Figure 9.1). INGOs

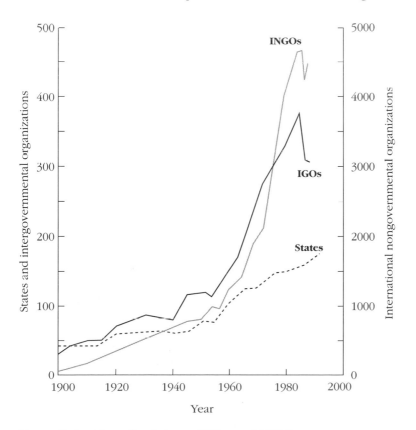

Figure 9.1 Growth of states, IGOs and INGOs
Source: Hughes (1993, p.45)

draw their membership from the private citizens of many countries and therefore reflect the idea of a civil society, operating at the global level (see Chapter 1). Their freedom to organize and lobby is a measure of associational autonomy within any society, and their ability to act internationally is a measure of the extent to which regional and global groupings of states respect this principle. Their role in geo-governance is a form of participatory, if not direct, democracy. It is a form of republicanism in which active citizens, through *internationally* active NGOs (i.e. INGOs) can lobby foreign governments, can donate monies above and beyond their taxes, and can participate in global conferences such as the 1992 Rio Earth Summit, which are themselves a typical feature of late twentieth-century geo-governance.

Elected governments may claim with some justification that they represent the electorate in bodies such as the UN. Authoritarian governments are obviously open to the charge of ignoring or misrepresenting their people's preferences. The NGO role is therefore participatory, and may even involve 'direct action' such as Greenpeace's obstruction of nuclear tests in the South Pacific in 1995. NGOs may *claim* to constitute 'we the peoples' (a much-abused quotation from the Preamble of the UN Charter), but as membership subscription organizations, and not *elected* representatives, their claim to be 'more representative' than elected governments is contestable. They are frequently more strident, and claim to occupy the high moral ground on single-issues, such as animal welfare and nuclear testing, but they do not have the responsibilities of elected governments, one of which is to balance the claims of interest groups and competing demands by citizens on different issues.

An advertising poster reproducing the Preamble of the UN Charter

---
Summary of Section 9.1 ───────
- International organizations are the most visible institutions of geo-governance. They sit at the formal, legal apex of an enormously complex pyramid of regimes, established between independent states for their mutual advantage. These extend over a range of issues, including security co-operation (that is, collective security and peacekeeping), functional co-operation, and regional co-operation.
- The technical, economic, humanitarian and environmental imperatives which between them created the post-1945 network of UN agencies are, under the impetus of globalization, now more intense than at any time previously.
- There are also significant mechanisms of informal geo-governance, such as the G7, and a plethora of non-governmental organizations which constitute an emerging global civil society.

9.2   The UN system and geo-governance

In the post-Cold War era, globalization and democratization combine to expose the limitations of the contemporary system of geo-governance more obviously than before. Limited by Cold War tensions, the efficiency and democratic credentials of the UN system were not exposed to full view.

The UN's political mandate

The UN (as well as the IMF and IBRD organizations) was created before the end of the Second World War, after an extended period of wartime planning amongst the allied powers. Its origins can be directly traced to the Atlantic Charter of 1941, and the term 'United Nations' was used as a synonym for the allied powers (UK, USA and USSR) during the latter years of the war. The UN Charter was first signed on 25 June 1945, six weeks before the bombing of Hiroshima and Nagasaki which concluded the war. The Charter entered into force in October 1945 and the first General Assembly was convened, in London, in 1946. This historical perspective is crucial to understanding the origins of the UN as an *instrument* of the wartime planning of the victorious

UK Prime Minister Clement Attlee addressing the first UN General Assembly, which opened on 10 January 1946

allied powers. The assumptions that underlay it were both partly democratic and partly based on power politics. The Charter was based upon three very specific assumptions, each valid in 1945, which were, however, rapidly falsified, and which in particular served to limit the credibility, effectiveness and democratic credentials of the global organization through its first twenty-five years until at least 1970:

- The organization was founded prior to the first use of nuclear arms; its provisions for legitimate military enforcement reflect this pre-nuclear naivety.

- It was founded prior to the Cold War, on the assumption of continuing post-war co-operation between the USA and the USSR in particular and the other Security Council members in general.

- It was founded when two leading members, France and UK, maintained extensive imperial territories and pretensions to continued colonial rule. Although the first steps to decolonization occurred in 1947, the 'process' was to take until the late 1970s to become general.

The UN, and the League of Nations which preceded it (1919), was founded upon the Wilsonian (liberal-internationalist) assumption (named after the US President Woodrow Wilson), that democratic states would conduct their foreign relations in a democratic manner – that is to say, by negotiation, by accepting international law to regulate disputes between states, and by self-restraint in the use of force. The Wilsonian analogy is to a domestic civil society which expects individuals to respect the 'rule of law'. Article 2 paragraph 4 of the UN Charter defines this obligation very clearly: 'All members shall refrain in their international relations from the threat or use of force against the territorial integrity or political independence of any state.'

It is one of the most ingrained assumptions of the late twentieth century, that 'democracies make good neighbours'. Problems in defining both 'democracy' and 'war' notwithstanding, it is hard to identify a single case of war between two democracies since 1945 (see Russett, 1993; Waltz, 1959). This 'democratic peace' thesis is, however, more often associated with regional rather than global co-operation. Fundamental to the EU, for example, is the assumption that there are no matters of dispute between its members that would justify the use of force to resolve them. The EU has become what Karl Deutsch called a 'security community' in which the members have long-term expectations of peaceful change and the rule of law.

Clearly wars between states *have* occurred, just as murder and civil violence occurs within civil society, contrary to laws concerning unlawful killing. The UN is not a Leviathan; it is not a supra-national authority or world government. From its earliest days the UN was inhibited in the field of international peace and security by Cold-War tensions and the paralysis of the infamous veto arrangements in the Security Council (discussed below). The UN has been *available* as a *forum* which many members have chosen not to use. It has been suppressed in this role by the use of the veto by the five major powers.

The original rationale for the veto was two-fold. As a mimic of the nineteenth-century Concert of Great Powers, the veto sought to protect the UN from adopting commitments that did not have the full support of the five powers whose resources of money and blood would be called upon to enforce collective actions to suppress aggression under the Charter. Secondly, the veto prevented the five (eventually) nuclear armed members from using the mechanisms of the Charter to declare war upon each other over some vital interest.

In practice, the veto has further illustrated the collision between democratic politics (the will of the *majority* of members) and power politics (the will of the five *permanent* members). By using the veto, a 14–1 majority vote of the Security Council can be nullified. This has served to protect the five permanent members in a wide variety of frankly indefensible situations such as the Franco–British invasion of Egypt in 1956, and the invasion of Hungary by the Soviet Union in the same year. The USA has similarly benefited from vetoing debate of cases such as the Vietnam War and the Grenada invasion of 1983. More typically, the US veto was cast to protect allies and friends, most significantly Israel and South Africa from the mid 1970s to the late 1980s. The figures showing the use of the veto over 50 years are illuminating (see Table 9.3).

Table 9.3 Vetoes cast in United Nations Security Council, 1946–95

China	3
France	18
USSR/Russia	116
UK	31
USA	70

Notes:
1 The figures refer only to the number of occasions when the veto has changed the outcome by nullifying the resolution under discussion (thereby excluding those occasions when a veto has been cast in support of a majority vote).
2 The first US veto was cast in 1970.
3 Only one veto has been cast since 1990 (by Russia on funds for the Cyprus peacekeeping mission, UNFICYP).

Source: International Research Unit, Foreign and Commonwealth Office, UK (January 1996, p.3)

The veto provisions are therefore deeply entrenched in the UN Security Council. The veto is the most obvious denial of democratic principles, and proposals for its reform are central to most contemporary calls for the reform of the organization. The veto was also responsible for the paralysis of the UN in acting upon its collective security mandate during the period of the Cold War. The suspension of the veto between 1990–95 is therefore quite remarkable. In the run-up to the use of force against Iraq in January 1991, sixteen resolutions, each more specific in denouncing some aspect of Iraq's actions (the occupation of Kuwait, the seizure of civilian and diplomatic hostages, etc.), were linked to increasingly severe sanctions on trade, air traffic and shipping, culminating in Resolution 678 giving six weeks notice of the use of force. These were all passed, some with Chinese abstention, but none subject to veto. Similarly, although in the 1990s the debates on Bosnia were affected by fear that Russia might cast its veto against enforcement measures should these damage Serb interests, in the event no Russian veto was cast, and Russian support for the Bosnian Dayton Peace Accords was secured in 1996.

Bloc politics

Beneath the rhetoric of North/South and East/West divisions in world politics is a complex and overlapping system of bloc politics in the UN. Bloc politics stimulates two opposed reactions. It *may* be seen as the very essence of democracy within the UN system, reflecting the diversity of cultural and political traditions within a universal membership organization, and resembling a party system. Alternatively, bloc politics *may* be represented as the *denial* of UN Charter principles because 'bloc voting' creates deals, trade-offs and cover for friends and allies in trouble, rather than judgements of complex and divisive issues on their merits according to the standards of the Charter.

The bloc structure has two, overlapping, political bases:

1   'regional groups' *geographically* defined in 1945, and

2   caucuses, or *political* groups, which have emerged later.

Regional groups are institutionalized within the UN Charter, and are used to routinely allocate committee and other positions on the basis of equitable geographical distribution (see Table 9.4). For example, the two-yearly rotating seats on the Security Council are allocated on a strict regional formula: five for Asia and Africa (informally two each plus one Arab state from either), two for Latin America, two for the incongruous West European and Other Group (WEOG) which includes Canada and Australia, and one for Eastern Europe. Each group decides internally, by a combination of arm-twisting and 'buggin's turn', to nominate the appropriate number. Nominations are only occasionally contested, as in the 1980s between Cuba and Colombia for a Latin American seat.

Table 9.4 Regional membership of the UN General Assembly and UN Security Council, 1995

Region	No. in UNGA	% total	No. in UNSC	% total
Africa	53	28	2 or 3[1]	13 or 20
Asia	44	24	3 or 4[2]	20 or 27
Eastern Europe	27	15	2[3]	13
Latin America	33	18	2	13
West Europe and others (WEOG)	27	15	5[4]	33
Total	184	100	15	100

1   the one Arab state may be North African or Asian
2   includes China
3   includes Russian Federation
4   includes France, UK and USA

Source: Bailey and Daws, (1995)

The inclusion of all the Soviet successor states in Eastern Europe, and of Australia and Canada within WEOG, shows that even this so-called 'regional grouping' in fact reflects certain political assumptions dating from 1945 which override strict geography.

The caucus system is much more explicitly political. Members of each group share certain ideological or religious affiliations. Table 9.5 indicates the major caucus groups.

Table 9.5 UN caucus groups

Group of 77 (G77)	128
Organization of the Islamic Conference (OIC)	41
League of Arab States	21
European Union	15
South Pacific Forum	15
Association of South East Asian Nations (ASEAN)	6
Gulf Co-operation Council	6
Nordic Group	5

Caucus groups are not exclusive. Malaysia, for example, caucuses within three groups: the Asian regional group, plus the OIC and ASEAN. Denmark is a member of the WEOG regional group, as well as the EU and Nordic groups. Some states are effectively barred from participation in their 'natural' groups. In their time, Israel, South Africa and Cuba have all been barred from their appropriate regional group. Traditionally, the USA has stood apart from the caucus system, but participates in WEOG. Some states can operate in more than one group. Turkey has at different times participated in the Asian and European groups. Japan is an observer at meetings of WEOG. Other informal groupings exist, such as the Commonwealth and the Portuguese- and French-speaking states, which may consult and co-operate with each other on particular issues. The Commonwealth has obviously had a major impact on political change in South Africa and was mobilized in 1995 to criticize and suspend Nigeria in respect of the absence of human rights.

Economic governance

The IMF and the World Bank were created by the Bretton Woods Conference of 1944. They are both headquartered in Washington DC, and are controlled by a voting system which does not give the majority of poorer debtors any pretence of one-member–one-vote control, but which ensures control by the richer creditor members. Voting rights are determined by the value of deposits in hard currency. (What bank would let its borrowers rather than its lenders determine its policy?)

Originally founded with very different purposes, the Fund and Bank have frequently been confused with each other, and misunderstood in their role. The IMF was originally mandated to 'manage' the Bretton Woods regime of fixed exchange rates (see Chapter 3). In the 25 years since 1971, years of 'floating' exchange rates, it has still lent money to countries that suffer balance of payments deficits. However, the former 'lender of last resort' of short-term liquidity has become transformed into a source of lending linked to long-term 'structural adjustment' of Third World, and now East European, economies.

The IBRD has undergone less change, but it always has been, and remains, a profit-making commercial lender, not an aid agency, despite many that imagine or wish that it were. The Bank has generally pursued conservative economic models, and was a net beneficiary of the 1980s debt crisis in the Third World. Like the commercial banking sector, it received more payments in interest than it extended in loans. The IBRD recorded profits of US $1,130 million (1.13 billion) in 1993 (YBIO, 1995). Table 9.6 shows the voting shares in the World Bank in 1992.

In comparison with the USA, the smallest constituency of 22 African countries could only muster 1.86% of World Bank votes. As Marc Williams has noted: 'US influence arises from the unwritten understanding that the president of the Bank is a US citizen chosen by the President of the United States. To date all eight Bank presidents have been US citizens and with three exceptions they have been selected from the banking community' (Williams, 1995, p.107).

Table 9.6 World Bank voting rights, 1992

USA	17.59%
Japan	8.01%
Germany	6.19%
France	5.93%
UK	5.93%
Five	43.65%

The management of the global economy is further dispersed among a number of less formal organs. The Group of 77 (which confusingly numbers 128 states) seeks to coalesce and represent the views of the developing countries. It was formed at, and took its name from, the 1967 conference of the United Nations Conference on Trade and Development (UNCTAD), and has pledged ever since to advance the so-called New International Economic Order (NIEO). The G77's influence was associated with the turbulent years of the 1970s and encouraged by the vogue for inter-vention, by rising commodity prices and low interest rates. It was thereafter doomed to marginalization through the trend towards privatization, marketization, declining raw material prices, rising debts and high interest rates which characterized the 1980s.

The G7, the economic and political opposite of the G77, was created by French initiative and convened at Rambouillet in 1975. The Heads of Government and Finance Ministers of France, Germany, Italy, Japan, UK and USA were joined for their now annual 'summit', in 1976, by Canada and in 1978 by the President of the European Commission. Occasionally expanded by invitations to the Netherlands, Belgium, Sweden and Switzerland, the re-shaping of the post-Cold War order was signalled, after 1993, by the admission of the Russian Federation to the annual deliberations. Associated with international financial co-ordination, such as supporting particular exchange rates, and co-ordinating the views of the world's largest economies in advance of other global forums, such as the GATT Uruguay round, the G7 has also acquired something of a reputation for being slow and unwilling to address the pressing issues of debt relief, environmental degradation, aid to Eastern Europe and Russia, and the West's own persistent recession after 1990. The G7 has also provided an informal forum in which the most influential members of the IMF and IBRD can formulate and co-ordinate their policies in these organizations with discretion. 'They sought to pre-empt discussion at the Executive Board and the Board of Governors and to move effective decision-making away from the institutional framework of the IMF' (Williams, 1995, p.68).

The final GATT agreement in December 1993, which concluded the so-called Uruguay round of negotiations, signalled the end of the General Agreement of Tariffs and Trade itself, and its transformation into the World Trade Organization (WTO). GATT itself was only ever envisaged as a stop-gap, when the US Congress rejected the original UN-related trade organization envisaged in the Havana Convention of 1948. GATT operated for over 40 years in a series of lengthy 'rounds', including the Kennedy round and Uruguay round, in which the enlarged membership, through extended horse-trading, reduced the average global level of tariffs on manufactured goods. Despite the rhetoric of free trade, GATT in fact excluded many sectors of trade, most obviously agricultural produce and financial services. It was also slow and resistant to opening trade in semi-manufactures and enlarging Third World market shares in manufactured exports, encouraging some to suggest that the semi-protectionist NICs (such as Korea and Taiwan) showed better growth than the devotees of free trade.

----------------- ***Summary of Section 9.2*** -----------------

- The UN and its system of agencies was created at a time of near Western hegemony in international relations, modified by the Soviet power of veto.

- Despite the doctrine of state sovereignty encouraging the one-member–one-vote principle, the UN and World Bank both depart markedly from this principle in important respects.

- The peculiar provisions of the Security Council have, in effect, 'frozen' the distribution of power as it existed in 1945. This has severely limited the relevance and ability of the UN to adapt to changes in the international system, most obviously the rise of Third World independence and the greater importance of economic management relative to military force in 'managing' the post-1945 system of states.

9.3   Democracy and geo-governance

The theoretical literature on international organization has always recognized the tension or, more correctly, degree of confusion between several roles that IGOs such as the UN can fulfil. Archer suggests that intergovernmental organizations may operate as *actors*, in their own right, or as an *arena* or *forum* in which members negotiate, and/or as *instruments* of the member-states' policies (Archer, 1984). These approximate to, but do not exactly map onto, the distinctions noted in Chapter 1 between radical and cosmopolitan, liberal-internationalist and realist accounts of world order respectively.

The idea that international organization might come to *replace* some part or all of the authority of the sovereign state, in a supra-national authority, is a familiar liberal-internationalist and cosmopolitan aspiration. In various forms the idea can be traced to Kant, the Abbé St. Pierre, William Penn and beyond (see Held, 1995). Whether inspired by some past model or hopeful of some future state, cosmopolitan accounts seek to overcome the negative, 'anarchic' features of the international system enshrined in the 1648 Treaty of Westphalia, replacing this with a system of cosmopolitan law binding on states, which would then cease to be fully sovereign. More modestly, liberal-internationalists regard the creation of international organizations and international law as logical extensions of domestic government and law, which attempt to serve the electorate. They would limit the authority of international organizations to activities governed by intergovernmental agreement. Realists are more limited in their enthusiasm for international organizations and seek to *use* rather than *be bound by* the organs of geo-governance. They are most keen to preserve rank, power and hierarchy within the organs of geo-governance, so as to replicate the power politics of the international system, of which international organizations are therefore conceived as a microcosm. Radicals seek to transform existing structures of geo-governance to reflect the interests of the world's peoples as opposed to the world's great powers.

The UN as an actor

The status of international organizations as actors is deceptive. IGOs have 'legal personality', a quaint expression meaning that they imitate many of the characteristics of states, the primary *actors* in international relations. They can sign treaties; their staff enjoy diplomatic immunity; agencies can apparently act in their own name. However, the UN (and its related agencies, such as UNICEF and UNHCR) has no means of raising its own revenue; it is funded by the membership subscriptions and voluntary donations of member-states. Its policies and decisions are created by the votes of its members, and it has no armed forces of its own. Despite appearances, namely blue-helmets and white paint, all UN peacekeeping forces are created ad hoc and rely entirely upon voluntary detachments of troops contributed by national armies. There is no standing force under the command of the Secretary General. The mandate of each force is typically highly restrictive, as shown most acutely in the Bosnian case, 1992–5.

The UN as an arena

IGOs also constitute arenas or forums in which sovereign states may compose, debate, vote upon and agree upon action on a lengthening agenda of global issues. Over the last 50 years a number of complex normative issues have been debated in the forum of appropriate international organizations. Many of the ideas and ideals that are now considered fundamental to our concepts of human rights (see Chapter 6), and key issues of international concern (see Chapter 5), have only acquired that status after 50 years of political agitation.

IGOs have played a significant role in the post-war global order. The most obvious transformation of the international political system in this time has been the decolonization of the European overseas empires. The UN General Assembly was a key forum for legitimizing the principle of self-determination. As a consequence, the international system has grown from 51 states in 1945 to 191 in 1995. Secondly, the imperative of economic development has led to the creation of many institutions of geo-governance, some with a managerial mandate like the IMF and IBRD, others like the Group of 77 with a Third World orientation demanding reform, or like OPEC attempting to create control of markets and resources by producer states, which have been historically exploited by colonial powers or transnational corporations. Thirdly, the recognition and protection of the *global commons*, such as Antarctica, Outer Space, the oceans and the ocean floor beyond the limits of national jurisdiction, has been promoted through a series of multilateral treaties which uphold the concept of the 'common heritage of mankind' (Vogler, 1995). Furthermore, campaigns against nuclear weapons proliferation and against apartheid, and, most recently, the promotion of environmental protection and *sustainable* development, have each been advanced through the UN General Assembly and its special conferences.

Non-governmental organizations (NGOs and INGOs) have also become a significant force in the politics of geo-governance. NGOs recreate the associations of civil society on a global or transnational basis. It is also a truth reluctantly conceded by some governments, that the NGO community has frequently acted in advance of, rather than in response to, governmental action. On a range of social and humanitarian issues, domestic governments are prompted to respond to lobbying. NGOs apply this logic to global issues. Natural disasters and their human complications have engulfed many parts of the world in the 1990s. In complex emergencies such as Bangladesh's recurrent flooding disasters and the Rwandan civil war of 1994–5, NGOs such as the Red Cross, Médicins sans Frontières, Christian Aid and Save the Children, have appeared first and best equipped at the scene. Similarly, in extended political campaigns on environmental issues and human rights abuses, NGOs such as Greenpeace International, WWF (on the conservation of endangered species) and Amnesty International (the protection of political prisoners) are more familiar to the public than the appropriate intergovernmental organs such as the UN Disaster Relief Organization, the Convention on Trade in Endangered Species (CITES) or the UN Human Rights Committee. IGOs and NGOs do co-operate. NGOs can acquire observer status within IGOs and indeed their representatives can speak in debates, but cannot vote. Article 71 of the UN Charter expressly encourages this role in the Economic and Social Council (ECOSOC).

In a plural society, leading INGOs such as WWF will effectively have two opportunities to influence policy. In their domestic lobbying of the British electorate and government (and other countries in which WWF operates), they can seek to influence the position that the UK will promote in international negotiations. Secondly, by their active presence as officially accredited observer organizations within the UN system, INGOs continue the process, frequently in coalition with others, and also by lobbying other delegations as well. The resources and sophistication of leading INGOs, such as Greenpeace, in a specific issue area such as the Rio Earth Summit (UNCED) of 1992, or that of the International Planned Parenthood Federation (IPPF) at the Cairo Conference on Population and Development, is substantial.

In a post-Cold War world it is tempting to view these developments as part of an unfolding democratization of diplomacy. The idea is not new: the League of Nations Association and the Union for Democratic Control were typical products of British liberal-internationalism in the 1920s. The rise of NGOs suggests a world of free and active non-governmental organizations making a popular response to globalization. Here is a democratic response to those forces of globalization typified until now by the rise of transnational corporations, deregulated markets and dominant cultures. These have enhanced the power of capital, and of managerial elites at the centres of global economic power, and in contrast fragmented and marginalized the poor, the consumer, and ethnic and cultural minorities.

In societies where NGO activity at the national level is subject to interference and control, INGOs assume a particular importance (and a fuzzy legitimacy), as they may lobby on behalf of causes, minorities and classes which are otherwise excluded from the political process. Recently this participatory approach has received official encouragement within the UN system. The 1992 Rio UNCED placed particular emphasis on the role of 'major groups' in implementing Agenda 21, a seven-year programme of action to implement the commitments to sustainable development made by the participants at Rio. Agenda 21 specifies the role that women, children, youth, indigenous peoples, NGOs, local authorities, farmers, workers and trade unions, business and scientists can play in implementation. The document is rare in deliberately reaching over the heads of governments to establish direct links between the UN and active citizens. The problem remains, however, that as unelected, activist-driven organizations these NGOs may in fact institutionalize an elitist, rather than a participatory, tradition. Who decides which 'major groups' are included? Who determines the right to observer-status within the UN? Does placing 'women' in a 'major group' assist their representation or consign them to a category of minorities? Again, the answer lies in the very different attitudes to women's rights (or youth, or indigenous minorities) maintained by different national governmental delegations. Women's groups, especially lesbian activists, were subject to harassment by the Chinese authorities organizing the UN Women's Conference at Beijing in 1995. Some delegations, women's groups and organizations promoting access to contraception and reproductive health care at the Cairo Conference on Population and Development were the target of denunciations by a coalition of states which included the Vatican and Iran, as well as American NGOs promoting the 'right to life' case against abortion. Certain observer groups at the UN have been barred entry to the US when scheduled to address UN meetings in New York. The most notable example was the exclusion of Yasser Arafat and the PLO in the 1970s.

The UN as an instrument

In the realist account, IGOs are the instruments of their members (or as shown in discussion of 'bloc politics', instruments of some combination of a majority of members). In some parts of the UN system, majority voting does *not* apply: the veto power of the five permanent members of the UN Security Council has been noted, whilst there are other anomalies such as the weighted voting used in the World Bank. Governments that oppress, torture and conduct genocide against their own people within the protection of their sovereign boundaries are not likely to embrace NGO participation in the organs of international government. Post-Cold War democratization, dramatic in Eastern Europe, and continuing steadily since the mid 1980s in South America, is far from comprehensive, let alone complete. 1.2 billion people still live under one-party rule in China. Across Africa democratization has been partial and in the Arab countries liberal democracy in its multi-party forms is still rare (Potter *et al.*, 1997).

UN Secretary General Boutros Boutros Ghali (centre, front row) poses with over 170 world leaders during the UN's 50th anniversary celebrations, 22 October 1995

That said, even in countries characterized as liberal democratic, democratization has never fitted well with traditional attitudes to making *foreign* policy, including policy in international organizations. Member states defend and advance their bargaining positions within international organizations by the conventional standard of national interests, executive privilege and confidentiality. The House of Commons does not expect to be briefed by ministers departing for Brussels or New York, revealing in advance, and in public, the limits to which the government will go to secure agreement in an EU or UN forum. There is even some expectation of cross-party support, or bipartisanship, suspending the critical role of opposition for one of support for the government in its dealings with foreign powers. Two assumptions underlie this attitude: one, that there are genuinely *national* as opposed to party interests in foreign policy, and two, that it is these which guide policy-making. Both propositions are contestable. Foreign policy has frequently created party-political divisions. The Suez crisis of 1956, the exit from ERM in September 1992, entry into the EEC in 1973, and the NATO nuclear deployment arguments in 1983–5, each divided the major British parties. However, even when lacking bipartisan support, the *right* of the executive to make foreign policy is not seriously challenged in the Western tradition of liberal democracy. This realist counterweight to the claims and activities of NGOs raises the final set of questions discussed in this chapter.

To a greater or lesser extent all traditions (radical, liberal-internationalist, realist and cosmopolitan) are dissatisfied with the current state of the UN system. Calls for reform are not restricted to critics of the UN. Advocates of an enlarged role for the UN, as well as those who seek to limit its growth, are dissatisfied with the system largely bequeathed by the 1945 settlement of international relations. Nearly all want reform – the disputes concern what direction that reform should take.

———————————————— *Summary of Section 9.3* ————————————————

- The UN, as with IGOs generally, can be understood as an independent actor, an arena, or an instrument of hegemonic powers.
- NGOs and INGOs are a significant force in the politics of the UN system.
- Cosmopolitans, liberal-internationalists, radicals and realists represent distinctive approaches to the UN and NGOs as forms of geo-governance.

9.4   Democratization of the UN system

There are far more unpalatable alternatives for the UN system than confronting reform. Marginalization and outright abolition both have their advocates, especially among American critics. The decision taken in the US Congress, in February 1995, to reduce the US contribution to peacekeeping funds demonstrates that even erstwhile supporters of global governance can set very demanding standards. It may be unfashionable to suggest that a degree of tension exists in the claims of democratic reform versus institutional efficiency. However, this is a central part of the conservative (or realist) case (Pines, 1984). In this view, the smaller forum and elite membership of the Security Council yields benefits in terms of speed and cohesion over the slower and more divisive debates of larger bodies. The domestic analogy would be to justify 'cabinet' decision-making on different criteria from 'parliamentary' debate. The argument concerns utility and the UN has to demonstrate its usefulness. Although the Charter curiously contains no provisions for withdrawal, membership of the organization is not *compulsory*.

It would be legally possible, if not politically feasible, to abolish the UN. That said, financial sanctions applied by the major donors would, practically, be an easier route than outright abolition for countries determined to limit the effectiveness of the organization. The period 1985–90 showed that the major donors are quite capable of freezing the funding of the UN and letting the organization wither. A hostile US Congress might still do this. Abolition would only solve one problem at the cost of creating others. Managing multilateral relations more effectively, rather than dis-inventing the multilateral agenda that all states must live with, is the serious task of politics.

A UN that atrophied would gradually come to resemble a weakened welfare net, rather than a major actor in global governance. This would be consistent with the neo-conservative critique of the *domestic* welfare state. It is no coincidence that the member states that have done most to dismantle the welfare state at home, particularly the USA and UK, have also done most to de-legitimate the claims of the UN to a global role. During the 1980s the USA and UK both pursued policies of donating less than the UN target of 0.7% of GDP as aid, both promoted zero-budgetary growth in the UN system, both withdrew from UNESCO, both declined to ratify the UN Convention on the Law of the Sea (which institutionalized the idea of the 'common heritage of mankind' to govern the sea-bed beyond national limits), and both acted to weaken the commitments of the parties to reduce carbon dioxide emissions in the Framework Convention on Climate Change adopted at the 1992 Rio UNCED.

The realists' agenda for reform: financial accountability

Realists are reluctant to concede *democratic* reform of the UN, and would argue instead for a greater correlation between financial responsibility and influence within the organization – that is, actually *enhancing*, rather than reducing, the elite privileges contained in the Charter. Conservative critics, such as the Reagan administration during 1981–88, its Congressional supporters such as Senator Nancy Kassebaum and even Democratic Party critics such as D.P. Moynihan, would point out that in contrast to the UN, which is in financial crisis, the EU is expanding, and even NATO is now embarrassed by the number of its former enemies that wish to join it (e.g. Poland, Czech Republic and Hungary). Even leading transnational corporations, such as Toyota, Siemens and ICI which outrank the UN a thousand-fold in financial resources, are actively courted by new states seeking inward investment, technology transfer, and modernization. These corporations offer more than the limited resources of the UNDP.

Table 9.7 indicates the extraordinary imbalances in contributions. Such imbalances are the means by which the larger donors may guide reform or, more probably, *prevent* reforms contrary to their interests. Proposals to democratize the UN, by enhancing Third World voting power, either by enlarging the Security Council or by limiting the veto, might provoke this response. More likely, such democratization would have to be linked to reforms which reallocated the burden of contributions to the UN. The American Revolution of 1776 was premised on the cry 'no taxation without representation'. The major donors in the UN system could reverse this call and block democratization on the grounds of 'no representation without taxation'. In other words, the poor majority would be required to show a greater willingness to contribute to the system before giving credence to their 'democratic' arguments for a greater role in the organization.

The concentration of financial responsibility in the hands of the five major powers is even clearer with respect to contributions to the peace-keeping budget (Table 9.8).

Table 9.7 Members contributing more than 1% of UN budget

			Major affiliations		
Member	% budget	P5	G7	EU	NATO
Australia	1.51				
Belgium	1.06			x	x
Brazil	1.59				
Canada	3.11		x		x
France	6.00	x	x	x	x
Germany	8.93		x	x	x
Italy	4.29		x	x	x
Japan	12.45		x		
Netherlands	1.50			x	x
Russia	6.71	x			
Spain	1.98			x	x
Ukraine	1.87				
UK	5.02	x	x	x	x
USA	25.00	x	x		x

Permanent 5 (P5) members of SC pay	43.68% including China at 0.95%
G7 pay	64.8% of regular budget
Top 14 pay	81.02% of regular budget
Remaining 176 pay	18.98% of regular budget

Source: Bailey and Daws (1995)

Table 9.8 Contributions of members to UN peacekeeping budget

China	0.93%
France	7.29%
Russia	11.44%
UK	6.1%
USA	30.38%
P5 pay	56.14%
22 OECD pay	41.42%
Thus, 27 countries pay	97.56%
Rest of world pay	2.44%

Source: Bailey and Daws (1995)

Both tables illustrate a head-on collision between voting power and financial power. Voting power can control *agendas*, but financial power determines programme implementation and outcome.

The USA *was* increasingly on the defensive after 1975 as the new Third World voting majority in the General Assembly led to a number of defeats for US resolutions. There is no veto in the General Assembly. The USA launched a vigorous defence and, indeed, retaliation in the period 1982–89. They accused the new majority of 'politicizing' the work of the UN, criticizing in particular the 'bloc politics' which dominated General Assembly debates. The new Third World majority was accused of practising the 'tyranny of the majority' or, more bluntly, of being a majority of tyrannies, quite devoid of domestic *democratic* credentials.

To the Reagan administration (1981–89), the presence of Third World communists, unfriendly dictators and military regimes discredited the claim that the UN was in some sense a democratic forum to be respected. The litmus test of American sensitivity was the infamous (and now repealed) General Assembly resolution which equated Zionism with racism and which therefore attempted to equate the state of Israel with Nazi practices. The US claims during this period would have rung more nearly true had the list of Western friends protected by the American veto not included such notorious authoritarians as the governments of El Salvador, Somoza's Nicaragua, and the Kuomintang regime in Taiwan, in addition to their one-sided support for South Africa and Israel, which attracted so much African and Arab anger.

This confrontational approach was associated with the years of the Reagan–Bush administrations and the Thatcher government's keen support. It involved the application of financial sanctions to recalcitrant, *dirigiste* or 'anti-Western' organs within the system, such as UNCTAD or UNESCO. A typical initiative was the implementation of the Kassebaum Amendment in 1985 to limit US contributions to the UN. Related US proposals led to reforms in the UN budgetary process and to Congressional oversight of the Administrative Committee on Co-ordination (ACC) and the Committee on Programme and Budget. These moves both extended US financial power over the UN and its agencies during the period. France and the UK have sought to limit criticism of their Security Council role by showing greater willingness to participate in peacekeeping operations and, in contrast to US financial sanctions, by maintaining full and prompt subscriptions.

Critics of the UN would suggest that this financial imbalance explains Western triumphalism in respect of the Gulf War and the sanctions maintained against Iraq after 1991. The UN may have already passed from a period of Cold War paralysis to one of elitist leadership by the USA and its allies. Has the UN thus already passed from being a democratic *forum* to a hegemonic instrument? This assertion rests on the passivity of other members, the veto powers of Russia, China and indeed any coalition of seven non-veto states to block the majority in the Security Council. (Even if the permanent five agree on an issue they must recruit an additional four votes to make the nine required to pass a resolution.) During the passage of the resolutions on the Gulf crisis, August–November 1990, the Security Council included Muslim Malaysia and 'radical' Ethiopia which both consistently supported the ultimatums against Iraq. Resistance to an enlarged UN role is therefore not the sole preserve of the USA. In the case of Bosnia, it was 'radical' China and India which consistently opposed expanding the UNPROFOR mandate to include humanitarian relief. Both countries viewed the Bosnian situation as an 'internal' matter and are opposed to the involvement of the UN in such situations (mindful of cases such as Tibet and Punjab).

The lesson of this period, however, is that the USA and its conservative allies have the capacity to block reform by financial sanctions, but only so long as the membership co-operate in a 'dependency culture' as welfare clients of global governance rather than as serious co-funders of the system.

Democratic reform?

The democratic reform of the UN is generally promoted by its middle-ranking members with a long tradition of commitment, service and sacrifice to Charter principles. Canada, Norway, Sweden and the Netherlands, for example, have all contributed greatly to peacekeeping forces, made voluntary donations to UN-aid agencies matching the 0.7 per cent GDP target, and at crucial times been prepared to resist abuse of power by the permanent five. Larger Third World countries such as India, Brazil and Nigeria have made the case for reform to reflect demographic realities.

The UN has undertaken partial democratic reforms in its time. In 1965, the Security Council *was* enlarged from twelve to fifteen members, to reflect growing Third World membership. In 1985, Bertrand proposed, unsuccessfully, to modify the UN along the lines of the EU's division of responsibilities between a Commission and Council. This was a curious choice in view of the democratic deficit which characterizes the EU (see previous chapter). Co-ordination has been a perennial pursuit. ECOSOC was created for the purpose of co-ordinating the disparate functional work of the UN. The Administrative Committee on Co-ordination (ACC) brings together all of the sixteen specialized agencies into a relationship with the UN Secretary General which was designed to improve efficiency and responsiveness to development priorities. Most recently, since 1992 the Commission on Sustainable Development (CSD) has advanced the combining of environmental and economic co-ordination in the concept of *sustainable development.* Agenda 21 and the environmentally driven reforms of the 1990s have been significant in encouraging domestic democratic participation through the enlarged role for NGOs. As well as creating the CSD, the UN has also improved funding for the Global Environmental Facility (GEF), which is jointly administered by the World Bank, UNEP and UNDP, and charged with the task of resourcing sustainable development projects.

Other reforms, consistent with enlarged participation, have focused on the Security Council. The accession of Japan and Germany to the Security Council as permanent members would constitute a rational adjustment or modernization of the system of global governance, rather like eliminating the 'rotten boroughs' in Victorian England. It would give two broadly liberal, internationally minded and economically more successful powers an overdue advancement within the global organization. Other Third World candidates have their claims to a permanent seat. Most regularly cited are India, Brazil, Mexico and Nigeria, on various grounds: population, regional leadership and loyalty to UN principles. If advancement was determined by showing willing and by taking risks, as in providing troops for peace-keeping, the case for reform would involve a large number of very small countries such as Fiji, Ireland, Ghana and the several Scandinavian powers. Since it is unlikely that France and the UK (who can veto any reform resolution) will relinquish their seats, enlargement, rather than replacement of members within the Security Council, is most likely.

The only attempt to implement some form of *direct* democracy within the UN system is a hybrid form of full voting rights accorded to trades unions and employers in the 'tri-partite' structure of the International Labour Organization (ILO), created in 1919. In this organization, each country's delegation comprises government, trades unions and management, each represented in the ratio 2:1:1. No other UN agency has adopted this model (Imber, 1989). The ILO is also unique in having adopted, as part of a reform package in the 1970s, provision for secret ballot procedures. This is itself an interesting example of how standards considered quite normal in domestic society, do not apply to the procedures of international governance.

Activists for liberal-democratic reform, such as the Campaign for a More Democratic United Nations (CAMDUN), have advocated an *elected* assembly ('we the peoples'), or at least an NGO assembly, to sit in parallel to the General Assembly. More exotically, world referendums and representation for indigenous and ethnic minorities have been canvassed. These rest upon an optimistic belief in the willingness of non-liberal governments to permit more liberal-democratic reforms of the UN than they would permit of their own domestic polity.

A yet more challenging ambition for democratic reform is the claim of cosmopolitans who want to transform the UN system in ways which would create a more nearly supra-national democratic institution. The cosmopolitan project also advances democracy in both its direct and representative forms. The end of the Cold War served to revive idealism in respect of the reform of global organizations. A similar wave of enthusiasm was present in 1919 and 1945. At their most ambitious the cosmopolitans view the end of the Cold War as the third opportunity in the twentieth century to re-cast the organs of global governance more consistently with the standards and aspirations of domestic 'good government'.

Cosmopolitans would also advocate greater legal powers for the UN, relative to the member-states. The most obvious would be to give General Assembly resolutions legally binding status, or to empower the General Assembly to adopt resolutions on security questions. At present, under Article 12 of the Charter, only Security Council resolutions are legally binding, and under Article 24, the General Assembly accepts that the Security Council 'acts on their behalf' (see Held, 1995).

Finally, Third World and Western radicalism, even when stripped of its overt Marxist analysis, continues to advocate structural reform to create an organization that is an *advocate for the poor*. Radical critics denounce the free-trade assumptions implicit in globalization, and the social (and environmental) casualties associated with IMF-administered 'structural adjustment policies'. The Third World's 'long march through the institutions' (a remark attributed to Lenin in another context) was near to fruition after obtaining a voting majority in the UN system after 1970. It has been postponed and vitiated by many events since. Majority voting in global forums has also been increasingly frustrated by consensus procedures. Majority control of the *agenda* of geo-governance has been shown above to be futile when a recalcitrant minority can control the UN's finance and policy *implementation*. Furthermore, the economic reversals of the 1980s, chronic indebtedness and the collapse of the USSR and its supportive aid, have blunted radical enthusiasm.

─────────────────── *Summary of Section 9.4* ───────────────────

- There is a tension between reform of the UN system and its democratization.

- Realists tend to seek a more efficient UN, responsive to the interests of the great powers and the organization's paymasters.

- Cosmopolitan, liberal and radical visions of reform sit uneasily with the veto and financial powers of the hegemonic states.

Conclusion

The remainder of the 1990s will see the extension of global governance and the reform of the UN debated within and between approaches identified above (realist, liberal-internationalist, cosmopolitan, radical). Each will invoke different principles of democracy to enhance their claim, be it the 'he who pays the piper calls the tune' of the Americans, the representative claims of Germany, Japan and the large Third World powers, the participatory claims of the cosmopolitans or the radical claims of the global dispossessed. In all probability the UN will be the beneficiary, if not the author, of the changes this debate will initiate. Despite its commitment to be 'a centre for harmonizing the actions of nations in the attainment of these common ends' (UN Charter, Article 1), the organization remains wedded to 'the principle of the sovereign equality of all its members' (Article 2). Ironically, therefore, the UN as an institution remains quite resistant to cosmopolitan arguments, and its many authoritarian member-states will resist its democratization. External forces and political debates will affect the UN. The external forces that will stimulate change are numerous: technological innovation, the activities of major transnational corporations, voters and activists in over 180 legally sovereign states, private and governmental think-tanks, and the decisions of six billion consumers, are amongst the most obvious.

The UN, in fact, may be the victim of its own globalist rhetoric. An extraordinary number of transactions in the global system do *not* involve *all* parties. The vogue for environmental issues to be promoted as global issues (climate change, ozone layer depletion, deforestation, transboundary pollution, etc.) masks the extent to which many of the most pressing environmental problems in the world are in fact persistently and stubbornly regional, national and even sub-national (i.e. within states). Over twelve million children die annually from preventable causes in Third World countries. The most persistent killer of children is water-borne infection from local sewage. 95 per cent of Third World sewage is discharged untreated into surface water. '80 per cent of all diseases and over one third of all deaths in developing countries are caused by the consumption of contaminated water' (UN, 1992, p.175). Deforestation and desertification occur in only a very small number of the world's 190 states. The second or third order *consequences* of these national regional disasters certainly have wider effects, such as mass migration and climate change. Regional defences against these consequences have been revived, as 'Fortress Europe' attitudes to migration and refugee status have shown. The so-called 'global village' is, in truth, a 'global city'. The 'Northern suburbs' of the world are no more likely to invite the people of 'cardboard city' to the dinner table, literally, in London and Los Angeles, than metaphorically, through expanded aid and immigration for the Third World.

The most realistic prospects for UN reform would therefore seem to be some grudging recognition of the representative claims of the major donors, most obviously Germany, Japan and the larger Third World states. The USA will perhaps concede these reforms in return for a redistribution of financial burdens. The claims of the global poor are not likely to be met. The cosmopolitans have the most eloquent case to be heard as we near the end of a century which has witnessed two attempts to create an organization for global governance. But a few simple statistics will demonstrate the gulf which exists between our willingness to be taxed for the defence of our domestic civil society, and the demands made on us to honour the call of a cosmopolitan global society. Global defence expenditure in 1991 ran to US $581 billion. The Agenda 21 programme of fully costed sustainable development was priced at $600 billion per annum, over seven years from 1992. Official aid from North to South amounted in 1992 to just $55 billion, compared to the UNCED declared target of $125 billion. Therefore, compared to the debates which dominate the domestic political agenda, concerning the relative distribution of public spending between defence, environment and the alleviation of poverty, the task at the level of geo-governance has only just begun.

References

Archer, C. (1984) *International Organizations,* London, Allen & Unwin.

Bailey, S. and Daws, S. (1995) *The United Nations: a Concise Political Guide,* London, Macmillan.

Bull, H. (1977) *The Anarchical Society,* London, Macmillan.

Falk, R. (1975) *A Study of Future Worlds,* New York, Free Press.

Held, D. (1995) *Democracy and the Global Order,* Cambridge, Polity Press.

Hughes, B.B. (1993) *International Futures,* Boulder, CO, Westview.

Imber, M. (1989) *USA, ILO, UNESCO and IAEA,* London, Macmillan.

Keohane, R. and Nye, J. (1977) *Power and Interdependence,* New York, Little Brown.

Mitrany, D. (1975) *The Functional Theory of Politics,* London, Martin Robertson.

Pines, B.Y. (1984) *A World Without a UN,* Washington DC, Heritage Foundation.

Potter, D., Goldblatt, D., Kiloh, M. and Lewis, P. (eds) (1997) *Democratization,* Cambridge, Polity Press.

Rosenau, J.N. and Cziempel, E.O. (eds) (1992) *Governance Without Government: Order and Change in World Politics,* Cambridge, Cambridge University Press.

Russett, B. (1993) *Grasping the Democratic Peace,* Princeton, Princeton University Press.

United Nations (1992) *Agenda 21,* UNCED.

Vogler, J. (1995) *The Global Commons: A Regime Analysis,* London, Wiley.

Waltz, K. (1959) *Man, the State and War,* New York, Columbia.

Williams, M. (1995) *International Economic Organizations and the Third World,* Brighton, Harvester-Wheatsheaf.

Yearbook of International Organization (Annual) Union of International Associations, Brussels.

Further reading

Archer, C. (1995) *International Organizations,* 2nd edn, London, Allen & Unwin.

Bailey, S. and Daws, S. (1995) *The United Nations: A Concise Political Guide,* London, Macmillan.

Falk, R. (1995) *On Humane Governance,* Cambridge, Polity Press.

Imber, M. (1994) *Environment, Security and UN Reform,* London, Macmillan.

Commission on Global Governance (1995) *Our Global Neighbourhood,* Oxford, Oxford University Press.

Conclusion

CHAPTER 10

Democracy beyond borders?: Globalization and the reconstruction of democratic theory and politics

Anthony McGrew

Introduction

Globalization presents modern democratic theory with a daunting task: how to reconcile the principle of rule by the people with a world in which power is exercised increasingly on a transnational, or even global scale. Since classical times the history of democratic thought has been a story of the successive re-thinking and re-grounding of the idea of democracy in contemporary historical conditions. Today the fate of democratic communities across the globe is becoming ever more tightly interwoven by patterns of contemporary globalization with the result that established territorial models of liberal democracy appear increasingly hollow. This invites a serious re-examination of the meaning of democracy to confront an epoch in which the scale of human social organization no longer appears to coincide with national territorial boundaries. What is, and what should be, the meaning of democracy under contemporary conditions of globalization are questions of the utmost importance to democratic theory and practice. A new agenda for democratic theory is called for: one which breaks with conventional accounts of democracy in which the nation-state is conceived as the only proper incubator of democratic political life. Central to this new agenda is a critical enquiry into the necessity, desirability, and possibility of 'global democracy' – that is, to democracy beyond borders.

The argument previewed

During the Enlightenment the great philosophers, amongst them Rousseau and Kant, sought to design the ideal form of international order – 'perpetual peace' – conducive to the entrenchment of republican (democratic) government. However, for much of the twentieth century, this tradition of normative thinking was wantonly abandoned as the academic study of politics embraced a form of 'intellectual apartheid', separating the analysis of modern political life into the domestic and the international spheres; into politics within and politics between states; into politics as government and politics between governments respectively. As a consequence normative thinking about the 'good political community' became divorced almost totally from theorizing about the 'global human condition', and vice versa. This is especially true of modern democratic theory which, despite its enlightenment heritage, for the most part, has bracketed the international in its elaboration and advocacy of the democratic project. But, in the late twentieth century, the international diffusion of liberal democracy and the globalization of social life have provoked a revival of normative theorizing, cutting across the disciplinary boundaries of political theory and international relations, concerning the nature of the 'good (democratic) political community' and the form of world order necessary to its cultivation.

Paradoxically, just as liberal democracy has become the 'universal political standard of civilization', democratic theorists are beginning to engage in a critical reinterpretation of the meaning of democracy in the context of late twentieth-century patterns of globalization. This rethinking of democracy, of democratic ideas and practices, is animated by a strong normative attachment to the 'democratic good' and to the conviction that, in an epoch of intense globalization, the vitality of democracy within nation-states is intimately connected to the democratization of world order, to an ideal of 'democracy beyond borders'. But such an 'ideal' is subversive of the existing international order; an order in which the struggle for power and security amongst sovereign states defines an amoral, anarchic system in which force is the final arbiter of the good.

Building upon the analysis of Parts I and II of this volume, this chapter will argue that contemporary globalization invites a significant rethinking of democratic theory, most especially in respect of traditional accounts of liberal democracy (qua national or territorial democracy). Accordingly, Section 10.1 of the chapter offers an explication, and critical assessment, of the challenges posed by globalization to the principles and institutional forms of liberal democracy. This culminates in a review of the argument that, under conditions of contemporary globalization, the realization of substantive, as opposed to simply procedural, democracy – that is, a polity cultivating the active citizen as opposed to the passive voter – demands the extension of democracy beyond the nation-state to bring to account those global and transnational forces which presently escape effective democratic control. But the argument for global democracy provokes a series of important analytical and normative questions, including amongst others: How would a democratic world order be constituted? Can democracy be 'transplanted' to the global domain? Is global democracy desirable? What kinds of normative principles would underpin a democratic world order?

Section 10.2 responds to these questions through a review of three 'models of global democracy': the liberal-internationalist; the cosmopolitan; and the radical communitarian. Each of these models represents a serious attempt to re-think and to reconstruct the idea of democracy to confront the challenges of globalization. Embodied in each is a distinctive normative vision embracing the essential conditions for, the key principles underlying, and the distinguishing features of a more democratic world order. But these models should not be interpreted as alternative futures, or trajectories of historical development, nor especially as preferred utopias devoid of an understanding of contemporary historical conditions. Rather, they represent distinctive 'thought experiments' upon the latent possibilities for the deeper entrenchment of democratic principles in the functioning and governance of the global system. Each of these 'thought experiments' is grounded in particular conceptual accounts of world order and traditions of democratic thought. Each exhibits, too, a powerful sense of the constraints upon, as well as the possibilities for, the democratization of world order. They fuse, in other words, an understanding of world order as it is with a normative analysis of what it might become, reflecting E.H.Carr's dictum that 'Any sound political thought must be based on elements of both utopia and reality' (Modelski, 1972, p.360).

But to conclude the analysis there would be to avoid the difficult questions posed by the sceptics. For the idea that democratic principles have a place in, let alone a relevance to, the conduct of international affairs is strongly contested by realist thinking in international relations. Orthodox realist accounts emphasize the 'natural' resistance of international political life to democratic practices since it is: devoid of any central authority or rule of law; dominated by great powers and power struggles; riven by entrenched hostilities and insecurities; and permeated by irreconcilable cultural particularities and civilizational differences. Realists recall the abject failure of the 'idealist experiment', during the inter-war period, which sought to 'make the world safe for democracy' through the reform of power politics. Any serious attempt to rethink democracy must therefore address the structural impediments to the democratization of world order. Section 10.3 therefore engages with the principal sceptical arguments concerning the idea of 'democracy beyond borders.

The sceptical account reflects a belief in the existence of categorical limits, whether ideological, institutional or political, to the 'reach' of the democratic ideal. But the assumption that world order is historically immutable neglects processes of historical change and the limited, although nevertheless significant, democratic developments which are highlighted in Part II of this volume. World order is a human construction, constantly being made and remade through the actions and inter-actions of a multiplicity of agents including states, diplomats, corporations, international organizations, social movements, non-governmental organizations, and individuals. In this respect it is best conceived as both a condition and a process; it is, to borrow a sociological term, 'socially constructed'. It is neither fixed nor immutable but in a constant flux of construction and reconstruction. Section 10.4 delivers a riposte to the sceptics and a more optimistic reading of the possibilities for 'democracy beyond borders'. This is not to argue that borders will be wholly irrelevant but rather that the 'deepening' of democracy within states has to be accompanied by a 'stretching' of democratic practices across states. Finally, the chapter concludes with a review of the key arguments and a reflection upon the requirements for a meaningful democratic theory today.

10.1 Globalization and territorial democracy

In the late twentieth century the formidable scale upon which many aspects of contemporary economic, social and political activity is organized makes territorial democracy appear increasingly impotent. Within Western liberal democracies this perception of impotence is linked to public anxieties about the declining effectiveness of governance, the growing fragmentation of civic communities, and paradoxically growing personal insecurity in an era in which, despite the end of the Cold War, national security appears unchallenged. Whether real or imagined these anxieties reflect a '...fear that, individually and collectively, we are losing control of the forces that govern our lives' and that this predicament is strongly associated with processes of late twentieth-century globalization (Sandel, 1996, p.3).

Of course, moral panics concerning the 'crisis' of liberal democracy have a respectable history in democratic thought. In the 1970s the work of radical critics of liberal democracy (including amongst others Habermas, Marcuse, and Offe) sought to expose the underlying 'legitimation crisis' of capitalist democracy. Unable to permanently resolve the fundamental contradictions between the operation of late capitalism and the logic of democracy the advanced capitalist state was confronted, it was argued, by a continual crisis of political legitimacy (Held, 1996). In contrast, conservative accounts diagnosed this 'crisis' as a result of 'overload', of big government and too many, rather than too few, opportunities for citizens to influence the decisions which shaped their lives. Fragments of these (and other) accounts can be detected in discussions about the contemporary democratic condition. But what is distinctive about this discourse is evidence of a convergence of views, amongst theorists representing very different traditions of democratic thought (republican, liberal, social democratic, socialist, and participatory), that a major culprit in the hollowing out of democratic institutions, and the growing incapacity of democratic states to direct their own future, is the intensity of contemporary globalization.

Sandel, a leading advocate of republican democracy, concludes that amongst the most fundamental obstacles to substantive democracy today resides in '...the formidable scale on which modern economic life is organized and the difficulty of constituting the democratic political authority necessary to govern it' (Sandel, 1996, p.338). From a radical democratic tradition, Walker observes that 'With the transformations in global political, economic, and cultural processes that are now underway, the possibility of democracy is especially problematic' (Walker, 1988, p.133). Whilst, from a broadly direct democracy tradition, Dryzek argues the liberal theory of democracy is critically flawed since, 'The liberal idea of democracy as preference aggregation also presupposes the notion of a self-contained, self-governing community. But in today's world, that notion is becoming increasingly fictional, as political, social, and especially economic transactions transcend national boundaries' (Dryzek, 1995). How do we account for this evident consensus?

Globalization and the emergence of the post-Westphalian order

There are powerful reasons for believing that globalization delivers a serious challenge to the Westphalian institution of sovereign statehood. In particular, while states still retain a legal claim to '...effective supremacy over what occurs within their territories' this is significantly compromised, to varying degrees, by the expanding jurisdiction of institutions of international governance and the constraints of, as well as the obligations derived from, international law (Keohane, 1995). As Goodman (Chapter 8) observes, this is particularly evident in the EU within which sovereignty is divided between national, international and local authorities. But even where sovereignty appears intact, states no longer, if they ever did, retain sole command of what transpires within their own territorial boundaries. Complex global systems, from the financial to the ecological, connect the fate of communities in one locale to the fate of communities in distant regions of the world. Although the intensity of global interconnectedness is most apparent in crisis situations, such as war or economic recession, everyday activities, from shopping to watching satellite television, offer reminders of how the local and the global are mutually constituted.

Furthermore, global infrastructures of communication and transport support new forms of economic and social organization which transcend national boundaries without any consequent diminution of efficiency or control. Sites of power and the subjects of power may be literally, as well as metaphorically, oceans apart. Decisions taken in the Seoul boardrooms of Korean electronic companies, for instance, are now vital to the prosperity of communities in the Neath Valley of South Wales. In this context the notion of the state as a self-governing, autonomous organism, appears to be more of a normative claim than a descriptive statement. The Westphalian institution of territorially circumscribed sovereign rule appears somewhat anomalous juxtaposed with the transnational organization of many aspects of contemporary economic and social life.

Contemporary processes of globalization, as Keohane argues, do not so much prefigure the demise of the Westphalian institution of sovereign statehood as its adaptation to new historical circumstances (Keohane, 1995). In this 'post-Westphalian' global order '...notions of sovereignty as an illimitable, indivisible and exclusive form of public power' are being displaced by a recognition that 'Sovereignty itself has to be conceived today as already divided among a number of agencies – national, regional and international – and limited by the very nature of this plurality' (Held, 1991, p.222). Accordingly, sovereignty is best understood as '...less a territorially defined barrier than a bargaining resource for a politics characterized by complex transnational networks' (Keohane, 1995). This is not to argue that territorial boundaries retain no political, military or symbolic significance but rather to acknowledge that, conceived as the primary spatial markers of modern political life, they have become increasingly problematic. For in a world of global connections, 'National communities by no means exclusively "programme" the actions, decisions and policies of their governments and the latter by no means simply determine what is right or appropriate for their own citizens alone' (Held, 1991, p.202). What are the implications of this for territorial democracy?

Globalization and the transformation of democracy

This displacement of the Westphalian norm of sovereign statehood has profound consequences for modern democratic theory and democratic governance which presuppose '...the territorial state as the highest unit of political loyalty, identity and democratic participation' (Connolly, 1991). This correspondence between liberal democracy and sovereign statehood is deeply rooted; for liberal democracy read the 'liberal-democratic nation-state'. Modern democratic theory too assumes a fixed '...correspondence among state, territory, nationality, sovereignty, democracy and legitimacy' (Connolly, 1991). However, by eroding the Westphalian institution of sovereign statehood globalization casts significant doubt on both the empirical and theoretical integrity of this presumed correspondence. This transformation of the normative and institutional foundations of modern liberal democracy is a pre-eminent theme in the discourse upon the condition of contemporary liberal democracy.

In his examination of the fate of the liberal democratic state in the context of patterns of contemporary globalization, David Held identifies significant disjunctures between the organizing principles of modern liberal democracy and the dense global and regional networks of economic, political, military, cultural and legal relations in which they are now embedded (Held, 1995). These disjunctures map the expanding gap between sovereign statehood and the effective sovereignty and autonomy of states operating in a densely interconnected global system. They highlight a growing asymmetry between the global and transnational scale of contemporary social life and the territorial organization of liberal democratic governance. In this sense they identify a growing contradiction '...between structures of power that seem to be increasingly internationalized, in some senses universalized, and processes of participation, representation, accountability and legitimacy that remain rooted in the institutionalized apparatuses of states' (Walker, 1991).

Such conclusions call into question the continuing capacity of liberal democratic states to function as autonomous, self-governing political communities. The very essence of democracy is 'rule by the people'. Constrained by global market forces and confronting problems which, like ecological degradation, deny purely national resolution, the liberal democratic state (as the chapters in Part I indicate) has only limited control over the forces which shape its destiny. Historically, this may always have been the case. What is new is the sheer density, as well as the magnitude, of existing patterns of global and regional interconnectedness. Contemporary globalization spills across every domain of social activity, from finance to sport, and generates complex interactions between these domains. In this context the capacity for self-governance is significantly constrained although it is far from extinguished. As Sandel observes, under conditions of globalization, liberal democratic states '...traditionally the vehicles of self-government, will find themselves increasingly unable to bring their citizens' judgements and values to bear on the economic forces that govern their destinies' (Sandel, 1996, p.339).

But if the idea of self-governance is made problematic by globalization so too is the modern conception of the 'demos'. Almost all conventional accounts of democracy conceive the political community, or the people, which exercises the right to self-governance as synonymous with the nation – the 'national community of fate'. Membership of the political community is thus defined almost exclusively in terms of the people within the territorial borders of the nation-state. But in the context of intense global and regional interconnectedness, the very idea of political community as an exclusive territorially delimited unit is at best unconvincing and at worst anachronistic. In a world in which global warming connects the long-term fate of many Pacific Islands to the actions of tens of millions of private motorists across the globe, the conventional territorial conception of political community appears profoundly inadequate. Globalization weaves together, in highly complex and abstract systems, the fate of households, communities and peoples in distant regions of the globe, such that real 'communities of fate' cannot be identified in exclusively national or territorial terms. The implication is that, under conditions of globalization, '...one cannot understand the nature and possibilities of political community by referring merely to national structures' (Held, 1995, p.225). This has profound implications for traditional accounts of consent and accountability which are central to modern liberal democratic theory and practice.

Without exception, democratic thinkers, from J.S.Mill to Robert Dahl, have assumed a direct symmetry between the institutions of representative democracy and the political community which they serve (Held, 1995).(Central to such accounts of liberal democracy are the principles of consent, legitimacy and accountability.)In these accounts government depends upon the consent of the governed. Citizens, through the ballot box, confer authority on government to rule in accordance with majority sentiment. Thus in theory government remains directly accountable to the 'demos' and rules in accord with general expressions of popular sovereignty. But this presumes a direct correspondence between rulers and ruled, a correspondence which is disrupted by the existence of global and regional networks and structures of power. In these circumstances governments may have no direct role in vital decisions which affect the very security or welfare of their citizens whilst equally the consequences of government decisions may have serious impacts extending well beyond their own territorial jurisdiction. In short, in a highly interconnected global system the exercise of power spills across territorial borders and lies beyond the reach of the relevant national mechanisms of democratic control and accountability.

Modern democracy, however, is not simply defined by institutions and procedures; it also embodies republican notions of the 'active citizen', of empowerment, participation and the 'virtuous community'. Substantive democracy – the realization of the 'good (democratic) society' – is an aspiration embodied in many traditions of modern democratic thought from the nineteenth-century 'developmental democracy' of J.S.Mill to the late twentieth-century participatory democracy of C.B.MacPherson (Held, 1996). But, as Cox notes in Part I, globalization is

also transforming the social and economic conditions under which substantive democracy might be realized (see Chapter 3).

Sandel argues that the growing sense of dis-empowerment which currently afflicts the public in many democratic states can be traced to the
fact that the ideal of liberal democracy '...and the actual organization of
modern social and economic life are sharply at odds' (Sandel, 1996,
p.202). Structures of public and private power have become increasingly
internationalized. International institutions, like the World Bank or the
WTO, and transnational organizations such as IBM or Hong Kong and
Shangai Banking Corporation, represent new agencies or sites of power
in the global order. Such power is also becoming more concentrated: in
1992 the world's top 100 multinationals controlled sales equal in size to
the entire US GNP and the top 300, 25 per cent of global productive
assets (Gill, 1995). Confronted by such enormous and distant
concentrations of power, citizens and communities in democratic states
especially experience an intense feeling of powerlessness. This is further
exaggerated by the inordinate complexity of public international decision
making which masks the location of power and undermines national
mechanisms of accountability contributing to a sense that 'Power is elsewhere, untouchable' (Walker, 1988, p.134).

This is compounded by the fact that in the last two decades the intensity of economic globalization, and associated restructuring of national
economies, have fuelled growing inequality within and between nations.
The gap between rich and poor societies, and the rich and poor within
states, is, to varying degrees in different regions of the world, widening
(Bradshaw and Wallace, 1996). In 1996 the total wealth of the world's
richest 358 individuals was in excess of the combined annual incomes of
nations with 45 per cent of the world's population (UNDP, 1996, p.2).
Every day 35,000 children die of preventable diseases. Economic
globalization is implicated in growing social polarization on both a global
and domestic scale. Within societies it fragments national and local communities, as some reap its rewards, others bear its costs and some survive
on its margins. This is nowhere so evident as in the citadels of global
finance where foreign exchange dealers in the City can earn in a week
what office cleaners earn in a year. This social polarization is associated
with an erosion of social solidarity, disillusionment with established forms
of politics, and de-politicization (Cox, 1996). In these conditions the
republican ideal of all citizens sharing in the governance of the political
community rings hollow since it '...requires political communities that
control their destinies, and citizens who identify sufficiently with those
communities to think and act with a view to the common good' (Sandel,
1996, p.202). Under conditions of globalization, the nature of democratic
citizenship and the enactment of popular sovereignty are thereby made
deeply problematic.

Contrary to these developments globalization is also associated with
processes of political empowerment and democratization. Huntington
observes that the 1980s 'wave' of democratization was reinforced by the
existence of a global media and communications infrastructure. By generating international awareness of political developments it facilitated a

US President Bill Clinton (left) shakes hands with Russian Prime Minister Viktor Chernomydin at the G7 meeting in Lyons on 28 June 1996. Also pictured are Japanese Prime Minister Ryutaro Hashimoto (rear, left), German Chancellor Helmut Kohl, French President Jacques Chirac and British Prime Minister John Major

kind of international 'demonstration effect' (quite literally) wherein knowledge of national struggles for democracy in one country encouraged the domestic mobilization of democratic forces in others. This was most conspicuous in the democratic revolutions of 1989 in Eastern Europe where national struggles for democracy generated a spontaneous mutually reinforcing effect – the political equivalent of a chain reaction.

Much more significant, however, has been the role of regional and global institutions in the consolidation of liberal democratic forms of governance. In Latin America, Eastern Europe, Asia and Africa, national transitions to democracy have been influenced by powerful external agencies. In particular the World Bank, the IMF and the G7 states have made economic and financial assistance to transitional states conditional upon both the process of 'democratic' political reform and economic liberalization. Whilst these objectives are often in conflict, this conditionality nevertheless amounts to an extraordinary internationalization of processes of democratic consolidation. Moreover, regional institutions such as the Organization of American States, Organization for Security and Co-operation in Europe, and the EU administer a vast array of initiatives and programmes designed to support and encourage democratic practices and reform within transitional states. Thus British universities receive EU funds to teach Red Army officers about the role of the armed forces in democratic societies. Alongside these public programmes there is also a vast proliferation of private initiatives by political parties, charitable foundations, human rights groups, and religious organizations seeking to encourage a flourishing civil society. These developments have been variously interpreted as a 'New Imperialism', renewed Westernization, or the triumph of democracy, whilst their impact has been highly uneven. But these labels fail to capture the diverse motivations and driving forces underlying a set of developments which, in combination, represent a significant explosion of global political activity.

This transnationalization of private political activity is reflected in the emergence of a 'global civil society' (Shaw, 1994, p.132). With the growth and technological advances in international communications has come a staggering expansion in the transnational organization and transnational activities of private associations and social movements in every region of the world. Amongst the most significant of these new transnational political forces are the environmental movement, peace movement, women's movement and religious movements. But, as in domestic civil society, there exist enormous inequalities between groups, both in terms of resources, support and access to sites of power, not to mention a proliferation of fundamentalist, anti-democratic, and anti-liberal organizations (Hurrell and Woods, 1995). Nevertheless, 'global civil society' constitutes a constellation of political forces which, through their individual activities, collectively seek to make states and other international actors more accountable for their actions (Shaw, 1994, p.132; Falk, 1987; Weiss and Gordenker, 1996). As both Walker and Linklater argue, the political practices of these progressive movements are constructing the foundations of a new model of citizenship which explicitly embraces the principle of 'duties beyond borders' (Linklater, 1996b; Walker, 1988). Just as sovereignty is being dispersed under the pressures of globalization so too is the idea of democratic citizenship becoming more differentiated since, 'Citizenship in a globalizing world is not the same as citizenship in a world that venerated the territorial principle' (Rosenau, 1992, p.287).

Liberal democracy today confronts an era of global organization. The contemporary scale of human social and economic organization is transforming the institutional conditions under which liberal democratic states operate. As Walker concludes: 'Although it is with respect to the state that we have come to understand what is meant by democracy, states are caught up in processes that make democracy more and more difficult to achieve' (Walker, 1988, p.83). However, democracy's predicament, suggests Sandel, is not entirely without historical precedent, for '...the challenge to self-government in the global economy resembles the predicament American politics faced in the early decades of the twentieth century' (Sandel, 1996, p.339). By the turn of the twentieth century, industrialization had transformed the scale of economic organization in the USA and created huge new concentrations of power. A significant disjuncture therefore existed between the 'nationalization' of economic activity and the capacity of local democratic political institutions to regulate it. For the progressive politicians of the era the solution lay in centralizing political power within the federal (national) government, creating a strong national state, and encouraging a potent sense of national identity and solidarity. Transposed to liberal democracy's present predicament this suggests a solution lies in the direction of formal world government. But the historical record also confirms that world government is neither a politically attainable nor a desirable arrangement. Instead we must acknowledge that '...contemporary conditions call for a radical rethinking of what democracy must involve' (Walker, 1991).

10.2 Rethinking democracy: models of global democracy

If the aspiration for substantive democracy is to be realized under contemporary conditions then liberal democracy must embrace those global and transnational spheres of modern life which presently escape its territorial jurisdiction. In this respect the democratization of world order and global governance promise not only a means to reclaim and regenerate the ethic of self-governance, which is at the heart of democratic politics, but also to harness the democratic energies of those progressive social forces which increasingly operate across, below, and above the nation-state. But such a project requires, in the first instance, a normative vision of 'democracy beyond borders', an account of what democracy might be or could become; a cogent rethinking of democracy. In this section we explore three quite different normative accounts or 'models' of global democracy: the liberal-internationalist; the radical communitarian; and the cosmopolitan.

Before elaborating these accounts a word of clarification is necessary concerning the nature of normative theory and these three models. Although normative theory is concerned primarily with explicating and analysing what is desirable, the principles underlying what ought to be or should be the case, it is neither necessarily wildly utopian in nature nor divorced from an understanding of contemporary historical circumstances. On the contrary it derives its intellectual credibility from an understanding of both '...where we are – the existing pattern of political relations and processes – and from an analysis of what might be: desirable political forms and principles' (Held, 1995, p.286). To discount normative theory simply on the grounds that it trades in ideas or projects which, under existing historical conditions, may appear politically infeasible is to accept a deterministic view of history. But '1989 and all that', completely unanticipated as it was, is a solemn reminder that prevailing assumptions about what appears politically feasible are often a feeble guide to history's possibilities. The ideals of eighteenth-century political theorists, often at the time treated with great disdain, are embedded in many of the routines of modern political life, from the language of rights to the institutions of liberal democracy, such that it is no exaggeration to claim that '...we live some [normative] theory – all the time' (Sandel, 1996, p.ix). As the accounts of global democracy discussed here exemplify, normative theory justifiably is concerned above all with the limits to and the possibilities of the politically desirable.

Although they offer different prescriptions for global democracy, the following accounts share a number of features in common. Firstly, an acknowledgement that globalization is transforming the conditions of liberal democracy. Secondly, a commitment to the widening and deepening

of democratic politics. Thirdly, a rejection of the idea of world government. Fourthly, a belief that new democratic arrangements for global
governance are necessary. Fifthly, and lastly, a conviction that political
ideas and ideals can, and do, shape political practice. However, each
account embodies a distinctive democratic ethic and reflects a unique
inheritance of ideas from different democratic traditions. Together they
represent diverse interpretations of the central questions of democracy:
How is the demos to be conceived? How is rule to be conceived? What is
the purpose of democracy? In the exegesis which follows the discussion
will examine, in each case, a specific prescriptive account of global
democracy which is representative of that normative approach, its underlying normative principles, its democratic heritage, and its limitations.
This analysis seeks to identify the normative theory which underpins each
account and thus establish the basis for comparing the democratic
principles and general features of each 'model' of global democracy. In
this context the concept of 'model' refers to a simplified and ideal-type
construction of a specific normative theory.

Liberal-democratic internationalism: 'neighbourhood democracy'

In late 1995 the Commission on Global Governance, an independent
international committee of senior statespersons, published its report *Our
Global Neighbourhood* (Governance, 1995). The report recognizes the
profound political impact of globalization: 'The shortening of distance,
the multiplying of links, the deepening of interdependence: all these
factors, and their interplay, have been transforming the world into a
neighbourhood' (ibid., p.43). Its main purpose is to address the problem
of democratic governance in this new 'global neighbourhood' acknowledging that the fate of national democracy, in an interdependent world, is
intimately tied to the prospects for the democratization of world order. As
the report asserts:

> It is fundamentally important that governance should be underpinned by
> democracy at all levels and ultimately by the rule of enforceable law ... As at
> the national level, so in the global neighbourhood: the democratic principle
> must be ascendant. The need for greater democracy arises out of the close
> linkage between legitimacy and effectiveness ... as the role of international
> institutions in global governance grows, the need to ensure that they are
> democratic also increases.
>
> (Governance, 1995, p.48 and p.66)

But the report is emphatic that global governance '...does not imply world
government or world federalism' (ibid., p.336). Rather it understands
global governance as a set of pluralistic arrangements by which states,
international organizations, international regimes, non-governmental
organizations, citizen movements and markets combine to regulate or
govern aspects of global affairs. In this sense there '...is no single model
or form of global governance, nor is there a single structure or set of
structures. It is a broad, dynamic, complex process of interactive decision-

The General Assembly of the United Nations in session

making that is constantly evolving and responding to changing circumstances' (ibid., p.4).

To achieve a more secure, just and democratic world order the report proposes a multi-faceted strategy of international institutional reform and the nurturing of a new global civic ethic. Central to its proposals is a reformed United Nations system buttressed by the strengthening, or creation, of regional forms of international governance, such as the EU. Through the establishment of a peoples' assembly and a Forum of [Global] Civil Society, both associated with the UN General Assembly, the world's peoples are to be represented directly and indirectly in the institutions of global governance. Moreover, it proposes that individuals and groups be given a right of petition to the UN through a Council of Petitions, which will recommend action to the appropriate agency. Combined with the deeper entrenchment of a common set of global rights and responsibilities the aim is to strengthen notions of global citizenship. An Economic Security Council is proposed to co-ordinate global economic governance, making it more open and accountable. Democratic forms of governance within states are to be nurtured and strengthened through international support mechanisms whilst the principles of sovereignty and non-intervention adapted '...in ways that recognize the need to balance the rights of states with the rights of people, and the interests of nations with the interests of the global neighbourhood' (ibid., p.337). Binding all these reforms together is a commitment to the nurturing of new global civic ethic based upon '...core values that all humanity could uphold: respect for life, liberty, justice and equity, mutual respect, caring, and integrity' (ibid., 1995, p.336). Central to this global civic ethic is the principle of participation in governance at all levels from the local to the global. As a serious, as well as systematic, attempt to 're-think' the conditions of democracy and to establish a set of normative principles and institutional arrangements by which to entrench democratic politics within all levels of governance the Commission's report represents a remarkable achievement.

Richard Falk has referred to the Commission as the 'last of the great liberal commissions' since underlying its carefully argued report is a normative theory of global governance which is rooted in liberal-internationalist approaches to world order and liberal models of democracy (Falk, 1995). Liberal-internationalism has its origins in the thinking of enlightenment philosophers. Given their faith in progress and human rationality, liberal-internationalists, since the last century, have argued that creating a peaceful and democratic world order is far from a utopian project but, on the contrary, a necessity in a world of growing interdependence. As a normative theory of world order it is concerned with how to *reform* the system of states with the aim of abolishing power politics and war (Long, 1996).

Three factors are absolutely central to this theory: growing interdependence, democracy and global governance. Cobden and Bright, leading liberal-internationalists of the nineteenth century, argued that economic interdependence generates propitious conditions for international co-operation between governments and peoples (Hinsley, 1967). Since their destinies are bound together states, as rational actors, come to recognize that international co-operation is essential to managing their common fate. In turn international co-operation to deal with collective problems, alongside the international diffusion of prosperity brought about by global commerce, makes war both increasingly irrational as a means to achieving political goals and increasingly unnecessary (Mueller, 1989). Secondly, democracies are constrained in their actions by the principles of openness and accountability to their electorates In these conditions rational governments are less likely to engage in war (Howard, 1981). Accordingly, the spread of democracy establishes a framework for international peace. Thirdly, through the creation of international law and institutions to regulate international interdependencies, world harmony can be maintained. Moreover, in an increasingly interdependent world the political authority and jurisdiction of these international institutions has a natural tendency to expand, at the expense of state sovereignty, as the welfare and security of domestic society becomes increasingly bound up with the welfare and security of global society. Although a simplification of liberal-internationalist theory, this summary sheds light on its underlying utilitarian logic.

In the twentieth century, liberal-internationalist ideology has played a critical role in the design of historical world orders, specifically under US hegemony, in the aftermath of both the First and Second World Wars. The creation of the League of Nations, and a 'world safe for democracy', was effused with such ideology, as was the UN system. In the context of the post-Cold War New World Order, liberal-internationalist ideas have acquired renewed vitality but adapted to fit 'new times' (Long, 1995). Whilst still remaining faithful to the liberal 'emancipatory' ideal – '...to subject the rule of arbitrary power ... to the rule of law within global society' (Governance, 1995, p.5) – contemporary thinking, as reflected in the Commission on Global Governance report, is decidedly reformist rather than radical.

Reformist in this context refers to incremental adaptation of the institutions and practices of global governance, as opposed to reconstructing or abolishing them. Thus the Commission proposes reform of traditional geo-political forms of international governance by means of a more representative and democratic UN system. But even in this arrangement the great powers and states are to retain their primacy in systems of global governance. The proposed People's Assembly is to be constituted in the first instance by an assembly of national parliamentarians. This tension between state sovereignty and popular sovereignty, which is evident in liberal theories of national democracy, is more explicit in liberal-internationalist thinking about the democratization of world order. So too is the liberal fascination with constitutional and legal solutions to problems which are essentially political in nature. Moreover, as might be expected, whilst the Commission's report documents a host of reforms to the political arrangements for global governance it is more circumspect with regard to reform of the global economy – 'In some cases, governance will rely primarily on markets and market instruments, perhaps with some institutional oversight' (Governance, 1995, p.5). Yet, as noted previously, economic globalization is deeply implicated in the transformation of modern liberal democracy. This ambivalence reflects conventional liberal thinking which separates the economic from the political and restricts democracy to the political sphere.

Implicit in liberal-internationalist discourse is an assumption that political necessity will drive forward the democratization of global governance. Avoiding global ecological crisis and managing the pervasive social, economic and political dislocation arising from contemporary processes of globalization '...will require the articulation of a collaborative ethos based upon the principles of consultation, transparency, and accountability. ... There is no alternative to working together and using collective power to create a better [democratic] world' (Governance, 1995, pp.2 and 5). But this ignores the central fact that growing interdependence is also a significant source of global conflict.

In key respects liberal-internationalism is a normative theory which seeks to transpose a weaker form of domestic liberal-democracy into a model of democratic world order (Clark, 1989, p.215). Its contemporary proponents are seeking to construct an ideal of 'democracy beyond borders' upon the theoretical foundations of modern liberal-democratic thinking including the developmental democracy of J.S.Mill and the pluralist democracy of R.A.Dahl (Held, 1996). But there is a real paradox here: for just at the historical moment when liberal democracy is being transformed by the forces of globalization it is proposed to erect a version of it at the global level.

Radical communitarianism: demarchy

Whereas liberal-internationalism emphasizes the *reform* of existing structures of global governance, the radical project stresses the creation of *alternative* forms of global social, economic and political organization based generally upon communitarian principles: that is principles which emerge from the life and conditions of particular communities, from local communities to communities of interest or affection e.g. environmentalists, religious, gender. It combines a commitment to direct forms of democracy and self-governance together with new structures of functional governance. It rejects existing structures of global governance since they are conceived as priveleging the interests of the wealthy and powerful and excluding the possibilities of more humane and democratic forms of governance. As Burnheim states, 'Democracy hardly exists at the international level, and it is difficult to see how it could in the context of existing institutions and practices' (Burnheim, 1986, p.218). The radical project is therefore concerned with establishing the necessary conditions which will empower people to take control of their own lives and to create 'good communities' based upon ideas of equality, the common good, and harmony with the natural environment. Unlike liberal-internationalism this necessarily involves the transformation of existing forms of social and economic organization to ensure a correspondence with democratic principles of governance. In this regard the radical project does not seek to transpose domestic democracy into the global domain but rather to transcend it. It is animated by a rethinking of existing '...political categories through which political practice is constituted' (Walker, 1988, p.136).

Radical thinking is reluctant to prescribe substantive constitutional or institutional blueprints for a more democratic world order since this represents the centralized, modern 'top down', statist approach to political life which it rejects. Accordingly, the emphasis is upon identifying the normative principles upon which 'democracy beyond borders' might be constructed irrespective of the particular institutional forms it might take. One significant attempt to identify such principles is Burnheim's normative theory of 'demarchy' (Burnheim, 1985). Central to this model of global democracy is the principle that democratic governance should be organized along functional (e.g. trade, environment, health), as opposed to territorial lines, and that such functional authorities should be directly accountable to the communities and citizens whose interests are directly affected by their actions. Thus '...democracy and democratic legitimacy are not to be sought in geographically-bounded entities like nation-states, but rather in functional authorities of varying geographical scope run by individuals selected by lot from among those with a material interest in the issue in question' (Dryzek, 1995). The spatial jurisdiction of these authorities would reflect the spatial scope of the problems and activities they seek to regulate or promote. According to Dryzek, 'The point is that the reach of public spheres [authorities] is entirely variable and not limited by formal boundaries or jurisdictions, or obsolete notions of national sovereignty. And they can come into existence, grow and die along with the importance of particular issues' (Dryzek, 1995).

Each authority would be managed by a committee, chosen on the basis of a statistically representative sample of those citizens and communities whose interests are implicated in its decision making. This would ensure that those with a stake in the decisions of each authority would have a voice in the governance of that functional domain of social life '...to the degree that they are materially and directly affected by decisions in that domain' (Burnheim, 1995). Thus, for instance, global environmental problems would be dealt with by one set of authorities whilst specific regional, national and local ecological problems would be regulated by other authorities. But each authority would be governed by representatives of the relevant political communities affected by its decisions. The co-ordination of decision making between these various authorities would be managed by committees organized on the same principle of representation so ensuring that they '...are not representative of states but of the kinds of people affected by their decisions' (Burnheim, 1995). Demarchy, as a principle of global governance, seeks to facilitate and encourage '...the active participation of people in decision making, sometimes as representatives of specific interests they themselves have, but often too as the trustees of interests that cannot speak for themselves' (Burnheim, 1995).

Demarchy is subversive of existing forms of global governance since its objective '...is to chip away and ultimately destroy sovereignty at all levels of social life' (Burnheim, 1995). Its radical agenda is influenced by a political philosophy which asserts that one of the '...great fallacies of political theory is the assumption that a centralized management of power ... is necessary to assure political order' (Burnheim, 1986). It ultimately aspires to the 'end of the nation-state' as a liberation from power politics and the inadequacies of territorial forms of liberal democracy. In its place it offers a vision of a proliferation of diverse, overlapping and spatially differentiated self-governing 'communities of fate' in which there would be multiple sites of power but no 'sovereign' or centralized structures of authority of any kind. Such a vision entertains the possibility of a '...massive shift in power in favour of the disadvantaged, which would eventually result in radical change in the overall pattern of [global] society' (Burnheim, 1986, p.238).

But how is such a radical re-structuring of global power relations to be achieved? For many radicals the agents of change are to be found in existing (critical) social movements, such as the environmental, women's and peace movements, which challenge the authority of states and international agencies as well as orthodox definitions of the 'political'. Through a politics of resistance and empowerment these new social movements are conceived as playing a crucial role in global democratization similar to the role of the (old) social movements, such as organized labour, in the struggle for national democracy. In 'politicizing' social activities and eroding the conventional boundaries of political life (the foreign/domestic, public/private, society/nature) social movements are defining a 'new progressive politics' which involves '...explorations of new ways of acting, new ways of knowing and being in the world, and new ways of acting together through emerging solidarities' (Walker, 1988, pp.147–8). As Walker suggests '...one lesson of critical social movements is that people are not as powerless as they are made to feel. The grand structures that seem so distant and so immovable are clearly identifiable and resistible on an everyday basis. Not to act is to act. Everyone can change habits and expectations or refuse to accept that the problems are out there in someone else's backyard' (Walker, 1988, pp.159–60). These new social movements are engaged in mobilizing transnational communities of resistance and solidarity whose activity, according to Falk, '...may remain largely "underground" until it erupts at an opportune moment to reshape the relationship of forces in many parts of the world' (Falk, 1987). Those opportune moments tend, in radical accounts, to be associated with impending global ecological and economic crisis (Chase-Dunn, 1986; Deudney, 1994).

Water cannon is sprayed round Brent Spar to stop Greenpeace from boarding to occupy.

Underlying the radical model of global democracy is an attachment to normative theories of direct democracy and participatory democracy (Held, 1996). There are echoes here of Rousseau's 'general will' and New Left ideals of community politics and participatory democracy. But the radical model also draws upon neo-Marxist critiques of liberal democracy, as is evident in the language of equality, solidarity, emancipation and transformation of existing power relations. Democracy is conceived as inseparable from the achievement of social and economic equality, the establishment of the necessary conditions for self-development, and the creation of self-governing communities. In this regard the radical model connects with the civic republican tradition of democratic thinking which conceives '...individual freedom is embedded within and sustained by a [strong] sense of political community and of the common good' (Barns, 1995). Encouraging and developing in citizens a sense of simultaneous belonging to overlapping (local and global) communities of interest and affection is central to the politics of new social movements as well as the search for new models and forms of social, political and economic organization consonant with the principle of self-government. As Sandel concludes:

> Since the days of Aristotle's polis, the republican tradition has viewed self-government as an activity rooted in a particular place, carried out by citizens loyal to that place and the way of life it embodies. Self-government today, however, requires a politics that plays itself out in a multiplicity of settings, from neighbourhoods to nations to the world as a whole. Such a politics requires citizens who can think and act as multiply situated selves.

(Sandel, 1996, p.351)

The radical model of 'democracy beyond borders' is a 'bottom up' theory of the democratization of world order. It represents a normative theory of 'humane governance' which is grounded in the existence of a multiplicity of 'communities of fate' and social movements as opposed to the individualism of liberal-internationalism and the '...abstract diversions in the ideas of ... "global cosmopolitanism" currently in vogue in political theory' (Matthews, 1995).

Cosmopolitanism: 'cosmopolitan democracy'

Recent years have witnessed what Linklater calls the 'cosmopolitan turn' in thinking about democracy (Linklater, 1996b). Its resurgence, in part, arises out of a conviction that, 'Today the territorial/security state forms the space of democratic liberation and imprisonment. It liberates because it organizes democratic accountability through electoral institutions. It imprisons because it confines and conceals democratic energies flowing over and through its dykes' (Connolly, 1991). Cosmopolitan thinking has a heritage stretching back to the Greek stoics and reflects a faith in the idea that humankind is bound together morally, if not materially, in a politics of 'spaceship earth'. Immanuel Kant, the eighteenth-century German philosopher, was a powerful advocate of the cosmopolitan ideal, observing that the '...greatest problem for the human species, whose solution nature compels it to seek, is to achieve a universal civil society

administered in accord with the right' (Kant, 1784, p.33). For Kant the solution to this problem lay in the development of republican states –
'democratic' government – and their association within a peaceful union
of states, and civil societies, operating under the rule of a cosmopolitan
law (Kant, 1795). Inspired by Kant's cosmopolitan thinking and commitment to democratic ideals, the 'cosmopolitan turn' has generated a distinctive normative approach to the contemporary problems of liberal
democracy under conditions of globalization. David Held's model of
'cosmopolitan democracy' speaks to these problems directly (Held, 1995).

At the core of this model is a belief that contemporary patterns of
globalization and regionalization are undermining existing national forms
of liberal democracy. In this context '...national democracies require an
international cosmopolitan democracy if they are to be sustained and developed in the contemporary era' (ibid., p.23). The cosmopolitan model
of democracy attempts to specify the principles and the institutional basis
upon which democratic governance within, between and across states is
to be expanded. This model is underpinned by an ethic of democratic
autonomy which Held distinguishes from the self-interest of liberal individualism since it refers to '...a structural principle of self-determination
where the "self" is part of the collectivity or "majority" enabled and constrained by the rules and procedures of democratic life ... Hence, this
form of autonomy can be referred to as "democratic autonomy" – an
entitlement to autonomy within the constraints of community' (ibid.,
p.156). To achieve this, under contemporary conditions, requires the
embedding of democratic practices more deeply '...within communities
and civil associations by elaborating and reinforcing democracy from
"outside" through a network of regional and international agencies and
assemblies that cut across spatially delimited locales' (ibid., p.237). By
such means those global sites and transnational networks of power which
presently operate beyond the scope of territorial democratic control will
be brought to account, so establishing the political conditions befitting
the realization of democratic autonomy.

Central to the achievement of democratic autonomy is the necessity
for a cosmopolitan democratic law, that is, law which '...transcends the
particular claims of nations and states and extends to all in the "universal
community"' (ibid., p.228). Although this idea of law comes close to
existing notions of international law, such as that concerning universal
human rights, it involves a more powerful and radical notion of legal
authority which '...allows international society, including individuals, to
interfere in the internal affairs of each state in order to protect certain
rights' (Archibugi, 1995). Accordingly, the principle of democratic autonomy depends upon '...the establishment of an international community of
democratic states and societies committed to upholding a democratic public law both within and across their own boundaries: a cosmopolitan
democratic community' (Held, 1995, p.229). This does not require the creation of world government, nor a federal super-state, but rather the establishment of a '...transnational, common structure of political action' – a
transnational structure embracing all levels of, and participants in, global
governance, from states, multinational corporations, international

institutions, social movements, to individuals. In this way the cosmopolitan model builds upon the post-Westphalian conception of global order as '...a global and divided authority system – a system of diverse and overlapping power centres shaped and delimited by democratic law' (ibid., p.234). It defines a complex structure of political authority which lies between federalism (as in the USA) and, the much looser arrangements implied by the notion of, confederalism. For it requires '...the subordination of regional, national and local 'sovereignties' to an overarching legal framework, but within this framework associations may be self-governing at diverse levels' (ibid., p.234). The realization of 'cosmopolitan democracy' would thus deliver the ultimate triumph of democracy, as the global 'political good', for it seeks '...the recovery of an intensive and participatory model of democracy at local levels as a complement to the public assemblies of the wider global order: that is, a political order of democratic associations, cities and nations as well as of regions and global networks' (ibid., p.234).

The implications of this model for the nation-state and individual citizenship are profound. It proposes the end of sovereign statehood and national citizenship as conventionally understood and their re-articulation within a framework of cosmopolitan democratic law. Nation-states would 'wither away' only in the sense that they would clearly '...no longer be regarded as the sole centres of legitimate power within their own borders' (ibid., p.233); but they would not be redundant. Whilst, as Linklater argues, citizenship would involve a recognition that individuals '...can fall within the jurisdiction of several authorities; they can have multiple identities and they need not be united by [national] social bonds which make them indifferent to, or enemies of, the rest of the human race' (Linklater, 1996b).

The entrenchment of 'cosmopolitan democracy' within the global system requires, in the first instance, a process of *reconstructing* the existing framework of global governance. This is to involve both short- and long-term measures in the conviction that, through a process of incremental change, geo-political forces will come to be socialized into democratic practices. These measures require that international organizations and the UN system be made both more representative and accountable. Thus functional international institutions, such as the WTO or the World Bank, would have elected supervisory boards whilst the UN General Assembly would be complemented by a directly elected 'assembly of peoples' which would form a 'second chamber'. Referenda would reinforce the voices of the world's peoples in these structures as would the exploitation of new communication technologies such as the Internet. Alongside these global structures regional forms of governance, with associated regional parliaments and executive authorities, would be expanded or developed. Moreover, the incorporation of cosmopolitan democratic law into the constitutional and legal frameworks of governance at all levels is central to this process of reconstructing global governance. An International Human Rights Court would dispense justice, in relation to human rights abuses, on a global scale. In addition, the cosmopolitan law would require the backing of coercive force at all levels of governance through the creation of new internationalized and accountable military structures. Finally, the institutions and operation of the global economy would be subject to democratic intervention to embed the principle of democratic autonomy in the structures and functioning of global market capitalism.

'Cosmopolitan democracy' proposes an enormously ambitious agenda for the institutional and political reconstruction of global governance. Nevertheless, its utopian vision is reflected in a variety of contemporary developments, from the 'big' structural shift towards a post-Westphalian international order, to the 'micro' level development of 'European citizenship' in the context of the EU. Crawford, too, identifies in international law a formal commitment to democracy '...which a generation or even a decade ago would have been regarded as political or extra-legal' and which more importantly is '...entering into the justification of legal decision making in a new way' (Crawford, 1994, p.14). Over the last half-century the number of national referenda on foreign and international issues has grown considerably in all regions of the globe (Rourke *et al.*, 1992). Linklater, moreover, argues that cosmopolitan democracy '...expresses important if challenged trends within Europe which favour the greater democratization of international life' (Linklater, 1996b).

Such trends, by themselves, do not necessarily portend dramatic change. Advocates of cosmopolitan democracy remain extremely aware of the fact that '...it is precisely because our current social and political institutions are a reflection of political values and preferences that ideas of the future can be instrumental in bringing about qualitative change' (Clark, 1989, p.52). Normative thinking, in this view, is not simply an analytical account of the 'good political community' but also an intellectual activity which identifies the political possibilities inherent in the present. In this sense it is both a reflection upon the contemporary historical condition and also constitutive of it, promoting the '...theorist as advocate, seeking to advance an interpretation of politics against countervailing positions ... [creating] ... the possibility of a new political understanding' (Held, 1995, p.286).

In comparison with the radical and 'neighbourhood' models of global democracy the cosmopolitan model reflects an eclectic democratic heritage, in that it has strong links to a variety of traditions of democratic thought. Whilst it draws considerable inspiration from modern theories of liberal democracy, it is also influenced by the thinking of contemporary theorists of direct democracy and civic (republican) democracy. This is reflected in the emphasis upon the principle of democratic autonomy and participatory democracy. In some respects it combines aspects of both radical communitarianism and liberal-internationalism. However, unlike liberal-internationalist theory it is not concerned with the *reform* of global governance *per se* but rather with its *reconstruction*. It seeks to replace the primacy of power politics in the conduct of global governance with the primacy of democratic decision making. It also seeks to address the democratization of global economic relations and forms of governance. It embraces a stronger commitment to self-governance in comparison with the top-down model proposed by the Commission on Global Governance. Moreover, it distinguishes itself from radical models of global democracy

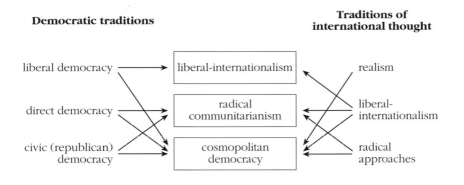

Figure 10.1   Models of global democracy: an intellectual genealogy

with its recognition of the centrality of law and public authorities as necessary conditions for the establishment of a more democratic world order. But the idea of cosmopolitan democracy is not without its critics.

Sandel argues that, 'Despite its merits ... the cosmopolitan ideal is flawed, both as a moral ideal and as a public philosophy for self-government in our time' (Sandel, 1996, p.342). This, he argues, is because at the core of cosmopolitanism is a liberal conception of the individual which neglects the ways in which individuals, their interests and values, are 'constructed' by the communities of which they are members. Accordingly, democracy can only thrive by first creating a democratic community with a common civic identity. Whilst globalization does create a sense of universal connectedness it does not, in Brown's view, generate an equivalent sense of community based upon shared values and beliefs (Brown, 1995). Thus cosmopolitan democracy, as global democracy, lacks the normative and moral foundations for its effective realization. The model is also criticized for its emphasis upon a constitutional-legal approach to the democratization of world order which fails to specify a convincing rationale for how cosmopolitan democratic law can be institutionalized in the absence of a global authority or without resort to coercion. Finally, it might be argued that without stronger mechanisms for taming the power of global capital the idea of cosmopolitan democracy remains seriously deficient.

This section has explored three normative accounts, or models, of global democracy. These are summarized in Table 10.1. There are significant differences, as well as similarities, between these three models of global democracy. Moreover, they are the product of quite distinct combinations of democratic traditions and reflect the influence of different schools of international relations theory (see Figure 10.1). All three offer a vision of a more democratic world order, although based upon quite different normative principles. But is the project of global democracy itself necessary, desirable or even feasible?

Table 10.1 Models of global democracy: a summary and comparison

	Liberal internationalism	*Radical communitarianism*	*Cosmopolitan democracy*
Who should govern?	The people through governments, accountable international regimes and organizations.	The people through self-governing communities.	The people through states, associations, international organizations, all subject to cosmopolitan law.
Form of global governance?	*Polyarchy* – pluralistic fragmented system, sharing of sovereignty.	*Demarchy* – functional democratic governance, devoid of sovereignty.	*Heterarchy* – divided authority system subject to cosmopolitan democratic law.
Key agents/ instruments, processes of democratization	Accelerating interdependence, self-interest of key agencies of power in creating more democratic/co-operative forms of global governance.	New social movements, impending global ecological and economic crises.	Constitutional and institutional reconstruction, intensification of globalization and regionalization, new social movements, impending global crises.
Traditions of democratic thought	Liberal democratic theory – pluralism and protective democracy, social democracy, reformism.	Direct democracy, participatory democracy, civic republicanism, socialist democracy.	Liberal democratic theory, pluralism and developmental democracy, participatory democracy, civic republicanism.
Ethic of global governance	'Common rights and shared responsibilities.'	'Humane governance.'	'Democratic autonomy.'
Mode of political transformation	*Reform* of global governance.	*Alternative structures* of global governance.	*Reconstruction* of global governance.

10.3   Global democracy: the sceptic's response

'How often have statesmen been motivated by the desire to improve the world, and ended by making it worse?' asks Morgenthau in response to advocates of a new world order (Clark, 1989, p.80). 'Realists', such as Morgenthau, remain intensely sceptical of normative thinking about international relations since they understand the 'real' world as a historic 'struggle for power and peace' between nations. International relations, in this realist account, is a self-help system, a Darwinian struggle for mastery and control, in which security and peace cannot be guaranteed by anything other than the always precarious balance of power. As the recent experiences of Bosnian-Serbs and Chechnians affirms, there is no external authority upon which any nation can automatically rely to guarantee its own security. The contingency of peace and order in world politics thus leads realists to seriously doubt whether even if (and it is a highly sceptical 'if') 'global democracy' may be regarded as historically necessary, it is either desirable or feasible under present conditions.

Although realists recognize that accelerating globalization has significant implications for world politics, and the autonomy of states in particular, they remain deeply unconvinced of the argument that it is transforming the Westphalian order of states (Gilpin, 1981). Krasner notes that, historically, sovereign statehood always has been compromised by external forces such that arguments about its demise, under conditions of globalization, are neither novel nor terribly convincing (Krasner, 1995). Thus, whilst most realists readily accept that international conditions and forces do constrain liberal democracy they tend to reject the notion that it is being undermined or transformed by global and regional interconnectedness. Similarly, the argument for a more inclusive and extensive democratization of world order is implicitly contested through a strong attachment to geo-political principles and norms of global governance. Furthermore, realists point to the already existing democratic practices in global governance, including human rights and mechanisms of national accountability and representation which allow citizens through their governments a voice in world politics, so disputing the view that the contemporary world order is entirely devoid of a democratic ethic.

More significantly realism tends at best to be ambivalent to, at worst dismissive of, the greater democratization of global governance. This is for four reasons. Firstly, history demonstrates that in a politically turbulent and volatile world the wisest principle remains *si vis pacem para bellum* – peace rests upon preparation for war. But by preparing for war states induce insecurity amongst their neighbours. This consequent security dilemma demands rational management of foreign policy, as well as of the balance of power between states, if conflict is to be avoided. On occasions, governments may be required to take decisions or pursue policies which, although designed to avoid conflict, are inimical to the direct material interests of, or prevailing opinion amongst, their citizens. In these circumstances democracy presents a danger since '...where foreign policy is conducted under the conditions of democratic control, the need to marshal popular emotions to the support of foreign policy cannot fail to impair the rationality of foreign policy itself' (Morgenthau, 1967, p 7). For many realists liberal democracy has the great potential for undermining national security by bringing irrational and emotive prejudices to bear upon vital decisions which require rational deliberation and often secret diplomacy. This 'democrat's dilemma' defines an irreconcilable tension between liberal democracy and national security (Ullman, 1975). A dilemma which cannot be resolved even within the context of global democracy; if anything the contradictions would become even more acute.

Secondly, whilst the historical evidence appears to confirm that democracies do not engage in military conflict with other democracies for many realists a more democratic world order would not necessarily produce a more peaceful world (Russett, 1993; Brown, 1996). For such an argument assumes that the origins of conflict are to be located in domestic politics: the political form of the nation-state (e.g. authoritarian, monarchical, democratic etc.). Yet one of the key insights of realism is its account of war as a systemic phenomenon: as a product of the anarchic system of states itself. As Rousseau despairingly observed, 'It is quite true that it would be much better for all men to remain always at peace. But so long as there is no security for this, everyone, having no guarantee that he can avoid war, is anxious to begin it at the moment which suits his own interest' (quoted in Clark, 1989, p.76). Given this, there is no reason to assume that a more democratic world order would necessarily create a more peaceful order. Indeed, the only certainty is that '...international peace cannot be permanent without a world state, and that a world state cannot be established under present moral, social, and political conditions' (Morgenthau, 1967, p.495).

Thirdly, ideas and power are inseparable in realist discourse. The global spread of democracy in recent years cannot therefore be dissociated from Western dominance of global power structures and the global diffusion of Western values. Whilst democracy, as a political form, may have an innate universal appeal, nevertheless, taken as a global 'standard of civilization', it is an expression of Western economic and political hegemony. Global democracy has connotations of a 'New Imperialism' in which world order is to be remade in accordance with Western political principles. Realists might therefore pose the crude question: would such proposals appear so benign to the West if the call was for an Islamic world order? In international politics the struggle for power is conducted not only through military means but also, as the 45 years of the Cold War showed, through the battle of ideas and abstract principles. 'International order', writes Carr, 'and "international solidarity" will always be slogans of those who feel strong enough to impose them on others' (Carr, 1981, p.87).

Fourthly, and finally, realism proclaims a normative case against global democracy which derives from a strong attachment to the rational ordering of international society. As Buzan observes, realism '...retains a powerful, and often neglected, normative attraction of its own' (Buzan, 1996, p.62). This normative attraction is associated with the defence of certain values, including '...ideological and cultural diversity political independence and self-reliance, and economic de-centralization' (ibid., p.62). As a normative discourse, realism can be understood as a strong defence of the nation-state as the only proper home or site for the effective realization of political community and democratic politics (Brown, 1995; Rengger, 1996).

Within realist discourse the very idea of a 'democratic world order', for the reasons just elaborated, represents a deeply undesirable political end (perhaps literally) for humankind. But the realist critique is not simply concerned with the necessity or desirability of such a project but also with its political feasibility. For in Morgenthau's view, one of the quintessential characteristics of realist thinking is its '...sharp distinction between the desirable and the possible – between what is desirable everywhere and at all times and what is possible under the concrete circumstances of time and place' (Morgenthau, 1967, p.7). In this respect realism condemns normative thinking about world order as utopian. As a 'science' of international politics it seeks to describe and understand the world, not to speculate upon its normative possibilities. Thus by drawing upon the historical record, most especially the failed attempt to reform world order in the inter-war period (through the League of Nations) realism seeks to prove the fallacy and naivety of well-meaning contemporary projects for a 'new world order'. Accordingly, in relation to the prospects for the democratization of world order realism is especially sceptical. Indeed, as many of the chapters in Part II highlight, the principle of legal sovereignty still remains a critical barrier to effective global governance, let alone global democracy.

Moreover, even though processes of globalization may be physically uniting the globe they are not necessarily engendering that sense of global community upon which the legitimacy of global democratic governance depends (Brown, 1995). Indeed, many realists argue that accelerating globalization merely intensifies and generates conflicts as the nations of the world seek to secure their interests in the 'global neighbourhood'. This fragmentation of the world into nations, regions, cultures, and communities inhibits the possibilities for a trans-cultural foundation for a global democratic politics. In Asia-Pacific the 'Asian way' of democracy is championed, whilst in Africa indigenous democratic traditions and ideas of human rights are being re-invented. Growing nationalism and global inequalities reinforce cultural divisions and global fragmentation. Cultural relativism too, increasingly a hostage to authoritarian politics, undermines the basis of common agreement on democracy as a global ethic. Within realism the contemporary international system is understood in terms of endemic conflict and inequality mitigated by fragile and limited attempts at global governance which lack the coercive means to ensure order. In short: global anarchy.

The crux of the realist critique of the 'global democracy' project revolves around the issue of power: of might versus right. In a world in which the USA annually spends as much on defence as the next ten states in the global pecking order combined, why would it desire a democratic world order in which its hegemonic power would be curtailed? Who or what is going to convince it that such a project is in its real interests? This dilemma illustrates a fundamental and more general point about the political feasibility of global democracy. In an international system dominated by a few great powers how, in the absence of any international coercive apparatus, is a transition to a more democratic world order to come about without their tacit approval? For even though such an order may be in their long-term interests, it is unlikely ever to be in their immediate interests. Global democracy may be a rational and desirable project but, as the pre-eminent sceptic Rousseau observed over two centuries ago, 'If ... the project remains unrealized, that is not because it is utopian; it is because men are crazy, and because to be sane in a world of madmen is itself a kind of madness' (Clark, 1989, p.75).

10.4 Prospects for global democracy: the advocate's riposte

Despite its evident ambivalence towards the democratic ideal, realism considers the 'last best hope' for democracy to reside within the secure shell of the nation-state. But, as already noted, for advocates of global democracy the conditions which historically made that union desirable are being transformed by the processes of globalization documented in Part I of this volume. Moreover, the advocates argue that realism fails to acknowledge the fundamental changes underway in world politics and so is too uncritically dismissive of the desirability and necessity of 'global democracy'. But what about the political feasibility of this project: are these normative models of global democracy simply wildly utopian visions? Must we be resigned, as realists imply, to the immutable realities of world politics? What are the prospects for a more democratic world order?

For advocates of global democracy there are three significant reasons for tempering the pessimism of realist scepticism with a cautiously optimistic reading of present possibilities: firstly, there is evidence of change in a more democratic direction; secondly, political ideas and concepts both reflect and shape contemporary political conditions; and thirdly, democracy is itself a 'transformative' political practice. Accordingly, there is, as Connolly suggests, every good reason not to assimilate uncritically the sceptic's case which '...no longer responds sufficiently to the democratic aspiration to have a hand in shaping fundamental patterns that constitute and enable, and endanger global life' (Connolly, 1991).

As already discussed in Section 10.1, immense shifts are underway in the structure of global politics brought about by the intensity of globalization. Whilst there is contemporary disagreement about the precise nature and eventual consequences of these changes the outlines of a post-Westphalian order are beginning to emerge. As the chapters in Part II suggest, there are immanent tendencies in this new order, from the globalization of human rights to the politics of the EU, which reflect a progressive politics imbued with a democratic spirit. Such democratic tendencies are also evident in many other contemporary political developments amongst which the following five are especially significant to the advocates of global democracy:

–   The consolidation, in the post-war era, of the 'Western' or 'Atlantic' collective of nations has evolved into ' a community of peoples and states' which Keohane refers to as a 'zone of peace' (Keohane, 1995). Within this 'security community' the conduct of power politics is significantly mitigated by a dense web of interconnectedness across every domain, adherence to democratic values and principles, a rule of law, and the resolution of conflicts through peaceful means. Such a 'zone of peace' appears detached from the 'anarchy' or 'right versus might' conceptions of world politics associated with the sceptics. Indeed, it represents an emerging 'democratic' order of states and underlines existing democratic tendencies in the contemporary world order.

A man at the Earth Summit at Rio de Janeiro in 1992 signs the Earth Pledge to 'help make the Earth a secure and hospitable home for present and future generations

– The enormous growth in progressive social movements (embracing ecological, labour, cultural, democratic, peace and feminist movements) defines a new 'life politics' which seeks through persuasion to transform how we live (life-styles) in the desire to create a more democratic, equitable, and peaceful human condition. Such movements connect directly the politics of life-styles to the global politics of trade, the environment, exploitation, human rights, and arms control, amongst other issues. Although separately they have limited political power, and depend upon the ability to mobilize political opinion, collectively they represent '...modes of radical engagement having a pervasive importance in modern social life, social movements provide significant guidelines to potential future transformations ... glimpses of possible futures and ... in some part vehicles for their realization' (Giddens, 1990, pp.158–61).

– The '1980s Wave' of democratization means that for the first time in history democratic and semi-democratic states constitute a virtual majority in the global system. The spread and consolidation of democracy across the globe suggests that democracy as a political practice, as opposed to its particular institutional realization, is more universal in its appeal than the sceptics or cultural relativists assume. Moreover, as Russett concludes, 'if enough states become stably democratic in the 1990s, then there emerges a chance to reconstruct the norms and rules of the international order to reflect those of democracies in a majority of interactions. A system created by autocracies centuries ago might now be recreated by a critical mass of democratic states' (Russett, 1993, p.138). Whilst the evidence for this is debatable, democratization has been associated with more 'democratic' foreign policy behaviour in regions as diverse as Latin America, Southern Africa, and Eastern Europe.

– Globalization is contributing to the emergence of a 'global risk society': life-styles and the security of households and communities across the globe are becoming increasingly enmeshed within complex transnational systems and markets, from global production, finance and exchange, to food chains and air transport systems. Disruptions to, crises or failures in, one part of these systems can cascade through the global system with enormous consequences for all concerned. Moreover, in an interconnected world some hazards, such as nuclear war, environmental pollution, a collapse of the world banking system, define global catastrophes from which few could escape the consequences. As a result, global and regional mechanisms of functional governance have expanded enormously to manage many of these risks. But the success of many of these agencies depends in part upon establishing and maintaining public confidence and trust in both the systems they regulate and also their own regulatory activities. This has encouraged the emergence of more democratic and open styles of decision making including the growing participation of NGOs in policy formulation and implementation (Weiss and Gordenker, 1996).

– Finally, in the contemporary political debate about the reform of the UN there is a growing political awareness, amongst the major powers, that issues of representation and democratic accountability can no longer be ignored.

These five factors together constitute a less pessimistic reading of the democratic possibilities expressed in contemporary developments. But associated with these 'empirical' claims advocates of global democracy also champion a particular view of the relationship between normative thinking and the 'real world'.

A continuous theme in the recent annual summits of the G7 nations, the 'global directorate' of great powers, has been the reform of global governance. At issue is the nature of global governance in the twenty-first century. A struggle between a more democratic vision of global govern-ance and a vision which consolidates the power of states and geo-politi-cal forces is underway. As Mark Imber notes this is a political struggle with immense implications for the world's peoples (Chapter 9). It is in the context of this on-going contest between geo-political interests and pro-gressive forces that the academic debate about global democracy acquires crucial significance. Advocates of global democracy have a particular understanding of the nature and role of normative theory. This is best expressed in the concept of 'reflexivity' (Giddens, 1990, p.36). What does it mean?

'Reflexivity' is a term which acknowledges that theorizing is an inte-gral part of the 'real world' rather than a practice which stands outside or above it. Thus to use a game analogy, the theorist should not be equated with the role of the cricket commentator, interpreting for the general audi-ence the events of the game, but with the player in the match who has to understand (theorize) the game in order to play it or explain it to others.

Thus, political and international theory can never deliver an objective, purely scientific account of political life since theorists are themselves agents engaged in contemporary political life. This does not mean that theory necessarily becomes a purely subjective exercise only that however rigorous and systematic it might be theory is always for 'someone and for some purpose' (Cox, 1981). For instance, Morgenthau's realist theory of international politics dominated the thinking of the architects of the USA's Cold War strategy and in so doing contributed to the shaping of the post-war world order. As Clark comments realists therefore '...are the truly successful utopians because they have created a world after their own image' (Clark, 1989, pp.88-9). Theory can thus help 'construct' the world in a very material sense; even the '...sovereign state had to be invented' (Spruyt, 1994, p.17). Accordingly, theory is best understood as being 'constitutive' of the social and political environment we inhabit. In this respect we all live some aspect of theory every day. As Giddens observes:

> The lay individual cannot necessarily provide formal definitions of terms like 'capital' or 'investment', but everyone who, say, uses a savings account in a bank demonstrates an implicit and practical mastery of those notions. Concepts such as these, and the theories ... linked to them, are not merely handy devices whereby agents are somehow more clearly able to understand their behaviour ... They actively constitute what that behaviour is and inform the reasons for which it is undertaken.

> (Giddens, 1990, p.41)

The idea of 'reflexivity' captures this essential inter-relationship between 'theory' and political practice.

For advocates of global democracy the notion of 'reflexivity' is crucial to understanding the 'practical' value and purpose of normative theorizing since it affirms that, although insufficient by itself, '...the reconstruction of knowledge is an important part of the process of social reconstruction' (Scholte, 1993, p.142). Without an understanding of how global democracy is to be constituted or understood how can it be constructed? Without some theory of the form of, and possibilities for, a more democratic world order '...alternative paths of historical development which can be explored through collective political action might also fail to be identified' (Linklater, 1996a, p.283-4). Advocates of global democracy conceive world politics and history as much more contingent, more susceptible to human political agency, and far less immutable than the sceptics admit. In this sense the events of '1989 and all that' are testament to this view. So too is the evolution of the states system which itself developed out of the transformation of the medieval European order brought about by the actions of monarchs and princes seeking to secure supreme authority within their own territorial domains. As Walker reminds us, 'Once upon a time, the world was not as it is' – or even now how the sceptics might want it to be (Walker, 1994, p.179). Acknowledging this, and the significant political developments described in both parts of this volume, suggests that the prospects for global democracy are not as utopian as the sceptics might seek to persuade us.

Conclusion: reconstructing democratic theory and practice

This chapter has argued that globalization is associated with the emergence of a post-Westphalian world order in which the institution of sovereign statehood is being reconstituted. Building upon the discussion of Part I, it was further argued that globalization, alongside this restructuring of sovereign statehood, has immense consequences for liberal democracy. Indeed, liberal democracy is being transformed as the global scale of modern economic and social life subverts the historic correspondence between territorial democracy and the sovereign nation-state. In these novel circumstances the very idea of democracy has to be re-thought to confront an age of global and transnational organization. Such re-thinking demands a vision of 'democracy beyond borders'. Indeed, the democratization of world order promises the only means to bring to account those forces which presently bypass mechanisms of national democratic control, and also to harness the political energies of those progressive social forces which increasingly operate across, below, and above the nation-state for the democratic good. Accordingly, three models of global democracy – the liberal-internationalist, radical communitarian and cosmopolitan – were elaborated alongside the normative theories from which they are derived. These models, and the project of global democracy, were subjected to a critical interrogation. Finally, in response to the sceptic's critique, the prospects for 'global democracy' were assessed (building upon the discussion in the chapters of Part II) through an exploration of the latent political possibilities evident in contemporary developments. In this context it was concluded that the political feasibility of the 'global democracy' project is perhaps less utopian than the sceptics might care to acknowledge, since history and world politics are far more contingent, and much less immutable, than they care to admit.

Can any general conclusions be derived from this analysis? Two, in particular, appear incontrovertible. Firstly, contemporary democratic theory has to continue to explore the consequences of globalization and the dissolution of the historical identity between democracy and the sovereign nation-state. If it fails to do so, it is in danger of encouraging what Connolly calls a 'homesickness' or '...a nostalgia for a time when a coherent politics of place could be imagined as a real possibility for the future' (Connolly, 1991). This 'homesickness' pervades world politics today and its more extreme, rather than benign, consequences are articulated in the horrors of ethnic cleansing, virulent nationalism and genocide. Democratic theorists must continue to avoid such nostalgia through continuing to reconstruct accounts of democracy to accord with the historical conditions of globalization and an expanded vision of the 'good community'. A theory of global democracy today also requires a theory of global politics. In this respect, democratic theory has begun to reconnect with its past and thus to overcome the modern separation of political theory from international political theory, the separation of a theory of the good life within the state from a theory of the good life for humankind.

This is welcomed by Linklater who identifies in this new intellectual synthesis a critical theory of democracy which can '...play a leading role in envisaging principles of political life which might not simply improve the lives of citizens within the supposedly more malleable world of the state but ameliorate the condition of the weak within world society as a whole' (Linklater and MacMillan, 1995, p.14).

Secondly, democratic theory and democratic practice are organically connected. The reconstruction of democratic theory is inseparable from the rejuvenation of democratic political life and vice versa. In this sense democratic theory is a form of 'transformative political practice'. As Walker comments '...if we are all democrats today ... then we are all engaged in a problematic, in an ongoing struggle, rather than a finished condition' (Walker, 1991). The reconstruction of democratic theory is crucial to that 'struggle' and so, in a 'shrinking world', also to repairing '...the civic life on which democracy depends' (Sandel, 1996, p.351).

REFERENCES

Angell, N. (1933) *The Great Illusion*, London, William Heineman.

Archibugi, D. (1995) 'Immanuel Kant, cosmopolitan law and peace', *European Journal of International Relations*, vol.1, no.4, pp.429–56.

Barns, I. (1995) 'Environment, democracy and community', *Environment and Politics*, vol.4, no.4, pp.101–33.

Bradshaw, Y.W. and Wallace, M. (1996) *Global Inequalities*. London, Pine Forge Press/Sage.

Brown, C. (1995) 'International political theory and the idea of world community' in Booth, K. and Smith, S. (eds) *International Relations Theory Today*, Cambridge, Polity Press.

Brown, C. (1996) 'Really existing liberalism, peaceful democracies and international order' in Fawn, R. and Larkins, J. (eds) *International Society after the Cold War*, Basingstoke, MacMillan.

Burnheim, J. (1985) *Is Democracy Possible?*, Cambridge, Cambridge University Press.

Burnheim, J. (1986) 'Democracy, nation-states, and the world system' in Held, D. and Pollitt, C. (eds) *New Forms of Democracy*, London, Sage.

Burnheim, J. (1995) 'Power-trading and the environment', *Environmental Politics*, vol.4, no.4, pp.49–65.

Buzan, B. (1986) 'The timeless wisdom of realism?' in Smith S., Booth, K. and Zalewski, M. (eds) *International Theory: Positivism and Beyond*, Cambridge, Cambridge University Press.

Carr, E.H. (1981) *The Twenty Years Crisis 1919–1939*, London, Papermac.

Chase-Dunn, C. (1986) 'Comparing world-systems', mimeo.

Clark, I. (1989) *The Hierarchy of States: Reform and Resistance in the International Order*, Cambridge, Cambridge University Press.

Coates, R.A. (1996) 'The UN and Civil Society', *Alternatives*, no.21, pp.93–133.

Connolly, W.E. (1991) 'Democracy and territoriality', *Millennium*, vol.20, no.3, pp.463–84.

Cox, R. (1981) 'Social forces, states and world orders', *Millennium*, vol.10, no.2, pp.126–55.

Cox, R. (1996) 'Globalization, multilaterlism and democracy' in Cox, R. (ed.) *Approaches to World Order*, Cambridge, Cambridge University Press.

Crawford, J. (1994) *Democracy in International Law*, Cambridge, Cambridge University Press.

Deudney, D. (1994) 'Global environmental rescue and the emergence of world domestic politics' in Lipschutz, R.D. and Conca, K. (eds) *The State and Social Power in Global Environmental Politics*, New York, Columbia University Press.

Dryzek, J.S. (1995) 'Political and ecological communication', *Environmental Politics*, vol.4, no.4, pp.13–30.

Falk, R. (1987) 'The global promise of social movements: explorations at the edge of time', *Alternatives*, vol.12, no.2, pp.173–96.

Falk, R. (1995) 'Liberalism at the global level: the last of the independent commissions?', *Millennium*, vol.24, no.3, pp.563–78.

Giddens, A. (1990) *The Consequences of Modernity*, Cambridge, Polity Press.

Gill, S. (1995) 'Globalization, market civilization, and disciplinary neoliberalism', *Millennium*, vol.24, no.3, pp.399–424.

Gilpin, R. (1981) *War and Change in World Politics*, Cambridge, Cambridge University Press.

Governance, Commission on Global (1995) *Our Global Neighbourhood*, Oxford, Oxford University Press.

Held, D. (1991) 'Democracy, the nation-state, and the global system' in Held, D. (ed.) *Political Theory Today*, Cambridge, Polity Press.

Held, D. (1995) *Democracy and Global Order*, Cambridge, Polity Press.

Held, D. (1996) *Models of Democracy* (2nd edn), Cambridge, Polity Press.

Hinsley, F.H. (1967) *Power and the Pursuit of Peace*, Cambridge, Cambridge University Press.

Howard, M. (1981) *War and the Liberal Conscience*, Oxford, Oxford University Press.

Hurrell, A. and Woods, N. (1995) 'Globalization and inequality', *Millennium*, vol.24, no.3, pp.447–70.

Kant, I. (1784) 'Idea for a universal history with a cosmopolitan intent' in *Perpetual Peace and Other Essays*, NYC, Hackett Publishers.

Kant, I. (1795) 'To perpetual peace: a philosophical sketch' in *Perpetual Peace and Other Essays*, Indianapolis, Hackett Publishers.

Keohane, R. (1995) 'Hobbes' dilemma and institutional change in world politics: sovereignty in international society' in Holm, H.-H. and Sorensen, G. (eds) *Whose World Order?*, Boulder CO, Westview Press.

Krasner, S. (1995) 'Compromising Westphalia', *International Security*, vol.20, no.3, pp.115–51.

Linklater, A. (1996a) 'The achievements of critical theory' in Smith, S. Booth, K. and Zalewski, M. (eds) *International Theory; Positivism and Beyond*, Cambridge, Cambridge University Press pp.279–98.

Linklater, A. (1996b) 'Citizenship and sovereignty in the post-Westphalian state', *European Journal of International Relations*, vol.2, no.1, pp.77–103.

Linklater, A. and MacMillan, J. (1995) 'Boundaries in question' in MacMillan, J. and Linklater, A. (eds) *Boundaries in Question*, London, Frances Pinter.

Long, D. (1996) *Towards a New Liberal Internationalism*, Cambridge, Cambridge University Press.

Long, P. (1995) 'The Harvard School of Liberal International Theory: the case for closure', *Millennium*, vol.24, no.3, pp.489–505.

Matthews, F. (1995) 'Community and the ecological self', *Environmental Politics*, vol.4, no.4, pp.66–100.

Mitrany, D. (1975) 'A war-time submission (1941)' in Taylor, P. (ed.) *A Functional Theory of Politics*, London, LSE/Martin Robertson.

Modelski, G. (1972) *Principles of World Politics*, New York, Free Press.

Morgenthau, H. (1967) *Politics Among Nations*, New York, A.Knopf.

Mueller, J. (1989) *Retreat from Doomsday – The Obsolescence of Major War*, New York, Basic Books.

Rengger, N. (1996) 'A city which sustains all things? Communitarianism and international society' in Fawn, R. and Larkins, J. (eds) *International Society after the Cold War*, London, Macmillan.

Rosenau, J.N. (1992) 'Citizenship in a changing global order' in Rosenau, J.N. and Czempiel, E.O. (eds) *Governance without Government*, Cambridge, Cambridge University Press.

Rourke, J.T., Hiskes, R.P. and Zirakzedh, C.E. (1992) *Direct Democracy and International Politics*, Boulder CO, Lynne Reiner.

Russett, B. (1993) *Grasping the Democratic Peace – Principles for a Post-Cold War World*, Princeton, Princeton University Press.

Sandel, M. (1996) *Democracy's Discontent*, Cambridge MA., Harvard University Press.

Scholte, J. (1993) *International Relations of Social Change*, Buckingham, Open University Press.

Shaw, M. (1994) *Global Society and International Relations*, Cambridge, Polity Press.

Spruyt, H. (1994) *The Sovereign State and its Competitors*, Princeton, Princeton University Press.

Ullman, R.A. (1975) 'Washington, Wilson and the "Democrat's dilemma"', *Foreign Policy*, no.21, pp. 99–127.

UNDP (1996) *Human Development Report 1996*, Oxford, Oxford University Press.

Walker, R.B.J. (1988) *One World, Many Worlds: Struggles for a Just World Peace*, Boulder Co., Lynne Reinner.

Walker, R.B.J. (1991) 'On the spatio-temporal conditions of democratic practice', *Alternatives*, vol.16, no.2, pp.243–62.

Walker, R.B.J. (1994) *Inside/Outside*, Cambridge, Cambridge University Press.

Wapner, P. (1995) 'Politics beyond the state – environmental activism and world civic politics', *World Politics*, no.47 (April), pp.311–40.

Weiss, T.G. and Gordenker, L. (eds) (1996) *NGOs, The UN, and Global Governance*, London, Lynne Reiner.

Further reading

Axtmann, R. (1996) *Liberal Democracy into the Twenty-first Century*, Manchester, Manchester University Press.

Carr, E.H. (1939) *The Twenty Years Crisis 1919–1939*, London, Macmillan.

Commission on Global Governance (1995) *Our Global Neighbourhood*, Oxford, Oxford University Press.

Falk, R. (1995) *On Humane Governance*, Cambridge, Polity Press.

Held, D. (1995) *Democracy and Global Order*, Cambridge, Polity Press.

Acknowledgements

Grateful acknowledgement is made to the following sources for permission to reproduce material in this book:

Figures
Figure 4.1: Rowlands, I.H. (1995) *The Politics of Global Atmospheric Change*, Manchester University Press; Figures 5.1, 5.2, 5.3: UNDP (1995) *Human Development Report 1995*, Oxford University Press, Inc. Copyright © 1995 by the United Nations Development Programme; Figure 9.1: Hughes, B.B. (1993) *International Futures*, Westview Press, Boulder, Colorado.

Tables
Tables 9.4, 9.7: adapted from Bailey, S. and Daws, S. (1995) *The United Nations: A Concise Political Guide*, Macmillan Press Ltd.

Photographs
Cover: Greenpeace and Associated Press; p.1: Press Association; p.4: Bildarchiv Foto Marburg; p.30: Hulton Getty; p.42: United Nations/J. Isaac; p.60: Popperfoto/Reuters; p.65: Popperfoto/AFP; p.84: John Wells/Science Photo Library; p.89: UN/Prendergast; p.101: Jorgen Shytte/Still Pictures; p.108: UN/DPI. Photo by Milton Grant, © United Nations; p.129: European Court of Human Rights; pp.133 and 135: Popperfoto; p.138: UNICEF/ Mushtaq Khan; p.164: Popperfoto; p.176: Courtesy of the European Parliament; p.188: Courtesy Parlament de Catalunya; p.192: Courtesy of ETUC; pp.204, 208, 210, 211, 221: United Nations; p.239: Popperfoto; p.243: United Nations; p.248: Greenpeace/Sims; p.259: United Nations/R. Marklin.

Index